TROUBLING MASCULINITIES

TROUBLING MASCULINITIES

Terror, Gender, and Monstrous Others in American Film Post-9/11

GLEN DONNAR

UNIVERSITY PRESS OF MISSISSIPPI / JACKSON

The University Press of Mississippi is the scholarly publishing agency of
the Mississippi Institutions of Higher Learning: Alcorn State University,
Delta State University, Jackson State University, Mississippi State University,
Mississippi University for Women, Mississippi Valley State University,
University of Mississippi, and University of Southern Mississippi.

www.upress.state.ms.us

The University Press of Mississippi is a member
of the Association of University Presses.

Copyright © 2020 by University Press of Mississippi
All rights reserved

First printing 2020

∞

Library of Congress Cataloging-in-Publication Data

Names: Donnar, Glen, author.
Title: Troubling masculinities : terror, gender, and monstrous others in
American film post-9/11 / Glen Donnar.
Description: Jackson : University Press of Mississippi, 2020. | Includes
bibliographical references and index.
Identifiers: LCCN 2020011869 (print) | LCCN 2020011870 (ebook) | ISBN
9781496828576 (hardback) | ISBN 9781496828583 (trade paperback) | ISBN
9781496828590 (epub) | ISBN 9781496828606 (epub) | ISBN 9781496828613
(pdf) | ISBN 9781496828620 (pdf)
Subjects: LCSH: Masculinity in motion pictures. | Motion pictures and men.
| Motion pictures, American—21st century. | BISAC: PERFORMING ARTS /
Film / History & Criticism
Classification: LCC PN1995.9.M34 D66 2020 (print) | LCC PN1995.9.M34
(ebook) | DDC 791.43/652110973—dc23
LC record available at https://lccn.loc.gov/2020011869
LC ebook record available at https://lccn.loc.gov/2020011870

British Library Cataloging-in-Publication Data available

For Carla, Gildon, and Feylan

CONTENTS

3 **Introduction**
Remasculinizing American Cinema Post-9/11

29 **1. "Shielding Us from What We Are Not Yet Ready to See"**
The Uniformed Hero as Victim and in Masquerade

65 **2. "I Don't Know Why This Is Happening"**
Shamed Everymen and America's Own Unknowable Monsters

103 **3. "I Can Still Fix This"**
Restoring Protective Masculinity and/but Becoming a Monstrous Savior

143 **4. "A Variation of Vengeance"**
The Inadequacy of Revenge in Remasculinizing the Nation Abroad

185 **Conclusion**
"How Do You Love Your Family and Leave Them to Go to War?"

195 Notes

213 Filmography

217 Works Cited

231 Index

TROUBLING MASCULINITIES

INTRODUCTION
Remasculinizing American Cinema Post-9/11

"It's Just Like a Movie!": American Cinema, 9/11, and Spectacle

In the almost two decades since 9/11, it is easy to forget just how comprehensive the relation to cinema, genres, and film masculinities was in the attacks' immediate aftermath.[1] Hollywood cinema, key film genres, and Hollywood masculinities were prominently mobilized in configuring and understanding the attacks—in which nineteen terrorists hijacked four domestic passenger planes, flying two into the World Trade Center and one into the Pentagon and killing more than three thousand people—proposing the desired national response, and advancing and conducting the succeeding "war on terror."[2] As it has often done in times of turmoil, America fell back on reassuring Hollywood narratives to displace the overwhelming impact of 9/11 and deal with its attendant traumas. The attacks also engendered heavily gendered ideas of national crisis and proposed national recovery. American national identity, notions of manhood, and expressions of hegemonic masculinity are often linked, especially in periods of perceived crisis. Each was widely considered to have been damaged by the attacks on, and consequent collapse of, the Twin Towers of the World Trade Center in New York. The attacks were persistently figured in gendered terms, and the political, military, and cultural responses equally so, diagnosing perceived gender deficiencies, valorizing particular "heroic" and "professional" masculinities, and promoting the return of "traditional" masculinity and "strong father" figures.

Although 9/11 was widely described as unimaginable and unprecedented, the attacks were widely configured through insistent allusions to American cinematic history and Hollywood genre. The attacks were likened to Hollywood science fiction and disaster movies and, perhaps exacerbated by pre-dating millennial concerns, clearly framed in apocalyptic tones. Eyewitnesses assimilated the attacks—commonly described as "just like a movie!"—through filmic experiences of catastrophe and spectacle. Scholars readily noted that it was as if Hollywood disaster movies had "premediated" the attacks—virtually fantasizing and imagining the wholesale destruction of key American symbols *into being*.[3] And the revered director Robert Altman excoriated Hollywood's "irresponsible" passion for the spectacle of disaster: "The movies set the pattern, and the [perpetrators] have copied the movies" (qtd. in Bell-Metereau 143).[4]

Hollywood has long offered extravagant spectacles of the fantastical destruction of America's major cultural and economic urban centers, with New York and Los Angeles as its preeminent targets. Both cities share significant similarities in the cultural imagination of disaster and apocalypse. Their iconicity and distinctive geographies make them persistently vulnerable *and* attractive to natural disasters, invading giant monsters and aliens, and man-made catastrophes. According to the cultural historians Max Page and Mike Davis, this fascination reflects a long-held cultural ambivalence toward each city. They equally invoke long-standing cultural "apocalyptic strains" in American religious life and popular literary culture, articulating deeply held desires to "witness" their imagined destruction while simultaneously celebrating their greatness and power. The continuing American fascination with witnessing New York's destruction, in particular, paradoxically reinforces its preeminence. The city stands in for (American) civilization itself, representative *and* exemplar. Any attack on it targets a specific idea(s) of America, and yet the city is in some sense *also* viewed as separate from alternate conceptions of America. Its iconic skyline inspires veneration, fear, and resentment in equal measure, symbolizing not only economic and political power but also arrogance and decadence. The city's (cinematic) strengths are also its weaknesses. It is a historic immigration entry point, associated with openness, cosmopolitanism, and racial diversity; yet its skyscraper heights and island iconicity are ever vulnerable to a multitude of external threats, and its sprawling, urban indifference ever affords anonymity and concealment to subversive threats within.

Time and again, postapocalyptic Hollywood science-fictional cityscapes offer ideal spaces to indulge American ambivalence about its great cities and revel in the imagined cinematic destruction and punishment of New York and Los Angeles. Hollywood apocalypses routinely deploy the trope of the city as a space in which to exhibit (and warn of) the corruption of contemporary society, and exercise/exorcise the desire to judge, punish, and exact retribution. Popular apocalypse and disaster narratives about New York and Los Angeles also articulate and salve fears associated with immigrants, racial diversity, and external threats. Indeed, Davis observes that the "abiding hysteria" of all such fiction seems "rooted in racial anxiety" (281), whether foreign anxieties about "alien invasion" or domestic ones about increased black urbanization.[5] These narratives articulate perceptions of cultural threat and announce prohibitions on supposedly undesirable contemporary social conditions and changes, exposing before annihilating monstrous and alien threats to restore and enshrine the cultural status quo (read: white institutions).

The desire (even need) to fall back on cinematic referents in the wake of 9/11 seemed to serve a specific purpose. In 1965, Susan Sontag famously wrote of the undeniable appeal of this "imagination of disaster," the strange pleasure in watching cities and humanity destroyed in Cold War science fiction cinema. Such cinematic spectacles typically provide audiences a privileged position, maximum visual pleasure, and an all-encompassing perspective on disaster and apocalypse so that they can securely—unaffected and detached—delight in catastrophe largely emptied of identifiable death. Nick Muntean contends that the immediate employment of cinema referents after 9/11 sought "to disarm the terrifyingly uncertain nature of the attacks by making them knowable through a mode of familiar, safely mediated spectacle that so often reaches a definite conclusion" (51). Yet, as Christina Rickli observes, 9/11 offered a "defective reference," especially unsettling given that not adhering to narrative conventions refused a sense of catharsis. The attacks did not conform to Hollywood cinematic narrative conventions such as "good" defeating "evil": 9/11 was clearly not a movie. Hollywood's penchant for spectacular destruction had long been criticized for proffering images absent of meaning.[6] Ironically, however, such pleasure in disaster spectacle came to be criticized after 9/11 because these supposedly hollow cinematic fantasies of destruction had become *saturated with meaning*.

Later it became Hollywood's prospective role in representing the events of 9/11 that would cause significant public consternation. Dominant critical consensus swiftly concluded that Hollywood would need to invert or transcend typical approaches to the "imagination of disaster." John W. Jordan's assessment of *United 93*'s (Greengrass 2006) early critical reception found that commentators and filmgoers were highly doubtful about Hollywood's capacity to represent the attacks accurately or authentically. Yet equally—and ambivalently—many commentators also "agreed that the cultural memory of 9/11 would be incomplete until" Hollywood responded (Jordan 205). These anxieties only superficially seemed to entail that the understanding of 9/11 would be irrevocably violated by Hollywood's commercial imperatives (or insensitivities) or that Hollywood would dishonor the victims of the attacks. Rather, the chief concern seemed to be that cinema's singular capacity to *make* events spectacular via projection would enshrine, even enlarge, the day's original fear. Such debates prompted scholars and social commentators alike to speculate that Hollywood spectacles of destruction would cease post-9/11 or at least be subdued. The initial response certainly seemed to witness a somewhat changed attitude to representing destruction and catastrophe, one that paradoxically withheld spectacle *and* evoked the fears engendered on 9/11. Yet, as Page notes, the prediction that Hollywood would refrain from visualizing New York's destruction was swiftly disproved. Evidence at least of the city's continued symbolic significance in the American imagination, many films would soon imagine it variously as the target of environmental, apocalyptic, alien, and monster attacks.[7]

◆ ◆ ◆

The rhetorical response to 9/11—which targeted the twin centers of American economic and military might—expressly conflated gender and national identity in portraying the attacks, connoting national crisis *as* masculine crisis. The attacks reanimated and codified long-standing ideological and cultural concerns about a supposed decline in "traditional" American masculinity—capable, competent and strong, and prepared for violence if necessary. The attacks not only diagnosed supposed masculine inadequacy but were blamed on others than the perpetrators. Julie Drew's feminist rhetorical analysis of media discourse and presidential speeches in 9/11's aftermath found that each explicitly gendered American national identity, characterizing the nation as emasculated and feminized. The breach of America's defenses and subsequent emasculation figured in the collapse of the Twin Towers destabilized national-masculine identity and threatened prevailing American narratives of national invulnerability (see also Baudrillard; Žižek; Nayak). Blurring the national and the personal, according to Drew, the news media feminized victims—including in oft-replayed images of male panic and fear at the Pentagon—first to signal the nation's "violation" and second to rhetorically define injury and trauma as both feminine and symptomatically weak. Conservative commentators lamented that the alleged loss of traditional masculinities had imperiled national security. This dominant post-9/11 discourse asserted not only that the attacks feminized the nation but that America was *already* feminized. The attacks had not so much damaged America as symbolized due punishment for the perceived devaluing and recession of normative (read: white) American masculinity.

This exposed national vulnerability demanded an emphatic response and mandated national retributive remasculinization (read: by individualist, transgressive male "warriors"). The attacks thus presented a supposed opportunity to recuperate traditional gender roles to redress America's international position. Matthew Hannah's identification of the "prominence of themes of *violation* and *penetration*" (551) in media commentary and policy pronouncements perhaps best signals this two-step classification, first of the attacks and then of the necessary (ideal) national response. Julie Drew argues that the pervasive desire to (re)masculinize, as well as enabling a shift to a more muscular, interventionist foreign policy, also constituted a response to the shame of such globally public emasculation.[8] Not only were particular types of male performance or masculinity valorized in the wake of the attacks, but political and news media rhetoric repeatedly advanced the necessity of "remasculinizing" American identity, actively invoking genre and gender codes from westerns and action cinema to advocate (desired and actual) appropriate responses.

Hollywood Masculinities: (National) Crisis and (National) Recuperation

The aftermath of 9/11 swiftly initiated a process of defining the attacks as *both* unprecedented *and* revisiting previous moments of national testing. Political and news discourse produced and then reinforced a new political paradigm: "9/11 changed everything."[9] The historian Richard Slotkin ("Our Myths of Choice"), writing in 9/11's immediate aftermath, suggests that when America suffers "an event that upsets its fundamental ideas," particularly of self, "its people look to their myths for precedents, invoking past experience." The Bush administration and conservative commentators simultaneously invoked Pearl Harbor, World War II, *and* Hollywood genre and gender codes in characterizing the desired ideal national response.[10] This discursive construction represented a tangled attempt to define a supposedly unprecedented present *and also* articulate a nostalgic future.

Scholarship on Hollywood representations of gender has long emphasized its prominent ideological role in the resolution of male crisis. Hollywood film is typically considered to recuperate threatened hegemonic masculinities through an arc of crisis, recuperation, and resolution. Such protagonist arcs are evident both in individual films and across particular genres, and particularly so in the conspicuous melodrama of "male action" genres, most often action films, war movies, and westerns. Mark Gallagher, who briefly discusses post-9/11 action films, also implicitly advocates this understanding, observing how "issues surrounding masculinity are raised and resolved" in Hollywood action films (5). Gallagher also observes the *continued* construction of violence as redemptive and regenerative. This tendency is especially palpable in periods of American national uncertainty or turmoil.[11] Historically, supposed crises in American masculinity (invariably though implicitly also presented as white) are equated with—even characterized as—crises of American national identity, including after Pearl Harbor, post–World War II, during the Cold War, and post-9/11. Yet the fundamental crisis of (white and institutional) masculinity in modern

American society is most often pinpointed to the 1960s and 1970s and slated to the cumulative impacts of feminism, civil rights, and the Vietnam War.[12] Crises temporarily destabilize and decenter normative masculinity's dominance, requiring its symbolic recuperation. Perceived changes in or threats to American identity/masculinity in turn generate a distinct cultural response in cinematic representations of masculinity. Fintan Walsh, examining a wide variety of performance case studies, propounds a "recuperative" understanding of masculinity, where national crises are followed by periods of remasculinization across the culture. According to Walsh, crisis as a period of disorder precedes restructuring and reestablishment, with the exposed vulnerability of emasculated and victimized masculinities provoking recuperative violence. In cinema, such remasculinization through redemptive violence can occur via a return to traditional masculinities or in recentering masculinity by focusing on the hero's bodily suffering.

Even a cursory review of scholarship on masculinities in recent decades, in society and in cultural representations, makes it perhaps more pertinent to ask when (normative) masculinity is *not* in crisis. As Walsh observes, given that masculinity is never stable and always being renegotiated, crisis is in a sense a persistent condition *of* masculinity—as it is of gender more generally. The cultural uniformity of the resolution of "crisis" raises suspicions about whether claims of persistent masculine or male crisis are disingenuous, suspicions that also indubitably associate individual masculinities with the power of the state. For example, Wendy Brown suggests that state power and masculine performance similarly offer insincere repudiations of their power to conceal dominance and reinforce privilege, with "power and privilege operat[ing] increasingly through disavowal of potency" (194). However, there remains a tension between the insincere and what is *perceived* to be real. Sally Robinson observes that "the persistent representation of white male wounds and ... masculinity under siege offers ample evidence of what is felt to be [its] *real* condition" in contemporary American culture (6, emphasis in original). Regardless of any association with tangible threats to power and dominance, hegemonic masculinity is both always in crisis *and* always (being) recuperated or recentered.

Even scholarship that critiques the recuperation of screen masculinities understands that this may not diminish hegemonic masculinity's power. Robinson, arguing from the perspective of the American cultural upheavals of the 1960s, sees evidence of "an ongoing process of remasculinization" in the final decades of the twentieth century but also finds narratives that require a different interpretation. The pervasive "rhetoric of crisis" that she identifies "accommodate[s] a range of narratives," variously characterized by competing interests and intentions. She identifies competing "fictions of crisis," which aim either "to heal a wounded white masculinity [and] remasculinize America" or "to dwell in the space of crisis" and reimagine (dominant) masculinity (11). Regardless, male crisis need not signify male disempowerment, for "there is much symbolic power to be reaped from occupying the social and discursive position of subject-in-crisis" (9). This sentiment is reflected in recent scholarship on post-9/11 American cinema, with Casey Ryan Kelly asserting that "representations of male victimhood enable white men to disavow" hegemonic white masculinity's persistent power (161). Kelly concludes that hegemonic white masculinity's "unintelligibility" and "incoherence," far from marking its decline or demise, strategically function to masculinize victimhood and evade indictment. Crisis certainly (re)centers dominant masculinity, yet Robinson, while not wanting to discount the persistent power of masculinity, concludes that its power is neither absolute nor secure. Yet the very persistence and saturation of claims of a loss of power require fulsome address.

Hollywood Genre Masculinities and 9/11: Crisis, Violent Suffering, and Remasculinization

This book builds on key scholarly examinations of particular periods in American cinema, which strongly inform key claims about post-9/11 representations of masculinity. Cinema's capacity to visualize and display is integral to the dramatization of crises of masculinity, and cultural criticism recognizes the polysemous, at times contradictory, complexities of male representation in American cinema. For example, Gallagher identifies an increased deployment of melodrama—a mode typically associated with "women's films"—in male-oriented action film. Earlier, Steven Cohan and Ina Rae Hark's influential anthology *Screening the Male* variously considered masculinity in terms of display, feminized males, masquerade, masochism, and "becoming" mother. The critical focus on muscular bodies and projects of violent remasculinization in 1980s action movies encourages a tendency to focus on the male body in writing on cinematic masculinity, both as an ideal marker of strength and capability and as a figure of vulnerability and humiliation. Steve Neale's *Screen* essay on the display and spectacularization of male stars—a partial response to Laura Mulvey's famed essay on the cinematic gaze—observes that male stars, particularly action stars, have long been objects of the cinematic gaze ("Masculinity as Spectacle"). The camera invites us to look at the male body—and the star body—as a marker of ideal masculinity, but in gazing at it, the audience also objectifies it; *as* spectacle, the male body is to be looked at by others, connoting its vulnerability.

American cinema routinely constructs victimized or masochistic masculinities as part of the "recuperative" arc typical of Hollywood screen masculinities.[13] David Savran, whose work focuses on constructs of victimization as a means to control and regulate hegemony, observes that American cultural texts that emphasize "masochistic masculinities characteristically conclude with an almost magical restitution of male power" (37). That is, Hollywood films destabilize dominant or hegemonic masculinities to reinforce and recuperate them and reinstitute a perceived cultural ideal. Of course, the prevalence of sequels—beyond an industrial mandate—suggests that the anxieties such films supposedly redress remain unalleviated, requiring seemingly endless repetition. Yet even the incessant need to call attention to and then resolve crisis serves to strengthen and naturalize masculine power.

Arguments about the post-9/11 remasculinization of American society, politics, and popular culture dominated scholarly responses to the attacks. This scholarship implicitly assumed that a Republican presidency post-9/11 would encourage political and cultural responses mirroring Reagan-era America, rather than Cold War or Vietnam-era America. Although the initial construction focused on perceived national humiliation and effeminization, the presumed reinvigoration of "muscular" 1980s action film gender codes in redressing prior (national) wounding and suffering dominated political and news media discourses post-9/11. Spectacles of bodily suffering and (consequent) violent remasculinization accelerate (to the point of exhaustion) in the hypermasculine masochism of action star bodies in 1980s action cinema. This period generated numerous highly influential analyses of action film hypermasculinities, particularly Susan Jeffords's *Hard Bodies*, Tasker's *Spectacular Bodies*, and Cohan and Hark's anthology. These analyses famously tie the spectacle of muscular, "hard-bodied" action stars like Sylvester Stallone to the remasculinization of Reagan-era American politics after Vietnam. However, while 1980s action heroes foreground "the spectacle of the male body in action and pain" (11), Gallagher asserts that they "bear few of their [Vietnam-era] predecessors' scars" (18). While this perhaps too easily discounts psychological scars, visible bodily suffering is often temporary, serving to recenter masculinity and justify retributive ultraviolence.

By *again* equating American national crisis with masculine crisis, American culture after 9/11 discursively initiated the political *and* cultural recuperation of hegemonic American masculinities, either via recentering them through depictions of endured suffering or via revalidating traditional masculinities (invariably through violence). This response was not unprecedented, with Jeffords identifying how a militaristic foreign policy was twinned with domestic values centered on hypermasculinity, father figures and family life, and nostalgia during the Reagan era. This echoes Susan Faludi's description of American political and news media efforts post-9/11 to restore broken national myths of (male) invincibility and (male) impregnability via a return to supposedly traditional American gender types. According to Faludi, the attacks prompted nostalgia for cinematic conquest and triumph from "classical" westerns. Although betraying a simplistic view of the genre, political and news media in the wake of 9/11 repeatedly and nostalgically cited Hollywood western and 1980s action film codes of the avenging, righteous hero needed to eradicate the shame and emasculation of the attacks. The discursive promotion of traditional (white, paternal, violent) masculinity was allegedly echoed in American cinema. Numerous scholars and commentators suggested this was realized via a (call for the) return to traditional gender codes, roles, and spaces, which mandated the consequent subordination of women and demonization of foreign Others.[14] Faludi claims that when threatened, American popular culture's consistently reactive promotion of hypermasculinity turns to Hollywood western myths and tales of heroic or "manly" men *saving imperiled women*. The recuperation of the father is a proclaimed trend in film and television post-9/11, across action films, serial television action-fantasy, and science fiction–alien invasion films. Yvonne Tasker and Diane Negra observe that both the state and popular culture likewise "offer[ed] fantasies of patriarchal protection" after 9/11 (qtd. in Godfrey and Hamad 160). Scholars also contend that post-9/11 film valorizes (invariably white) male sacrifice and suffering to recuperate damaged—and supposedly disavowed—traditional masculinities. In linking the hero's and the nation's suffering, American national identity is equally remasculinized through violence. The restoration or redemption of a father figure after familial or societal crisis is an acknowledged and persistent staple of American cinema, and post-9/11 Hollywood cinema supposedly redeployed images of strong fathers, helpless daughters, and absent mothers to facilitate (national) remasculinization.

Exemplifying American cinema's historical capacity to remasculinize male protagonists in the advent of a "crisis moment," representations of catastrophe, disaster, and apocalypse often become a vehicle to restore or reinvigorate masculine authority (and the status quo) through the mythic figure(s) of the "avenging hero" or the "strong father." This opportunity to redress perceived social ills by reinvigorating dormant but desirable human qualities *after the end* is typically considered to support conservative ideologies. Mick Broderick finds that the return of the strong father not only promotes "renewal" through heteronormative articulations of the couple, the family, and the community but reinforces the symbolic order and conservative social regimes through the restoration of the archetypal Father and patriarchal law. Mathias Nilges further contends that when America—or, rather, dominant conceptions of it—feels threatened, popular cultural representations of the postapocalypse typically reinstate traditional masculinities, with "moments of national instability . . . regressively equated to threats to masculinity" (31). As Nilges argues, because of the post-9/11 loss of traditional notions of stability and protection associated with the "logic of fathering," the cinematic "return to paternalism and the restoration of the strong father becomes positively associated with the rejection of an unpleasant present" (31). Nilges is one who counters the consensus opinion on the recuperation or remasculinization of primarily traditional or hegemonic masculinities post-9/11. He argues that the crisis of the "loss of traditional forms of stability and protection" is most obvious in "the figure of the white male action hero," who is increasingly unable to avert threats to family, community, and nation (28). Nilges nonetheless contends the narrative of the absent, troubled, or impotent father is frequent post-9/11, with paternal deficiencies resolved in response to a larger crisis. Sean Redmond develops this line, arguing that the white hero in post-9/11 apocalyptic science fiction film embodies white masculinity "on the cusp of its own expiration," suffering "a terrifying identity crisis over [his] place within the social and economic order" ("Nowhere Left to Zone" 299). Not unlike Nilges, Redmond ultimately finds that these films' "final solution may well be whiteness inspired" (304), with the white salvific hero ultimately privileged, rather than superseded.

Susanne Kord and Elisabeth Kimmer, examining science fiction and apocalypse-disaster films, likewise note that a global crisis repeatedly initiates a transition from diminished, inept "actual" fathers to symbolic "ideal" fathers. The crisis must be solved by the father, often by means of violence, justified because enacted to protect the family. Extending Jeffords's identification of the increasing tendency to define heroic masculinity through fathering into late-1990s cinema, Kord and Kimmer even suggest cultural representations of crises in masculinity invariably morph into crises in fatherhood in 1990s and 2000s cinema, with the father "an ideal vehicle for national myths." Exploring the co-optation of femininity, they contend that subsuming "mother" within the father's personality becomes a general trend in another alleged period of "sensitive" men and masculinities in American cinema.[15] As much as dwelling in crisis or remasculinization through violence, such co-optation not only signals the availability of feminine qualities to male characters but preserves and extends (white) male hegemony. Hollywood apocalypses, as much as delivering spectacular judgment and punishment, thus often represent—in gendering concepts like "order" and "control"—a nostalgic restoration of an *idealized, imagined past*, particularly through (reinstated) gender roles and the return of the Father.

A significant offshoot of this paternal emphasis is articulated in Sarah Godfrey and Hannah Hamad's analysis of "protective" masculinities, typically embodied in former policing or covert protective services, in post-9/11 action film. They outline this promotion of "protective" masculinities as a conflation of "public/private sphere paternalism" allied with post-9/11 ideals of masculinity (164). In connecting fatherhood and public-sphere work, Godfrey and Hamad argue films like *Taken* (Morel 2008) redeem "failed domestic fatherhood via [the] triumphal resurgence of public protective paternalism" (161). This hybrid masculinity, which has its roots in 1980s action films such as *Die Hard* (McTiernan 1988), deploys public-professional work to (re)validate previously derided or devalued performances of traditional masculinity and the redemptive violence of the strong father. Such protective professional-fathers symbolically connect national and familial security, mirroring the domestication of 9/11 evident in the collapsing of public and private boundaries through televisual mediation and subsequent political characterization. Godfrey and Hamad further note that the conservative-professional recuperation of paternalism is likewise tied to the imperiled daughter, depicting the resolution of threats to females through righteous, redemptive paternal violence. The cinematic redemption of fathers seemingly requires female helplessness (as daughters) or absence (as mothers). Cinematic representations of the transgressive hero-father's use of protective skills *outside* his sanctioned professional role stand apart from how protective *uniformed* roles and performances were celebrated in 9/11's aftermath. Politicians and popular media repeatedly valorized particular types of men and masculine performance in the wake of 9/11 and the succeeding war on terror, most notably firefighters, police officers, and soldiers.

Everywhere and Always: Domesticating Terror and Invoking Homeland (In)Security

Although commonly described through Hollywood genre film referents, the aesthetic of the day's horrific imagery was also decidedly televisual. This, in part, is why the attacks were so widely anxiety inducing, unsettling distinctions between private and public, inside and outside. Despite its uncanny, unsettling evocation of spectacular Hollywood imagery, 9/11 as an event was defined just as much by its televisual mediation, predominantly constructed and witnessed via television. In the hours, days, and years after 9/11, television screens helped *domesticate* the terror. Ambivalently, television screens managed the spectacle of terror, rendered the American home vulnerable, and promoted individualized security regimes.

The event's sheer excess, scale, and horror, in concert with the immediacy, extent, and endless repetition of live televisual coverage, arguably signaled—and perhaps augmented—its trauma. Garnered from amateur footage, this imagery diverged sharply from disaster genre codes, offering a limited rather than omniscient perspective. Indeed, Muntean observes that "perhaps one of the most terrifying aspects of 9/11 was . . . [how it] . . . momentarily disrupted any and all conceptions of 'secure' seats of spectatorship" (52). Although 9/11 afforded a superabundance of images, from a multiplicity of perspectives, its televisual mediation offered no master (i.e., Hollywood) perspective and therefore no "safe" viewing position. The unceasing media coverage and excessiveness of events exacerbated the sense of audience impotence; audiences were compelled to watch but remained largely helpless.

Television screens confirmed the veracity (if not the nature) of the terror threat and frighteningly blurred boundaries between home, nation, and battlefield. This anxiety was augmented by political and media rhetoric, with the attacks symbolically configured as both national *and* domestic, linked to breaches of national borders *and* the American home. The Bush administration rhetorically defined 9/11 as both an act of war and a symbolic attack on the American home. Live televisual mediation facilitated the Bush administration's invocation of national crisis and existential threat via a rhetorical collapse of boundaries: the nation as attacked, the city as a battlefield, and the home as vulnerable. President Bush even opened his address to the UN General Assembly in 2003 by declaring that on 9/11 "New York became a battlefield, and a graveyard, and the symbol of an unfinished war."[16] The notion of a threat to the American home was reiterated frequently, as Susan Faludi observes, with Bush stating in his fifth anniversary speech in September 2006: "We face an enemy determined to bring death and suffering into our homes." Extended into the ensuing war on terror, home and "homeland" were readily conflated, with Donald Pease observing, "It was the efficacy of its absence from any locatable place within the symbolic order that enabled the homeland to determine the entire structure of assigned places" (qtd. in Dawes 287). As much as signaling the administration's political desire to deflect accountability, such rhetorical moves further extended the attacks' into and onto the American home, attacks represented as not only having breached America's borders but threatening everyday American domestic life.[17]

The attacks encouraged a reassertion of America as an idea(l) in first advancing and thereafter prosecuting the ensuing war on terror. Yet they also triggered a "turn inward," and a desire to (re)consolidate physical and conceptual borders. The discursive collapse of distinctions between "foreign" and "domestic-home" characterized the terror threat as both everywhere *and* always. This legitimized the administration's foreign-military and domestic-policy responses but also emphasized the nation's fragility and aggrandized the terror threat.[18] In this sense, James Hay and Mark Andrejevic attest that administration policy rhetorically defined the post-9/11 threat to domestic daily life as dispersed *and* proliferated. Terror could strike anywhere and anytime. This was precipitated by the administration's portrayal of terrorism's threat as existential—with (Western) society imperiled and in a struggle for its very survival.

Terrorists *as* Monsters *as* Terrorists

A muscular, militaristic response—the so-called war on terror—prefaced rhetorically on Hollywood genre and gender codes mandated not only reasserting wounded American national/male identity but Othering. Political and news media rhetoric also advanced American remasculinization in the wake of 9/11 through binary constructions of the terrorist threat as wholly Other, inhuman and monstrous. It is not unusual for a foreign enemy to be "created" to reaffirm and solidify social and political boundaries. Meghana Nayak observes that ongoing state identity production often encourages construction of the very differences that supposedly threaten so as to sanction the state's protection against threat (45).[19] Employing Nayak's use of "Arab/Muslim," which serves to "politicize and denote the conflation . . . [of Arab and Muslim] into a singular entity" (58), numerous scholars also identified an insistent conflation of "Indians" and "Arab/Muslims" after 9/11; the foreign was again made domestic.[20] For example, Matthew Hannah claims that post-9/11 discourse was reminiscent of "centuries of stereotypes of Indian combat" and Hollywood western iconography, recalling both a cowardly enemy opposed to civilization itself and an unyielding retributive hero (558). Post-9/11 rhetoric and policies also reinvoked a "frontier" desire to violate boundaries and to tame and defeat the "terrorist-Other," seeking to secure American identity and recuperate traditional masculinity, both in rendering the Other monstrous and in imagining his ultimate, violent annihilation.

The history and genre tropes of Hollywood westerns were repeatedly invoked post-9/11, in combination with Orientalist imagery and frontier discourse, to construct the modern terror threat. Richard Slotkin asserts that, in the aftermath of the attacks, along with the myth of the "good war," associated with Pearl Harbor and World War II, America invoked the myth of "savage war," based on the frontier myth ("Our Myths of Choice"). According to Slotkin, this myth is called on when American identity or manhood is perceived to be profoundly threatened or injured to rationalize a limitless, violent, and "perhaps irrational use of force." Terrorist figures were configured in relation to cinematic history and in contrast to ideal American masculinity and the Hollywood avenging hero.[21]

Highlighting the deep synchronicity of public discourse and later popular cultural representations, Godfrey and Hamad similarly identify tropes associated with westerns in the construction of the "Arab Other" in post-9/11 action cinema. Post-9/11 political and cultural remasculinization of normative American masculinities was regularly associated with westerns and in American cinema largely occurred in relation to the terrorist-identified Other, whose defeat facilitates the hero's recuperation. Nayak similarly claims that 9/11 led to a wider Orientalist discursive and military project, "forcefully coding constitutive differences" between dominant Self and subordinate Other, to "resurrect" American identity as strong and impenetrable (42–43). However, she vitally observes that Orientalism also effectively "reflects insecurity about the Other becoming an actor rather than object" (45). As she recognizes, American Orientalizing efforts also "reveal that fear has always been necessarily present in the relationship" between America and its "constitutive others," even before 9/11 (44). Allegorical monsters, which offer instruction on how a culture sees not only its Others but itself, mirror discursive constructions of the modern terrorist threat.

This mirroring of monster and terrorist—personifications of evil, characterized as malevolent, without rationale or purpose—is especially evident in the deliberate yet indiscriminate targeting of civilians.[22] In *Monster Theory*, Jeffrey Cohen outlines "a method of reading cultures from the monsters they engender" (3), contending that monsters are local, culture-specific manifestations of the attitudes and fears of a particular society at a particular time. Cinematic monsters, not so much discovered as made, articulate our anxieties and forbidden desires, and their typical annihilation at least temporarily exorcises those fears or suppresses those desires. Cinematic monsters also accumulate meaning intertextually via the monsters that precede them. Writing about Cold War science fiction–horror, Steffen Hantke observes that such films offer "a space for reifying, manifesting and confronting, and thus for exorcizing" sexual anxieties, racial fears, and national traumas, and reasserting individual, collective, or institutional control ("Historicizing the Bush Years" 240–41).[23] In relation to this, Adilifu Nama argues that blackness in post-9/11 science fiction cinema functions "to promote an image of a racially integrated America" and "to assure a nation grappling with post-9/11 paranoia . . . that patriotic solidarity transcends racial loyalty" (40–41).[24] Thus anxieties about *domestic* racial difference are assuaged through "multicultural fantasies" that function to transcend or contain race, subordinating it in the service of nation or displacing it onto the alien-monster Other. In so doing, such films typically depict the reinvigoration of society and the status quo and a return to some form of normalcy, however fragile. In this sense, arguments about the rhetorical and formal containment of monsters and terrorist-Others—including in cinema—typically downplay how each is stimulated by fears and anxieties *of the Other* and *about the Self*, an oversight this book concertedly seeks to avoid.

The Overall Approach and Structure

This book represents an opportunity to examine cinematic depictions of the relationship between hegemonic masculinity and its many Others during an especially febrile period in American history. It interrogates critical presumptions about the extent and success of American cinema's widely presumed remasculinization, and American national identity and manhood alike as muscular; whether cinema promoted a return to traditional gender roles; and whether it elevated certain expressions of masculinity valorized in the wake of 9/11, including the strong father. Outwardly, and perhaps unsurprisingly, the films I examine place normative masculinity into crisis before seeking to recuperate and reassert it. Yet the redemption of American masculinities in encounters with terror and terror-identified Others is more ambivalent and uncertain.

Masculinity as Relational

In examining whether and how remasculinization is complicated or thwarted in post-9/11 American film, I emphasize gender's relationality to link Judith Butler's seminal work on gender performativity with Raewyn Connell's equally influential sociological work on hegemony, seeking productive complementarities in these distinct feminist disciplinary approaches. Connell, a pioneering sociologist, recognizes that masculinity is often popularly linked to the position of men ("Studying Men and Masculinity"), with masculinities predominantly aligned with men via a simplistic conflation of biological sex and gender. Gender is still popularly considered strongly relational to male and female biology— a "categorical" understanding. As Butler observes, this belief—which cannot account for gender complexities or the interplay of race, cultural difference, class, and sexuality—mistakenly implies that there is "an interior essence [to gender] that might be disclosed," with gender "a natural manifestation of sex or a cultural constant" (*Gender Trouble* xv, xxi). Likewise, Connell succinctly outlines the weaknesses of popular understandings of gender and gender relations ("Studying Men and Masculinity," *Masculinities*). Role theory, for example, which emphasizes gender roles and the performance of socially defined roles, like "father" or "police officer," does not account for issues of power or gender change across time and space.

Yet such popular understandings, terms, and values of gender remain culturally prominent, including in popular cinema, and so it remains important to address them on their own terms. Mark Gallagher, for example, observes that popular film aligns itself "with perceived gender norms and ideals" and popular understandings of the relation between masculinity and male biology, or "maleness," for commercial reasons (13). In a study of representational practices of masculinities in mainstream narrative American cinema, it is important to avoid exclusively employing any single theoretical paradigm, which would unduly force cultural representations to fit within a particular conception of gender. Mainstream cinematic representational practices are complex and often present an at times contradictory combination of popular and theoretical understandings of gender. Accordingly, while I predominantly draw on contemporary theorizations of gender, I also refer to popular understandings of masculinity where pertinent.

Dominant theoretical understandings of gender across cultural studies and the disciplines it draws on treat gender as nonbiological, fluid, relational, and plural. Connell advocates a relational understanding of gender ("Studying Men and Masculinity"). Masculinity is not internal but a social construction, built from a configuration of everyday, embodied practices. Rather than individual, it is built through "a structure of social relations" and "shared symbolism" (45). Masculinities do not exist in isolation and only come into existence when people act in relation to others; masculinities are defined, constructed, and performed socially. Masculinity is unstable and changes with time and place, across different periods and different cultures and geographies. It is also nondiscrete, related to and shaped by sexuality, cultural difference, race, and class, all of which come into existence in and through relation to one another. Connell observes that we should more properly understand masculinity in the plural—that is, as *masculinities*—not only in modern multicultural societies but also within particular cultural settings.

Gender's relationality is equally evident in discursive approaches to gender, which remain ascendant in contemporary cultural studies of popular media and cinema. Aligned with Judith Butler's seminal text *Gender Trouble*, gender is here conceived as "a set of discourses that are contested, accepted and resisted within networks, rather than binaries" (Tasker, "Soldiers' Stories" 215). Butler's theory of performativity further describes gender as constructed, performed, and embodied in the world, "manufactured through a sustained set of acts" (*Gender Trouble* xv). In *Bodies That Matter*, Butler asserts that performativity "is not a singular act for it is always a reiteration of a norm or set of norms" that "conceals or dissimulates the conventions of which it is a repetition" (xxi). For Butler, gender has no origin but is an effect of institutions, repeated acts, practices, and discourses (*Gender Trouble* xxxi). In this sense, repetition seeks to render the performance of gender *and* gender itself as natural, innate, and stable. This desire to fix gender explains the continued resonance of popular understandings of gender, especially in periods of profound social or institutional change and turmoil. At the same time, the effort required to do so often throws gender's constructedness into sharper relief.

Masculinity is persistently negotiated in relation to and interaction with other genders and is tied to notions of desire and power. Equally, a relatively seamless reiteration of performative norms is necessary to create a comprehensible subject—to and for others. To become what Connell terms a "meaningful body," gender performance is constrained by and must generally observe dominant gender expressions within a group or cultural context. Masculinities are dynamic, complex, and changeable, "in which we make ourselves—and are made" (Connell, "Studying Men and Masculinity" 46), as the "social world" equally "defines, positions, empowers and constrains" (43). This capacity to define, constrain, and police gender is reinforced by institutions, which privilege particular gender expressions. Likewise, Connell contends that while particular acts, described as "masculine" or "feminine," characterize individuals, such acts are also sustained by institutions such as the military ("Studying Men and Masculinity"). In this sense, for example, some masculinities are privileged while others are marginalized, even excluded, particularly when they do not match the dominant group in terms of class, ethnicity, religion, or race. Connell describes masculinities that are privileged as hegemonic—that is, normalized in positions of authority and dominance, and a socially reinforced ideal. Hegemonic masculinities are highly visible, and they subordinate alternative masculinities, femininities, and genders, which are invisible or marginalized in contrast.

Cinema Studies, Masculinities, and Genre

The high visibility of hegemonic masculinity is often echoed in scholarly research on representations of masculinity in American cinema. Such critical focus has importantly exposed the negative impacts of hegemonic masculinity and patriarchy on women. However, it also supports Connell's observation that there has been much less focus on practices of power between men, and between hegemonic and less honored masculinities, including ethnic and minority masculinities ("Studying Men and Masculinity"). Thus, in focusing on gender as relational, there is significant value in surveying the relations of

American hegemonic masculinity with its Others, monstrous, terrorist, and female, beyond reiterating its supposedly one-way and one-sided impact on each.

Jeffrey Dennis's valuable survey of the literature on representations of masculinity in popular culture finds relatively little academic interest in masculinity in popular American cinema until the early 1980s.[25] Scholarly interest in representations of masculinity, including in cinema, increased markedly only from the early 1990s. Dennis discovers significantly less focus on mainstream film, in contrast to more celebrated films, such as *Brokeback Mountain* (Lee 2005) and *Full Metal Jacket* (Kubrick 1987) (115). Even when masculinity studies explore particular genres, Dennis finds they predominantly focus on the "male action" genres. This is perhaps unsurprising, given the privileging of individualistic heroes in westerns and action movies and the male-dominated cohorts of war films. These tendencies skew scholarly focus onto the representation of dominant or hegemonic masculinities and can overlook the heterogeneity of performed masculinities, an abiding concern this book seeks to redress.

Popular cinema and genre films constitute an integral part of the cultural response to periods of perceived change or moments of crisis, and are widely considered to represent, diagnose, explore, and shape contemporary sociopolitical fears and anxieties about American national identity.[26] Yet an implicit critical distinction between "serious" cinema and popular-genre film remains, as if a film's sociocultural and political currency is muted by its adherence to popular genre conventions. In contrast, Claire Sisco King, writing about male sacrificial victim-heroes in Hollywood film post-9/11, asserts popular films "invit[e] new understandings of American experience" by virtue of their supposed "emptiness," in their capacity to displace and then explore 9/11's trauma (164–65). Such an outlook no longer surprises. Popular-genre film can be as—if not more—revelatory than supposedly "serious" film, uncovering the key terms and conditions of hegemony *because of*, rather than in spite of, its seeming simplicity or obviousness.

Although scholarship on terror, cinema, and genre post-9/11 is substantial and continues to grow, the absence of a sustained, concentrated focus on American cinematic representations of masculinity in experiences of terror across film genres—outside of individual chapters in edited collections—remains a cultural blind spot. Scholarship has predominantly concentrated on direct representations of the war on terror, despite their uniform commercial and critical failure, or documentary, especially about the war in Iraq. Even examinations of indirect or allegorical narrative films—which, as Terence McSweeney observes in his collection *American Cinema in the Shadow of 9/11*, remain rare—predominantly focus on spectacular cinematic evocations of the "real," such as 9/11 imagery or rhetoric.[27] This lack mandates a sustained multigenre analysis of representations of American masculinities in encounters with, and experiences of, terror in contemporary American popular and genre cinema.

The challenges of a multigenre study are not insignificant, the danger of appearing overly schematic in outlining each (sub)genre's characteristics and cultural functions being most obvious. Analyzing a single genre may be more conventional and straightforward, yet a multigenre analysis can trace gendered responses to (perceived) terror threats in American cinema post-9/11 *within and across* genres.[28] While few popular narrative films directly represented the events of 9/11, its impact has been pervasive; American cinema constituted an important part of the cultural response to the attacks of 9/11 and the ensuing war on terror.[29] Hollywood cinema genre and gender codes—from disaster, science fiction, horror, westerns, and action—were repeatedly invoked in the mediated construction of 9/11, its subsequent interpretation, and the design and conduct of the war on terror. Given the immediate and pervasive configuration of 9/11 and the war on terror via Hollywood genre and cinematic heroism, this book examines the representation and presumed recuperation of American masculinities in crisis via close textual analyses of a diverse set of American narrative films and genres that offer a mix of direct, indirect, and allegorical representations and reimaginings of 9/11 and the war on terror.

Genres do not have fixed, identifiable boundaries but are fluid and overlapping. Rather than being designated by distinguishing characteristics or categories or a particular set of films, they cater diversely to assorted groups, particular places, and specific times. As David Bordwell and Kristin Thompson separately observe, Hollywood cinema has always exhibited a hybridity of sorts, mixing multiple and various genre elements. Rick Altman further argues that genres "serve diverse groups diversely" and "multiple conflicting audiences," from local and global audiences to producers and directors, critics and scholars (207–8). Mark Jancovich reminds us that genre designation is historically and socially specific, more often a matter of collective and commonsense consensus and, as such, is liable to change and shift over time. The particular social context in which texts are produced and received inevitably emphasizes certain generic tendencies and features. For example, science fiction creatures and monstrous bodies are also historically associated with horror film, particularly in 1950s Cold War giant-creature and invasion films and during a broader mixing of genres in the 1980s. There remains a certain generic legibility across time, space, and cultures, with designations also shaped by generic traditions. These traditions guide expectations that audiences and producers have of particular plotlines, narrative structures, and endings, but they also spotlight genre shifts. In light of Janet Staiger's observation that Hollywood films have never been "pure" or easily arranged into categories (6),

I discuss key films across a variety of (sub)genres, often examining them in relation to less obvious genres or generic characteristics to examine whether threatened American masculinities are redeemed and reinstalled following the violent incursion of a "terror-Other."

This book adopts a resolutely *contextual* approach to textual analysis, which remains the dominant approach in film studies. This approach builds on that of the media studies researcher Alan McKee, emphasizing the sociocultural, political, and cinematic conditions—including narrative, form (genre and style), historical, and industrial—that shape the production and reception of these films. Textual analysis provides cogent interpretations of texts, including their relation to broader cultural contexts and the particular genre codes used to generate meaning, to investigate the construction, meaning, and social significance both within and across texts. Miller and Kraidy further write that textual analysis offers an explicit consideration of "what happens in media texts and what happens to them as they travel" (145), as meaning is "remade again and again by institutions, discourses, and practices of distribution and reception" (152). Given this perspective, and because the interpretive nature of textual analysis prescribes numerous possible valid interpretations of a text (and equally discounts many), an explicit consideration of context anchors analysis and permits assertions about wider cultural impact and reception. This mandates detailing popular critical reception to place the films within the cultural context of their theatrical release so as to somewhat ameliorate our growing historical distance from 9/11.[30]

The Approach

This book explicitly examines whether and how post-9/11 Hollywood cinema seeks to remasculinize men in crisis encounters with terror via formal and narrational strategies of containment. Writing about the prevalent commercial failure of Hollywood's depiction of the war on terror, Garrett Stewart suggests it is "too shapeless for plot . . . [or] finding narrative drive or closure" (171). Simply narrativizing 9/11 earns a measure of control, making what exceeded comprehension *comprehensible* by imposing a beginning, middle, and end. Deploying genre tropes and fulfilling genre expectations arguably also overcome supposed shapelessness and excessiveness by providing familiar structures and reducing complexities.[31] Such strategies of containment, in some sense paralleling Cold War discursive efforts identified by Alan Nadel, seek to create space for the recuperation and remasculinization of threatened American masculinities. The films examined in this book—more mainstream and less overtly "political" than those Stewart discusses—seek to manage the chaotic threat of terror by variously containing (the) spectacle of 9/11, the irresolution of the war on terror, and the ongoing threat of terror. The films arguably do so by controlling or withholding otherwise overwhelming cinematic spectacle—rather than unabashedly celebrating it—and by adhering to conventional narrative structure and genre conventions, including gender codes, and film style.

Less heralded articulations of fractured, unstable masculinities in Hollywood film, beyond typical claims about the rejuvenation of 1980s action star masculinity or strong fathers, importantly inform the analysis of post-9/11 cinematic masculinities throughout the book. Hollywood cinema has reflected often on the impacts of social and economic changes on gender relations—and masculinities in particular. For example, Mark Gallagher detects how film noir and "women's pictures" each emphasize damaged or compromised masculinities in the 1950s (8). This complexity is even apparent in westerns post–World War II, popularly considered to communicate ideal, stable, and coherent ideas of American masculinity.[32] Kaja Silverman, writing about American film masculinities from a feminist psychoanalytic perspective, influentially identifies ambivalent, fractured, and unstable masculinities "at the margins" of post–World War II Hollywood war movies and film noir—popular cultural outliers in a sense. The focus on masculinities in crisis intensifies across 1960s and 1970s American film. Widespread protest from the mid-1960s and military defeat in the Vietnam War highlighted American (and masculine) vulnerability at home and abroad, and cinema reflected on this condition by emphasizing (white) masochism, suffering, and sacrifice. For example, Christopher Durham links key changes in male gender identities in westerns—including their relative decline—to this sociopolitical and cultural turmoil. Adilifu Nama also identifies representations of masculinity under threat in 1960s science fiction, with urban "racial paranoia" augmenting the perception that white masculinity and institutions were "under attack." Nama contends this foreshadowed "the narcissistic self-pity of white male martyrdom . . . that became a signature feature" in post-Vietnam American films (51). Gallagher, examining constructions of active masculinities in popular American action film and literature since the 1960s, argues that cinematic representations of "male action" compensate for real-world threats to masculinity in the workplace and the domestic sphere. Prominent male action stars in the 1970s, such as Charlton Heston, Steve McQueen, and Lee Marvin, are presented as conflicted but conventionally tough. Yet in the wake of the social unrest of the 1960s, they also reveal the work required "to maintain a functional male identity" (Gallagher 10). This visible labor seeks to recenter (white) masculinity through the male capacity to endure professional *as well as* (the spectacle of) bodily suffering. American cinema in the 1970s, however, registers the beginning of a cultural backlash, overturning the endured suffering of wounded, humiliated (white) American males through climactic violent remasculinization. This backlash includes a cinematic focus on the "sensitive male" and his final compelled (*and* desired) descent into "savagery," a development that the esteemed critic Dave Kehr ("Descending into a State of Nature") links to the moral effects of Vietnam. Violent action is more than a genre-typical masculine response to threat and victimization; it is deemed to be necessary.

This book, finally, explicitly responds to Raewyn Connell's long-standing call for greater and concerted focus on relations of power between men and masculinities ("Studying Men and Masculinity"). In concentrating on marginalized and Othered—as well as hegemonic— masculinities, I offer a nuanced revaluation of dominant arguments about the representation of masculinities in post-9/11 American cinema. The masculine Other's absence or weak characterization is typically considered to annihilate difference and preserve hegemony and dominance, falling back on caricatured and outdated tropes of cinematic villainy from 1950s science fiction to 1990s action films. Rather, I consider whether this connotes an unwillingness or inability to meaningfully grapple with radical and frightening difference, both highlighting the tendency for hegemonic masculinities to (re)establish their dominance at the expense of others and critiquing their capacity to do so. By alternately "drilling down" into and "pulling back" out from films all too often only superficially analyzed, I seek to avoid the inclination to reinstate hegemony and dominance analytically. More than simply considering meaning as polysemic and open-ended, I am avowedly interested in deconstructing and decentering gender and institutional power structures. Rather than presuming the power of hegemonic masculinities—typically white and male—over other genders, I especially interrogate dominant scholarly claims that post-9/11 American film represented and recuperated so-called traditional masculinities at the expense of monstrous Others, Orientalized males, and maligned women.

The Films

The broader scope of a multigenre analysis does necessitate delimiting the set of core films I examine. For this reason, I focus on films that directly depict encounters with "terror threats" against articulations of "America." This thematic focus largely shapes the concentration on films released between 2005 and 2010, at the bloody height of the conflicts in Afghanistan and Iraq. It also broadly concurs with Robert Cettl's analytical filmography of terror cinema post-9/11. Although focused on direct representations of terrorism, Cettl observes that—much as during the Vietnam War—American cinema largely avoided addressing 9/11 and the war on terror before a wave of "terrorist films" from 2006 and across the final years of the Bush administration. I concentrate on representational practices of gender in what I term "terror threat" films, exploring how and whether threatened American masculinities are recuperated and restored in these mainstream narrative films after the violent incursion of a terror-Other. These films diversely feature the 9/11 attackers, giant monsters, home invaders, vampire-zombies, imperialist aliens, Palestinian terrorists, and fictionalized "Arab/Muslim" terror masterminds. In each, the terror-Other is not only inhuman but monstrous, positioning terrorists as monsters and monsters as terrorists. The films also specifically represent terror attacks against ideas or notions of "America," whether as a community or nation or ideology, irrespective of particular geographical location.

These films represent a collection, rather than a cycle, of seemingly disparate films, but all variously represent encounters and experiences of terror. Specifically examining gendered experiences of terror, the book's chapters progressively address various temporal and spatial-geographical aspects of the *initial* encounter with, or *ongoing* experience of, terror, investigating the experience of terror both as an event and as a lived state. Structurally, each chapter moves progressively outward from 9/11, New York, and "Ground Zero" and onto the wider war on terror, isolated outposts, and articulations of America abroad. Although focused on specific key texts, the analysis importantly contextualizes the "terror threat" films in relation to American film history, genre, and gender representational practices during earlier periods of American national instability and turmoil. This approach contributes to concerted efforts (see McSweeney; Joyce) to critique the unquestioned deployment of "9/11 changed everything." Such framing, all too often echoed in film criticism, erroneously (and conveniently) constructs the attacks—and cinema's responses to them—as not only unprecedented but marking a decisive break from "pre-9/11" politics and culture. This book consciously disrupts ahistorical characterizations of the attacks and their impact in popular cinema.

Chapter 1 examines direct representations of the immediate experience of 9/11, of living within or *inside* a terror event. I concentrate on how *World Trade Center* (Stone 2006), a post-9/11 disaster film with elements of melodrama, represents the terror event and Ground Zero. I also touch on the imagined experience aboard the ill-fated United Flight 93 in *United 93* (Greengrass 2006) and the ambivalent association of male characters with Ground Zero and the Twin Towers in Spike Lee's *25th Hour* (2002).[33] *World Trade Center* seemingly satisfies critical assumptions about Hollywood masculinities: it formally and narratively works to restore normative masculinity through the restitution of male agency and the return to the home *and* through the remasculinization and remilitarization of uniformed masculinity (read: national identity). I particularly examine tensions between private and professional aspects of male identity via the father–police officer through the wearing of a "protective" uniform. An idea of work runs throughout the films, with the destabilization or loss of professional capacity, caused by terror, repeatedly threatening masculine identity. In going *inside* terror, these films seek to contain it. Here I examine an abrupt shift in midfilm subgeneric register from "disaster epic" to the "mine accident" movie. This shift provides a space for the symbolic restoration of the trapped men as husband-fathers and into the home, despite its pejorative gendering as feminine, confined, and fearful in the film. This, however, is undercut by concurrent *returns* to a uniformed protective role by rescuer-characters that seek to remasculinize normative American manhood (and American national identity). Examining the significance of the restitution of uniformed-protective masculinity through masquerade, the chapter finally considers how these tenuous recoveries and remasculinizations are irrevocably overwhelmed by a series of yawning absences, including that of the wholly unspecified and unrepresented terror-Other.

Moving from disaster film to science fiction–horror, chapter 2 concentrates on experiences of living *through* a terror event and how the violent eruption of terror overwhelms *less-than-ordinary* nonprofessional everymen. *Cloverfield*'s (Reeves 2008) amateur-footage aesthetic indirectly restages the mediation—and terror—of 9/11 via an innovative mix of a giant monster movie recast through realist horror. Locking the audience into its characters' highly mediated but inherently limited victim-perspective, absent both the reassuring omniscient camera and an "expert" protagonist, foregrounds restricted vision and limited knowledge. From the beginning, the power of looking through the camera and filming others is undermined by female characters who repeatedly "unman" the filming everymen, contesting the gaze of the male look and the/his camera. The chapter also explores the shame and emasculation of the overcivilized male in the home invasion horror film *The Strangers* (Bertino 2008) and the earned redemption of the working-class everyman in *War of the Worlds* (Spielberg 2005).[34] Provocatively, the "unmanning" of these everymen ostensibly invites or incites terror. Unable to counter the monstrous threat, the everyman's response to terror in *Cloverfield* must be displaced onto a heroic-redemptive quest, specifically the rescue of a prostrate "damsel in distress." The chapter also centrally explores notions of containment. The redemptive quest *Cloverfield* imposes a comprehensible narrative response and generic structure onto an otherwise *too large, too excessive* experience. However, confined to the limited and unsteady victim-perspective, and absent monster point-of-view shots, the giant monster, the film's massive terror-Other, exceeds the everyman's capacity to (visually) "capture" and "know" it and so remains frighteningly unknowable to the doomed male protagonists—and the audience. The excessive, elusive monster and limited camera alike fatally compromise the *already* disempowered everyman's quest to remasculinize, connoting his enduring vulnerability and inevitable doom. The film's divergences from genre conventions, the characteristics of the handheld camera, the unknowable and violently disruptive giant monster's undiminished Otherness, and the equally disruptive role of seemingly maligned females inevitably frustrate the hero's remasculinization—and finally identify him as the monstrous figure that requires annihilation.

Chapter 3 focuses on allegorical representations of living *with* terror—permanent and pervasive—after large-scale catastrophe, living in an unrelenting state of insecurity and vulnerability. The chapter primarily examines *I Am Legend* (Lawrence 2007), a postapocalyptic science fiction film (with horror elements), in sustained relation to both an earlier adaptation of its source novel, *The Omega Man* (Sagal 1971), and a touchstone text, *The World, the Flesh and the Devil* (MacDougall 1959), to contest dominant critical opinion about whether the film ultimately figures masculine and paternal redemption.[35] The three films each deploy their iconic male stars and the postapocalypse to represent American (and male) anxieties about race, class, and gender in periods of national instability and flux. In *I Am Legend*, paternal failure, embodied by the "muscular" military scientist in charge of the failed attempt to avert apocalyptic plague, is entwined with the breakdown of civil society. *I Am Legend* genders the apocalypse, establishing female culpability and repeatedly feminizing its "final man" in the succeeding postapocalyptic terror. It also seemingly assuages this professional-paternal "protective" guilt through redemptive male sacrifice that privileges militarized masculinity and a Christological worldview and recovers institutional masculinities as foundational in the nostalgic postapocalyptic restoration of America in a survivors' colony. The chapter examines how females are ultimately figured as redeemers and make male redemption *possible*—they symbolically and literally carry the cure—and the impossibility of remasculinization against the unsettling hybrid indeterminacy of the vampire-zombie terror-Other. In stark contrast to previous readings of the film, *I Am Legend* irrevocably undermines sacrificial paternal redemption in the hero's *becoming* America's most monstrous terror-Other, the suicide bomber.

Chapter 4 examines imaginings of the war on terror, the nation's reaction to 9/11, and the impacts of vengeance on male redemption. The chapter primarily explores the depiction of a response to coordinated terror attacks on an isolated American outpost in Saudi Arabia in the action-thriller *The Kingdom* (Berg 2007). The film initially reimagines the response to 9/11 as a measured forensic procedural. Yet American masculine identity is destabilized first by being ineffectually confined during the terror attacks, and second by subsequent curbs on American professional agency and mobility in an unwelcoming foreign environment, in which space is structured much like a frontier western. The film counters the twinned undermining of masculine identity and American sovereignty through a jarring genre shift in its final act to an over-the-top action-war revenge fantasy shoot-out. The abrupt return to arms and retributive destruction of the reviled Orientalized terror-Other mastermind nominally reinstitutes professional agency, reembodies militarized masculinity, and (re-)Americanizes foreign space. Violent revenge seemingly revises the shame of 9/11—and the irresolution of the war on terror—but *The Kingdom*'s uncertain conclusion recalls the equally ambivalent narrative coda in John Ford's cavalry western *Fort Apache* (1948). Female characters in *The Kingdom* and *Zero Dark Thirty* (Bigelow 2012) are incorporated into (female) military masculinity, but in each film, violent retribution results in melancholy rather than triumph.[36] Supposedly cathartic violent retribution in *The Kingdom* and *Munich* (Spielberg 2005) likewise extends the terror threat through blowback and fails to reinvigorate protective professional-paternal masculinity corroded by not only acting like, but being the same as, America's dark mirror, the monstrous terrorist.

The book closes with a conclusion discussing the seeming eradication of anxieties about paternal-military failings and redemption of American males *performing* protective roles in recent Hollywood film. *12 Strong* (Fuglsig 2018) superficially marks the overcoming and erasure of the sense of failure post-9/11 and the irresolution of the war on terror, especially in its obsessive emphasis on male promises of return.[37] The film's coda depicts the supposedly triumphant return of soldier-father heroes, paragons of idealized American masculinity, to the home. However, anxieties about paternal-protective failings persist in structural and narrative incoherences that invert the trope of the hero's homecoming, confirming just how pervasive and enduring this "gender trouble" remains in American cinema post-9/11.

1

"SHIELDING US FROM WHAT WE ARE NOT YET READY TO SEE"

The Uniformed Hero as Victim and in Masquerade

Oliver Stone's *World Trade Center* (2006) purports to be a film about revelation—both biblical and prosaic—unveiling, seeking truth, and overcoming. The attacks of 9/11 mark a radically refigured state of affairs for America and a new threat, but in *World Trade Center* they also reveal the spirit of American perseverance, community, and faith in response. The survival and rescue of the two Port Authority Police Department officers, John McLoughlin and Will Jimeno, from the ruins of Ground Zero equally represent a triumph. Yet perhaps Dave Karnes, an accountant who dons his former Marine Corps uniform to search for survivors and locates the trapped men, better summates the film's function. Upon seeing the thick cloud of smoke, ash, and debris that shrouds the rubble of the fallen Twin Towers, Karnes offers the transcendental declaration: "It's like God put up a curtain of smoke, shielding us from what we are not yet ready to see." Rather than revelation, *World Trade Center* attempts to shield audiences, formally and narratively, from the horror of attacks already over-represented in popular media and from their profound impacts on American national identity, uniformed masculinity, fathers, and the home.

Released five years after 9/11, the post-9/11 disaster film recounts the true story of the entrapment, survival, and rescue of Staff Sergeant McLoughlin (Nicolas Cage) and rookie Jimeno (Michael Peña), trapped in the collapse of the Twin Towers on 9/11.[1] After potential rescuers become victims after their entrapment in the first tower's collapse, *World Trade Center* introduces Karnes (Michael Shannon), who is based on a real-life participant. Karnes first watches news of the attacks at work in Connecticut, before visiting his church to seek guidance. The first shot shows a Bible, open to the book of Revelation to John (or Apocalypse), positioning the attacks as a time of tribulation for citizen and nation alike. In light of Revelation's significance, though, they likewise represent a revealing or unveiling and foreshadow a final victory and ultimate overcoming.

Spectacle is a long-standing, pervasive feature of the disaster genre, and the cinematic representation of disaster has reveled in the fantastical destruction of key American architectural sites, chief among them New York.[2] It also holds a key function in *World Trade Center* in the remasculinization of the trapped men. After 9/11, such unabandoned pleasure in spectacle was criticized because the previous hollowness of such spectacles was now *saturated* with meaning as a consequence of real destruction and terror. Given the well-documented critical and societal anxieties about Hollywood's proposed representation of 9/11, it is unsurprising that both *World Trade Center* and Paul Greengrass's *United 93* (2006) effectively *go inside* the terror event—inside the World Trade Center and Flight 93—to explore the immediate experience of 9/11. In this sense, the relative "unseen-ness," as Muntean describes it (55), of the respective subject matter in both films is telling, each electing to focus on "previously obscured and private details." While films that directly depict 9/11 both represent *and* respond—in the attempt to articulate and comprehend—they are also in part impotent and overwhelmed by the impossible task of representing the scale of the actual and symbolic loss that 9/11 represented. *World Trade Center* may be a direct representation of 9/11 but, unable to fully represent the *unrepresentable*, it is as defined by indirectness as are allegorical representations. In representing the experience inside what would become Ground Zero, *World Trade Center* offers a hyperlocalized account of what was largely unseen.[3]

These first post-9/11 Hollywood "imaginations of disaster" personalized the tragedy *and* avoided spectacle by primarily confining experience to the subjective, limited perspectives of characters (Keane). This approximated the mediated experience of 9/11 and the horrific, only partial experience of real disaster and terror, and stands in stark contrast to typical cinematic depictions of disaster. Compounding this, although the actual event of 9/11 is representable at some level, it seemed virtually unrepresentable cinematically for a number of reasons. First, Muntean observes that a sense of mastery or control over an event as massive and excessive as 9/11 is impossible (55). Second, the attacks seemed unrepresentable both because of the horrific invisibility or underrepresentation of most of the victims (before they could be memorialized), and because the attacks were in some sense already *overrepresented* as spectacle—rendering any fictional cinematic representation gratuitous. Perhaps for this reason, explicit references and clear evocations of 9/11 and imagery of the war on terror were roundly criticized, deemed unnecessary, distressing, and exploitative. In going *inside* terror and controlling cinematic spectacle—with all non-computer-generated imagery of 9/11 confined within TV screens—*World Trade Center* seeks to contain terror. This also offers a space for the trapped men to renegotiate their uniformed masculinity and symbolically restore them as husband-fathers to the (head of the) home—whose preattack neglect as husband is implied to be symptomatic of the American home(land)'s vulnerability. In this sense, the attacks are represented as catalytic rather than cataclysmic, and the men's wounding and entrapment necessary to reverse threatened male status and power, restore paternal authority to the home, and inspire the reconstruction of a reinvigorated America. Yet *World Trade Center* finally admits the failure of this project, clearly signaled in the pejorative gendering of space—Ground Zero is a masculinized space of search and recovery, and the home feminine, confined, and fearful—and in the film's need to concurrently stage numerous idealized returns to uniform.

Uniform(ed) Masculinity: Performance and the Schism between Wearer and Uniform

Fashion scholars predominantly posit a close relationship between what individuals wear, identity, and the communication of ideal masculine attributes. According to Jennifer Craik, uniforms serve as shorthand signifiers of the identity, characteristics, and role of the wearer and afford a "visible lexicon of [valued] social characteristics, skills, attitudes, and habits" ("The Cultural Politics of the Uniform" 132). Perhaps consequently, uniforms play a dominant role in defining and communicating modes of masculinity, with normative masculine roles and attributes—activity, competence, capability, and strength—typically inscribed in (certain types of) uniforms. Craik argues the spectacle of the uniform and its *display* of masculine attributes—both to the self and for others—combine in the performance of masculinity itself, particularly for uniforms emblematic of "doing" or action. Meaning resides primarily not in the body and what it does but in how it appears to others, appropriating power and authority from the uniform to the wearer. From the outset, *World Trade Center* intimately aligns men and masculinity with wearing a uniform and performing a protective role. Yet the film refigures Godfrey and Hamad's identification of "protective" masculinity—which emblematizes professional-paternal authority embodied in *former* policing or covert protective services—via its *uniformed* articulation. Additionally, masculine identity in *World Trade Center* subordinates the paternal within the professional in the wearing of uniforms and performance of a protective role. Protective uniforms are routinely portrayed as representative of institutional or national identity in narrative cinema—admittedly, not always for good.

Police and military uniforms connote collective strength, social status and authority, reliability, self-control, and commitment. Uniforms afford certainty about "the idea of identity sustained" by and through the uniform (Calefato 196). *World Trade Center*'s uniformed males thus appropriate, communicate, and reinforce the power and authority associated with their uniform *and* also offer reassurance to others. Uniforms erase markers of difference, literally making wearers the same. Yet in the context of 9/11 and the war on terror, uniforms also represent a positive marker *of difference*, related to being identifiable, in opposition to the treacherously hidden (and nonuniformed) terror-Other. Uniforms in *World Trade Center* make visible the performance of masculinity but also seek to naturalize or conceal it in rendering it *uniform*. Uniformed masculinity in *World Trade Center* is also repeatedly associated with paternal roles and attitudes, somewhat unusual given that the 9/11 attacks did not especially directly involve children on the day. This alignment of uniformed identity with a paternal bearing is associated with fellow officers when McLoughlin, standing behind reception at the Port Authority, raises his head from his morning reports and quietly observes another officer on bended knee, comforting a lost young girl.[4] A paternal role is further embedded within uniformed masculinity when, after being informed by an injured businessman that children are in the buildings, McLoughlin tells Jimeno, "Don't worry, they got them out." In *World Trade Center*, protective masculinity is both uniformed and paternal.

The conflation of uniform and wearer is variously privileged and problematized in *World Trade Center*, which aligns masculine identity with the attributes inscribed in uniforms. The film explicitly identifies McLoughlin with his uniform, the man possessing the attributes and modes of behavior that his uniform (and protective role) connotes. After the first plane hits Tower One, the PAPD officers are called back from their foot patrols to the Port Authority, and a team is chosen to assist in the tower's precautionary evacuation. McLoughlin is readily figured as highly competent and knowledgeable about the WTC complex, having worked at the towers when they were bombed in 1993 and consequently redesigning its safety and emergency protocols ("*World Trade Center* Production Notes"). Uniforms communicate identity but are equally transformative—and mark a sort of *becoming*. The identity of the younger PAPD officers in McLoughlin's unit, including Jimeno, is swiftly tied—for themselves and the audience—to their uniformed persona: their names only given (stamped on their lockers) *immediately after* they are in uniform and have figuratively "put on" their identity (figs. 1.1–1.2). Their locker-room banter also ceases as each adopts the uniform, as if marking a (performative) transformation from civilian-boy to police officer–man.

Figure 1.1. The rookie, Will Jimeno, "puts on" his identity.

Figure 1.2. Jimeno is only named after "putting on" the uniform.

Yet these same men hesitate when McLoughlin asks for a small group of volunteers before Jimeno, a rookie, volunteers. Two others—Rodrigues and Pezzulo—follow, moving to the front of the team. On entering the buildings, McLoughlin leads the team around the complex, collecting the necessary rescue equipment and breathing apparatuses before attempting to ascend Tower One: "We won't save anyone if we can't breathe." The scene showcases mobility and aligns it with professional and masculine identity.[5] In *World Trade Center*, the uniform incongruently mirrors the self—men *are* their uniformed identity—but equally *makes them* who they are. While the tension is not logically inconsistent, it does perhaps explain the film's ambivalence about the relation of men, masculinity, and uniforms—mirroring an unspoken tension evident in scholarship on uniforms and identity. The officers identify themselves with—and as—their profession, with its ideals and obligations embodied by *and* enacted through their uniforms. They represent *and* are represented by their uniforms. Yet the film also signals how putting on a uniform changes each man, becoming someone different and becoming linked to something greater. This tension between compulsion and choice, reflection and transformation, suggests a schism between uniform and wearer—and a gulf between the uniformed and nonuniformed self.

The uniformed persona is privileged and presented as ideal, but it also cloaks. While McLoughlin's acknowledged emotional (and physical) isolation is characteristic of stoic conventional masculinity, it also implies how he uses his uniform to shield himself (from others). Uniforms also repress or suppress (personal) characteristics discordant with their connoted ideals. In this sense, uniforms arguably offer a more complex relation of the body and masculinity. More than communicating the trained body and representing national idea(l)s, uniforms also cover and compensate for the wearer's individual failings or vulnerabilities.[6] "Protective" uniforms, more than merely making visible the performance of masculine ideals, can also conceal or repress wearer attributes and behaviors that contradict connoted ideals of the uniform and normative masculinity. While Craik claims that "dressing up" prefigures what lies underneath, intimately correlating identity and uniform, she acknowledges potential discrepancies between the gendered uniform and the gendered wearer/body. This ostensibly admits unremitting tensions between (the experience of) wearing a protective uniform and its ideal meanings and between the appearance and performance of protective uniformed masculinity. Early in *World Trade Center*, running toward the unfolding catastrophe and horror, McLoughlin is discernibly reluctant to enter the buildings but proceeds nonetheless. He shuffles toward the buildings, almost sidelong, repeatedly glancing backward to the space of relative safety, but resisting the desire to return in the direction in which civilians flee. A reverse shot, which reveals the look on his face concealed from the trailing volunteer officers, confirms his uncertainty and rising fear. McLoughlin's reluctance highlights the persistent discrepancy between uniform and man, the public-professional ideal versus the personal actuality. His continued procession toward the buildings shows how the obligations of the uniform shape certain actions and behavior, inducing him to endure, but his hesitance signals the excessiveness of events and the unrelieved tension between wearer and uniform.

Masochistic Masculinity as Insufficiency:
Entrapment, Emasculation, and Wounding

When he is finally ready to ascend, Tower Two begins to collapse. McLoughlin surveys the impending civilian victims in the background but is merely able to scream at his officers to run for the elevator shaft before the group is caught in the collapse. McLoughlin's knowledge and competence save his men, but the collapse renders his meticulous collection of rescue and breathing equipment redundant; competence becomes impotence. The collapse, like any traumatic event, "thwart[s] initiative and overwhelm[s] individual competence" (qtd. in Ozcan 211); no matter how knowledgeable and resourceful he is, McLoughlin's actions cannot affect the disaster. While his knowledge foregrounds McLoughlin *as* a hero, he is a hero *overwhelmed*, as events quickly exceed his ability to respond. The limits of McLoughlin's competence and knowledge—or, rather, how events will exceed them—are foreshadowed even before the PAPD officers arrive at the site, as McLoughlin paradoxically admits: "There is no plan. We planned for everything . . . but not this. Not something this big." The PAPD officers' impotence and impending immobility are immediately prefigured when they first disembark at the WTC complex. The horrifying sight of a body falling from the burning towers (the "falling man") foreshadows the trapped men's later fall. This depiction of fundamental vulnerability shows how it necessarily "implicates the subject of representation and the viewer" (Fitzpatrick 85)—both the officers and the audience—rendering the viewer speechless and helpless, despite wishing to act.[7] The officers debate their capacity to at least try, however futilely, to help people trapped in the towers, but they remain rooted to the spot until McLoughlin returns; their helplessness is rendered as paralysis.

Impotence becomes immobility as McLoughlin returns to consciousness after the tumult of the collapse, blinding light, and an abrupt cut to black. McLoughlin asks his men to sound out. Rodrigues and Chris, a former colleague of McLoughlin's who joins the group before the collapse, do not answer the men's plaintive pleas: "They're gone," Jimeno acknowledges.[8] With both McLoughlin and Jimeno pinned under debris, mobility is no longer professionally privileged for the surviving officers. Public-professional protective masculinity is threatened by the collapse of the Twin Towers and subsequent entrapment inside the wreckage of Ground Zero, as professional capacity is overwhelmed and masculine mobility erased. McLoughlin later acknowledges this perceived impotence—"What good did we do?"—the past tense reflecting the end of his policing-rescue role.

Professional-masculine identity characterized by inaction and impotence in their rescue effort is reinforced after the collapse via the men's immobility.

Uniformed masculinity in *World Trade Center* emblematizes the state of the nation throughout the day's attack, the men's entrapment inside the wreckage of Ground Zero—and the destabilization of normative masculinity—mirroring America's similar fall (into darkness). If uniformed masculinity is first defined through activity, as competent and capable, it is destabilized by the men's entrapment. The officers are emasculated when they are immobilized and incapacitated in the collapse and no longer able to sufficiently *perform* or *embody* the uniformed masculinity through which their identity is constituted.[9] The officers' failure to rescue anyone in the towers—even to ascend a single level in the building before the first collapse—casts the alignment of normative masculinity and a uniformed, protective role into question. The towers' collapse and the officers' consequent entrapment showcase male vulnerability, over capability, in the face of catastrophe. The officers' protective role flounders as disaster heroes *become* victims. In this sense, the uniform cannot cloak—or shield—individual insufficiency or the perceived vulnerability of normative masculinity. This vulnerability is mostly figured via the loss of control, highlighted in their entrapment and their initially helpless, narrow experience of the collapses, in cruel juxtaposition with the sense of control earlier connoted by their uniforms. The *appearance* of control is overawed, exposing the fragility and vulnerability of masculine-uniformed performance. While *World Trade Center* certainly implies that insufficiency is human and understandable, given the overwhelming nature of 9/11, it is nonetheless discomfiting.

Trapped and isolated, McLoughlin's and Jimeno's survival is initially experienced as suffering and punishment. Aligned with Sally Robinson, *World Trade Center* becomes a "masochistic narrative," figured through the trapped men's wounded bodies and *as* a loss of control, persistently highlighted in their passivity, limited vision, and restricted knowledge in the "hole"—the space within the collapse where they are trapped.[10] With the body the site of masculine performance and identity, notions of masochism are intimately tied to the spectacle of the visible, wounded body—the body and its pain fetishized for others. Following Gaylyn Studlar and Silverman, Robinson argues masochism is predicated on deferred resolution and release, theatricality and display. Masochistic narratives prominently feature the display of male wounds to evidence, "manage and/or heal the threats to a normativity under siege" through physically and emotionally wounded bodies (5). Echoing Robinson, *World Trade Center* offers a "language of crisis" through a vocabulary of blockage and release.[11] Uniformed masculinity in the film is, quite conventionally, defined by inexpressivity and the repression of speech and emotions; as McLoughlin observes, "I don't smile a lot," so "people don't like me." This blockage is literalized in the trapped men's immobility and incapacitation. The collapse of the second tower sends a fiery shower of rock into the "hole," crushing McLoughlin's legs and burning Jimeno. Both men scream repeatedly, yell at each other, and weep—their screams pointedly hysterical in the invisibility of their physical wounds. Having lost control not only of the rescue effort but *of themselves*, they (tear)fully and irrevocably shed their uniformed identity. McLoughlin's repeated screams symbolize the anguish that accompanies the destabilizing of his masculine-professional identity, the hysteria also a moment of release, as the symbolic blockages that each man's uniformed identity has both reinforced and concealed are painfully abandoned.

Their scream-punctuated "release" is also liberating and facilitates a reconstruction of masculine identity that eschews the uniform. Indeed, their entrapment and wounding compel the two officers to talk with each other for the first time *as* men, about their nonuniformed identity, family, and emotions. In concealing their wounded bodies under rubble, hidden from their families and colleagues—*and* the audience—*World Trade Center* partially confounds notions that masochism "must be made *visible*" and tied to the spectacle of the wounded body (Robinson 13, emphasis in original). Far from "displaying their wounds," the men can only reconstruct their damaged masculinity, previously predicated on notions of display through the uniform, in the concealment of the hole, *shielded by* darkness and rubble. The hole, the site of emasculation and incapacitation, here becomes paradoxically vital for the men's redefinition of their masculine identity. Rather than abject, it becomes a productive space, functioning as a boundary between masculine/feminine and public/private. The hole, which Stone describes as womb-like (Jaafar), is a feminine space that facilitates the men's symbolic rebirth, affording the men the psychological and emotional space and time required to confront the challenge to their uniformed-masculine identity. The hole as a contained space provisionally dislocates the trapped men from the chaos, fear, and horrific consequences of the attacks. The hole places distressing limits on perspective and knowledge, echoed in McLoughlin's repeated screams of "I don't know" as the attacks undermine his conception of self. Yet these limits on knowledge also shield McLoughlin and Jimeno from the site/sight of their professional failure as would-be rescuers cum victims. The hole is a productive space precisely *because* it conceals, including by concealing the sheer horror and magnitude of the attacks in withholding the site/sight of the building collapses from the men; Jimeno will even ask his rescuers where the buildings have gone after he is disinterred.

United 93 and the Ambivalence of Accurately Representing 9/11

Although discussing *United 93* as a Hollywood film is arguable—given its British director, lack of stars, and cinema verité aesthetic—John W. Jordan and Stephen Prince observe that the film was predominantly reviewed as a Hollywood production, possibly because it addressed a recent and traumatic American story. Jordan's review of *United 93*'s initial critical reception finds that commentators and filmgoers were skeptical of Hollywood's capacity to represent 9/11 accurately and authentically, without distorting the national trauma for dramatic purposes or exploiting it for commercial profit. Yet equally—and ambivalently—many commentators also "agreed that the cultural memory of 9/11 would be incomplete until" Hollywood responded (Jordan 205). Nonetheless commentators debated American audiences' preparedness.[12] In particular, cinema's singular capacity to enlarge and make spectacular via projection seemed to be reviewers' chief concern, fearing that it would enshrine and enlarge the day's original horror. The few who did consider Hollywood capable of "memorializing" the day attested that doing so would require a film to transcend or defer typical Hollywood approaches to the "imagination of disaster" (Jordan).

United 93 equally possessed the advantage of not representing events primarily and already known via their (tele)visual mediation, another example of *going inside* the terror event. Yet in *United 93* the most iconic moments of destruction are similarly contained, only shown on TV screens or as blips on air traffic monitors, confining the spectacle of terror to small screens and abstract representation. Yet television screens and monitors also exemplify the passivity of the people watching (especially in positions of authority), and an impotence horrifyingly extended to government, police, and the military. For example, the air traffic controllers and military observers in *United 93*—and the military and government in *Lions for Lambs* (Redford 2007), who witness the deaths of two soldiers stranded in Afghanistan via satellite imagery—all ultimately watch screens helplessly. Screens not only evoke 9/11's predominantly mediated experience but highlight the inability of governmental institutions on 9/11 and throughout the war on terror.

The emphasis on control in *World Trade Center*, and anxieties induced by its loss, is mirrored in *United 93*. As Ron Rosenbaum observes, *United 93* inevitably depicts how "frighteningly little control" air traffic and military control rooms had, the audience "constantly watching people watching screens, seeing the horror develop in what the screens reveal and conceal." The strategy to contain and delimit characters' helplessness is similarly evident in *United 93*'s final and complete shift to events on the hijacked plane, only after efforts to avert the attacks repeatedly fail and disaster becomes inevitable—exemplified in the despondent final admission of the head of ground operations, Ben Sliney (as himself), "That's it. We're finished here." Sliney's statement signals the moment *United 93* cuts away from these ground efforts and diverts focus onto the plane, relying on the actions of its passengers to individually reverse this professional, institutional, and national loss of control. Commentators commonly praised *United 93*'s supposed transcendence of Hollywood "type" in its authenticity and veracity. Yet rather than satisfy concerns, *United 93*'s so-called authenticity led to critical unease and resistance.[13] As Fran Pheasant-Kelly observes, *United 93* "stops rather than ends" in an abrupt cut to black before its tragic conclusion, which numerous commentators find dispiriting, rather than fitting ("Authenticating the Reel" 102).[14] *United 93* was paradoxically both *too real* in its claustrophobic evocation of events and *could never be real enough* as a Hollywood movie—one that ultimately exceeds the known public record but explains the perceived *need* to "go inside" the experience of 9/11.

Containing (the) Disaster: Cinematic Spectacle and Conventionality

Even greater public and media consternation greeted the confirmation that Oliver Stone was to make *World Trade Center*.[15] Stone's ambivalent representations of twentieth-century American history led numerous critics to fear (read: assume) he would dishonor the day's tragedy and its victims. His earlier presidential and Vietnam-era films—*Platoon* (1986), *Born on the Fourth of July* (1989), *JFK* (1991), and *Nixon* (1995)—also prompted presumptions that he would negatively represent the Bush administration's role or indulge his proclivity for conspiracy theory. Finally, his common stylistic flourishes led to expectations that "the usual Stone tics," such as shifts from color to black and white, repetitions of action or "explosions of light to italicize evidence of evildoing" (Alleva 24), would overpower, even consume, victim-survivor stories.[16]

World Trade Center ostensibly merits none of these concerns. Stone, like Greengrass, used survivor accounts to claim a measure of authenticity and veracity. These interviews, along with the involvement of participants as script consultants and extras, sought to affirm Hollywood's telling of their story; as Stone suggests, it "was crucial that it be responsible and accurate" (Jaafar). Each director's fervent assertions of adherence to the actuality of 9/11 ensured that the films could not be dismissed as "common entertainment" (Muntean 56–57). Yet *World Trade Center*'s conscious and concerted play at "authenticity" and verisimilitude paradoxically masks the film's formal style, its genre conventionality and "Hollywoodness." And while adopting a more conventional employment of stars, Stone attempts to conceal and contain markers of star performance. Numerous critics were concerned that Cage's complex star image and hyperbolic performance style would efface the real man and story. Yet many lauded how Cage subsumed his own star persona—his hysterical screams aside—in service of the account of McLoughlin's experience.[17] For the vast majority of the film, Cage as McLoughlin is virtually unrecognizable. Moreover, the star-hero is a victim who, unable to restore himself, let alone rescue others, must ultimately be rescued. *World Trade Center* hides its star beneath rubble and in darkness, subordinating the star to the story by dimming and immobilizing his star power. Cage sacrifices his star persona and often (at least in his later career) histrionic, idiosyncratic performance of screen masculinity in favor of an understated, grounded, and realist—though equally constructed—one.

World Trade Center seeks to contain (the) disaster and the horror of the attacks through narrative and generic conventionality. Atypically for Stone—and to the clear surprise of critics—*World Trade Center* is formally, narratively, and stylistically conventional.[18] It uses well-known actors and dramatic visual effects and score and, as Keane writes of disaster films, offers closure in focusing on a few "representative characters" who make their way toward survival. In contrast to commentators' oft-stated requirement that Hollywood transcend "type," it is *World Trade Center*'s classical narrative structure, its "Hollywoodness," that was consistently applauded as its most admirable and surprising feature. Stephanie Zacharek further testifies that if films about 9/11 must be made, then Stone's "old-fashioned dramatization" is perhaps "more honorable," in contrast to *United 93*.[19] Pheasant-Kelly ("Abjection, Trauma, Catharsis" 1) contends that *World Trade Center*'s conventional narrative structure, in offering closure and filling in narrative gaps about 9/11, "promotes catharsis." The film is consciously "a visual narrative of empowerment ... constructed to repair the American sense of self and restore national integrity" (Ozcan 207). Ironically, it is *World Trade Center*'s embrace of Hollywood style that seemingly most enables it to *mediate* 9/11 and facilitates the recuperation of wounded normative masculinity. Yet some commentators thought the film's embrace of "Hollywood" style ultimately unsettles its capacity to either afford catharsis or redeem wounded masculine and national identity, particularly in its too neat, almost pat epilogue.[20] *World Trade Center*'s conventionality and narrow personal focus also arguably "shield us from the true dimensions of the tragedy," the film thus becoming "a comforting diversion" that ultimately fails to satisfy (Rosenbaum). Nick Muntean also contends that containment within a known narrative—the promotional poster clearly signals the trapped men's survival—renders *World Trade Center* "inherently unable to re-present the chaos and anxiety—the initial failure of narrative" that made 9/11 so traumatic (58).

World Trade Center specifically uses narration and style to contain the disaster, its horror *and* its spectacle, using familiar genre cues and structure to manage and reduce the uncontainable horror of 9/11. The film's formal conventionality, in concert with its sentimentality, valorization of uniforms, reintegration of the family, and elevation of the father, seemingly reiterates conservative values. In focusing on two men's struggle for survival, Stone humanizes and personalizes what would otherwise only be mediated abstractly and epically in/as the collapse of two towers, but he also seeks to manage the day's chaos and gain a measure of control over it. Mastering a tragedy as massive and excessive as 9/11 may be impossible, but by imposing narrative film structure, genre characteristics, and a focus on one small story, *World Trade Center* does make what exceeded the capacity to comprehend *comprehensible* via a beginning, middle, and end (to the film, if not its story).[21]

World Trade Center formally, as much as narratively, creates space for the trapped men to renegotiate destabilized conventional masculinity. In the process, the film also subtly resignifies survival and redefines heroism. Stone also de-emphasizes spectacle by shifting register within the disaster subgenre midfilm. The film opens with shots of New York's daily awakening and the influx of workers from surrounding areas on public and private transport—the city's lifeblood flowing to its center. The omniscient camera and establishment of "ordinariness" are hallmarks of the disaster genre, and the epic disaster movie in particular. These opening shots also establish a "narrative of innocence," identified by Marita Sturken (qtd. in Dawes 289) as part of the process by which the WTC was transformed into sacred ground. However, this is similarly a trope of the disaster genre. Stone's early establishment of ordinariness and routine thus "merge[s] our memory of [9/11] with our memory of every [other] disaster movie" (Rich). After the collapse of the first tower (only thirty minutes in), the film contains the terror and veils the officers' professional failure through an abrupt midfilm subgenre shift, from disaster epic to the smaller, more intimate and claustrophobic "mine accident" movie. Although disaster epics also render the experience of disaster intimately, the hero's role is transfigured in a mine accident film. In *World Trade Center*, the trapped men's survival, in contrast to their original mission to rescue others, *becomes* their heroism.²² As abrupt and unsettling as this midfilm shift is—forcing changed audience expectations—it enables *World Trade Center* to satisfy genre conventions by shifting formal expectations from rescue to survival. In so doing, rescuer becomes victim, *but* survival becomes the mark of a redefined hero and subverts the men's seeming emasculation via entrapment.

World Trade Center also contains the disaster via visual sparsity, a willingness to forgo the temptation of spectacle, and a concentration on confined spaces, much like *United 93*. Stone's intention to de-emphasize spectacle to contain its horror is highlighted in his use of a 1.85:1 (Academy Flat) aspect ratio, as opposed to the more epic 2.35:1 ratio typical of contemporary disaster films; it "could have been spectacular, but . . . not in keeping of what [the film/story] is about" (Stone, qtd. in Gentry 58).²³ Similarly, he also drained color from the World Trade Center scenes after the first plane's impact. And each constricted, cramped space—not only the hole but also the homes—may be constraining and oppressive but equally contains and delimits the disaster's horror *and* characters' helplessness to a bounded, enclosed space. In *World Trade Center*, the primary experience of the attacks and the collapses is restricted to the narrow, limited experience of McLoughlin and Jimeno. While this approach is atypical in disaster movies, which traditionally favor omniscient narration, Stephen Keane observes that this is a telling feature of Hollywood "imaginations of disaster" early post-9/11. These elements enable Stone to personalize the tragedy *and* avoid spectacle by primarily confining himself to the subjective perspectives of characters.

World Trade Center further controls cinematic spectacle by largely mediating the day's horrific scenes via television screens—with all non-computer-generated imagery of destruction or death, including the "falling man," confined within TV screens. Although the imagery of 9/11 was routinely described as "just like a movie," Stone relies on television to restage it (fig. 1.3).²⁴ Like the men's wives and fellow officers, the audience's witnessing of the disaster(s) is largely restricted to TV news coverage—as indeed it was on 9/11. Again reflecting and reiterating the limited experiences of characters *who can only watch*, representing the day's most horrific images on television screens also frames and reduces their horror by limiting their scale.²⁵ By not showing, or only showing the spectacle on the small screen, *World Trade Center* "knits the audience back into the experience" of 9/11 (Rich).

Confining the horror to small screens does still figure the helplessness or impotence of those who watch. At the Port Authority, before heading to the site, it is only on televisions that the patrolling officers directly witness the aftermath of the first plane's collision, initially considered an accident (fig. 1.4).²⁶

Figure 1.3. The horror of 9/11 is similarly contained within TV screens in the officers' homes.

Figure 1.4. Confining the horror to TV screens also indicates the officers' powerlessness.

This withholding is in line with the subjective character points of view but also tacitly acknowledges the ubiquity of these images in media discourse. This hopelessly limited perspective, however, disturbs typical notions of uniformed officers possessing greater knowledge or privileged access to information. The limits on knowledge and dependence on the news media for information—in contrast to the self-sufficiency and privilege typically connoted by the police uniform—are underlined as the officers debate the early images. These limits on the officers' knowledge are accentuated by communication devices, and especially walkie-talkies, repeatedly demonstrated to be deficient, affecting their collective capacity to act and replaying the breakdown in communications that bedeviled first responders on the day.

Reimag(in)ing Masculinity: Restoring Agency, Fatherhood, and Rescuing the Self

When McLoughlin and Jimeno can no longer *perform* their profession, when their uniforms (can) no longer *represent* their identity, they must reconstruct, or reimagine, an alternative masculinity, foregrounding a (literal and figurative) return to the home. The *breaking down* of their uniformed masculinity refigures the relationship between professional and paternal, permitting the elevation of previously subsumed familial roles. The trapped men revalue conventional ideas of masculinity by substituting fatherhood for their uniformed identity. After his scream-filled "release," McLoughlin reimagines the film's opening scene, in which he privileged the uniform over the home. In his reconstruction, rather than rising from bed without turning toward his wife, McLoughlin rolls over and embraces his wife *before* rising and heading to work. Now privileging his role as husband and erasing his earlier inattentiveness, this reimagining commences McLoughlin's restoration to the home, nullifying his failure as hero-rescuer via his reestablishment as husband-father.

Stone's depiction of passive victim-heroes, arguably feminized by their entrapment, drew criticism, particularly given Stone's characterization of the hole as womb. Michael Lewis lambasts Stone's "skewed" choices of protagonists, asking why of all who entered the towers, Stone chose two men "whose chief distinction was to lie supine and immobilized for thirteen hours . . . [and] to depict only stoic, passive endurance" (43). Although Lewis makes an important observation on Stone's surprising narrative choices, the trapped men also represent other character virtues Lewis identifies, such as perseverance, courage, and sacrifice. More importantly, *World Trade Center* counters the trapped men's passive, wounded masculinity by (re)asserting their *continued agency*. Indeed, it is at their seemingly most vulnerable and impotent that the film foregrounds their (undiminished) reproductive potency *as* fathers. The paternal aspect vitally becomes the characteristic of uniformed-protective masculinity that does not fail—evinced by the successful evacuation of the children (by *other* uniformed males)—and fatherhood becomes the role through which the men's identity can be reconstructed.[27] Over two flashbacks during their ordeal in the hole and then the final epilogue—each saturated with light to resist the darkness of the hole—*World Trade Center* connects the men to each other, restores them to the home, and signals rebirth. The flashbacks—one for each man and his wife—detail advancing stages of pregnancy. In the first, McLoughlin and Donna discover they are unexpectedly pregnant. And in the second, later flashback, Jimeno and his heavily pregnant young wife, Allison, discuss baby names. Finally, personal and societal rebirth is signaled in the epilogue's final freeze-frame of (a nonuniformed) Jimeno raising his young daughter, unborn at the time of the attacks.

Along with a three-part structure approximating order–disorder–order restored, *World Trade Center* seemingly offers closure in an epilogue, a "thank-you" barbecue set two years after 9/11 that the men give to honor their rescuers. The scene was routinely criticized, deemed unnecessary and akin to a made-for-TV movie. Yet when Cage (as McLoughlin) and Peña (as Jimeno) embrace the men they portray, the "real" men affirm not only this telling of their story but Hollywood's right to tell it.[28] The epilogue, a scene of rebirth and reconnection for wider American society, cements a sense of revelation through McLoughlin's voice-over: "Coz I saw a lot of good that day." Slavoj Žižek asserts that a "utopian perspective" apparent in *World Trade Center* and *United 93* as disaster movies implies American society "need[s] a major catastrophe in order to resuscitate the spirit of community solidarity" (qtd. in Charles 3). The epilogue restores the men to home and family, seeking to erase the vulnerability and insufficiency evidenced when the attacks overwhelm the capacities of uniformed masculinity. The barbecue also figures as an opportunity for the rescuers and the men's families to celebrate the men's powers of survival. The epilogue superficially fulfills Claire Sisco King's claims about post-9/11 "sacrificial films," which imply America has not only suffered but been "redeemed and improved" through the traumatic, undaunted heroism of men (165). By foregrounding their identities as fathers and their (literal) role in the flourishing of society, the celebratory barbecue predominantly serves to complete the restoration of paternal potency to the previously passive, trapped officers.

As is typical in disaster and apocalypse films, the attacks destabilize preceding hierarchies. Initially the attacks solidify order and hierarchy: McLoughlin assumes the lead role, and Jimeno, the rookie, "babysits" the equipment cart while more experienced volunteers collect key equipment. Even after they are trapped in the collapse, screen space first communicates the separation between the trapped men, with McLoughlin unable to even see his officers. The surviving men's early conversations in the hole equally mark the divisions associated with their police rank, implying this is the first occasion McLoughlin and Jimeno have discussed their nonprofessional identities. However, screen space is progressively reconfigured to bring the two men together. The film collapses physical space in the hole to erase their emotional distance, presenting their conversations as steadily more intimate across a series of shot–reverse shots.[29] In this sense, Jimeno's and McLoughlin's masculinity, consciousness, and survival are entwined. Indeed, after their rescue, the two men lie side by side in their hospital room, united *and* equal. The interrelatedness of uniformed masculinity—and national identity—is foreshadowed in McLoughlin's mantra to "stay together!" upon entering the complex but is most heavily figured in the final rescue operation. Informed that McLoughlin may not survive, Jimeno tells one of his rescuers to cut off his leg, because "If he dies, I die."[30] These instances also foreground masculinity as sacrificial, with such self-sacrifice and shared service routinely embodied by uniformed masculinity in *World Trade Center*. The attacks reorganize implicit social and racial hierarchies, but Stone's narrational strategy also highlights *World Trade Center*'s concerted erasure of difference, most evident in relation to ethnicity. Ethnicity is at once clearly coded and superficially celebrated in the composition of Jimeno's family and various popular culture references but does not mark difference so much as demonstrate that Americans on the day were the same. The trapped men's relationship in some sense mirrors that of interracial buddy films.[31] While an erasure of difference is also typically and symbolically addressed in interracial buddy films, there is nonetheless a different tenor to *World Trade Center*'s representation of the trapped men's relationship, as if there never was any "real" difference. Yet rather than focusing on overcoming difference, on men who must cooperate across difference to survive, *World Trade Center* seeks to annul difference. For example, as McLoughlin's health slips, Jimeno, assuming a lead role in their refigured relationship, coaxes McLoughlin to talk to ensure he stays awake.

World Trade Center also restores the trapped men's agency by—quite extraordinarily—implying they *rescue themselves* through concerted focuses on survival and symbolic restorations of agency. The film emphasizes survival over rescue in both a narrative and a temporal sense. While this is not unusual in mine accident films, these survival narratives typically afford equivalent attention to the rescuers' stories, ordeals, and challenges. Yet the vast majority of *World Trade Center* depicts McLoughlin's and Jimeno's struggle for survival *before* their discovery and rescue. Their perilous and painstaking recoveries, which required approximately three hours for Jimeno and ten for McLoughlin, occupy little screen time. While the film's focus on the trapped men's experience—and therefore *their* sense of their recovery—makes this weighting logical, it significantly lionizes survival over rescue.

Such symbolic restorations combat the men's helplessness and incapacitation, suggesting they are to some degree responsible not only for their survival but for *their own rescue*. Likewise, when Jimeno is pulled from the hole by his rescuers, McLoughlin pointedly restores the trapped man's agency, calling out: "You done it, Will. You made it." This linguistic restoration of agency is redoubled in

McLoughlin's final hallucination before his disinterment, in which the rescuers tirelessly working to secure his recovery completely disappear. In it, Donna (Maria Bello) exhorts McLoughlin, now close to death, to "get unstuck" and to "get off your ass and come home." Donna's entreaty, as *his* hallucination, even implies he calls on himself to return home. The men apparently gain strength from the collapse of the towers and their ordeal. When the father of Allison (Maggie Gyllenhaal) tells her that Jimeno has been located alive, he opines, "He's made of rocks, is he not?!"[32] Ceylan Ozcan's observation that the film's official poster constructs a visual metaphor in which the two men are "miniatures copies" of the two towers is here brought into starker relief (209). More than merely copies, it is as if in *actually* ingesting the rubble—of towers representative of American power and identity—the men erase them as symbols of weakness and loss. Stone's use of the two men's story as a microcosm of the entire day thus attributes not only their trials but also their qualities—their resilience and courage—to those of the nation. The men's incorporation of the tower both figures their symbolic persistence and suggests that an equivalent strength of spirit constitutes every American (man). By redefining the men's masculine identity through fatherhood and restoring their agency, *World Trade Center* not only humanizes the nation's broader symbolic loss but also disavows its passivity and impotence. The film reestablishes the men *as* bodies of "doing," absolves their failure as hero-rescuers by restoring them as husband-fathers, and signals a symbolic return to the home.

Calling Father Home: Ambivalently Gendering Hole and Home

World Trade Center uses the men's entrapment to rework male-female relations to stage their recuperation and restore them to the home. Yet the representation of women in the home—constrained, tethered, helpless, and passive—also figures the ambivalence of gendered spaces in the film and serves to unravel the men's remasculinization via a symbolic return to the home. Only when the men break down emotionally does the film widen its focus onto the parallel experiences of their families and wives, waiting at home for news of the trapped men's fate. This widened attention—accompanied by flashbacks to family life, bliss, and routine shared by husband and wife—connects the men in their hole with the wives in their homes. While femininity is also associated with nurturing and caring, and women are represented as holding the family together, the repeated representation of the women in *World Trade Center* as hysterical is distinctly conservative. The conflation of biological sex (female) and gender (femininity), along with the persistent gendering of spaces, also signals the ambivalence of the trapped men's return to the home. As a feminine space in which the men were initially rendered immobile and passive, the connection of the home with the hole—the only Ground Zero space that women figuratively enter—begins to suggest an ambivalence toward femininity and alternative masculinities.

World Trade Center repeatedly identifies women as immobile or victims, where it does not exclude them entirely, especially evident in the depiction of the trapped men's wives and the male-only space of Ground Zero; only uniformed males physically enter the space of search and rescue.[33] The alignment of men, uniforms, and masculine attributes unsettlingly highlights the conspicuous absenting of women from particular *gendered* roles and spaces throughout the film, excluded from Ground Zero and active uniformed roles. The only female PAPD officer shown remains tethered to the reception desk, *always already* immobile. This overwhelming maleness effectively and inaccurately implies an all-male police force. In keeping with this perspective, males at the WTC site are persistently presented as protectors and women as victims, extended even to civilians.[34] The businessman who informs Jimeno about children possibly trapped in the complex is rendered as more-than-victim, exhibiting a protective-paternal capacity. However, a businesswoman—deemed by Stone to be a too intense and hysterical victim—who similarly implores McLoughlin to "do something" was deleted from the final cut, thereby excising her from the site.

The idea of the trapped men being called (to return) home is repeated numerously and heavily figured in their final recovery. The rescuers, an assortment of uniformed colleague-brothers, repeatedly declare, "You're almost home" and "We're gonna get you home" and after their recovery proclaim, "Welcome home." Stone claims that *World Trade Center* is more about light than containment (in interview with Gentry). Light, representing a tenuous but persistent connection to life, is immediately searched for by the men after the collapse. Light is also restored by the rescuers' flashlights after night falls, and even the fires at Ground Zero offer warmth and light rather than represent imminent danger. Yet the men's flashbacks, hallucinations, and visions most figure the hole as a sacred space filled with light. Just before being discovered, Jimeno's vision of Jesus reintroduces light into the darkness and perhaps most exemplifies the notion of being called home. Jimeno's vision finally merges with the light of the fires above the hole and Karnes's flashlight, when Jimeno is jolted back to consciousness. He plainly interprets his experience as a revelation, Jesus suffused with light and carrying a water bottle: "He's telling us to come home, John."[35]

Yet Stone's likening of the hole to a grave (B. Johnson) underscores the underlying ambivalence that dominates *World Trade Center*. The hole is as a

Figure 1.5. The hole is figured as a grave in indicating McLoughlin's symbolic resurrection.

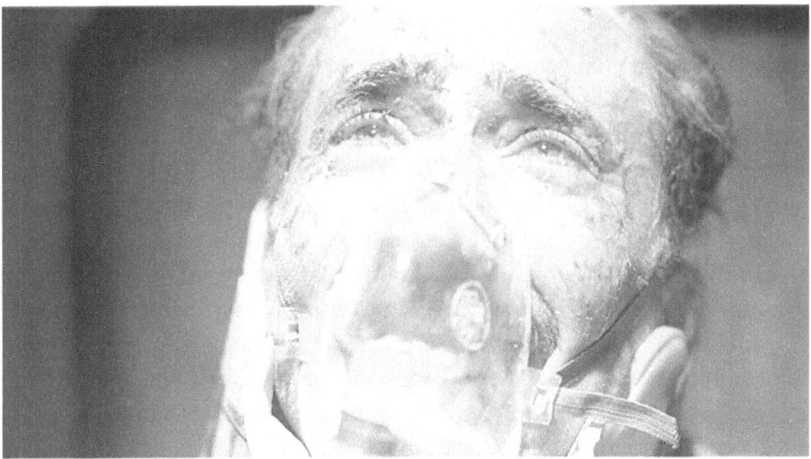

Figure 1.6. McLoughlin moves from total darkness and into a "heavenly" light.

grave for the trapped men—literally so for Pezzulo—and their recovery, like their return to consciousness after the collapse, signifies a return to life and resurrection without death. Most notably, as McLoughlin is disinterred, the hole is visually figured as a grave, a rectangular space cut into the rubble. As McLoughlin reaches the surface, his face passes from darkness to light; darkness, which was total in the hole, and which sought to (literally and figuratively) dominate light, is vanquished (figs. 1.5–1.6). Moreover, the camera continues to ascend toward the heavens, revisiting the film's early invocation of Apocalypse via McLoughlin's symbolic Rapturing.

While the hole vitally offers a space for the trapped men—and the nation—to renegotiate their identity, Stone cuts the screen time in the hole to avoid "oppress[ing] the audience" and uses the men's homes as "antidotes to the hole" (qtd. in B. Johnson 50). As much as *World Trade Center* connects and equates the spaces of the hole and the home, they are also opposite. In contrast to the home, the hole is a place of destruction and death, a horrific "nothing" space. As such, the film tries to transport the men from the hole to the home and thereby connotes a return to a reinvigorated, restored America. Yet, as J. Hoberman observes, the film *collapses* battlefield and home (front), recognizing a more figurative notion of home, but one equally threatened and vulnerable ("Fight Them over There"). The numerous flashbacks and hallucinations of life in the home are saturated with light, but Stone likewise—and somewhat incoherently—acknowledges how confining and oppressive the homes are: they "become like 'holes' as the light closes down and the day runs out" (B. Johnson 50). The space of the home is as constrained and ambivalent as the hole, equally functioning as a sort of cage for men *and* women. Indeed, the frame presses against characters in the homes, tightly constraining them within. The trapped men's helplessness is equally mirrored in the restricted perspectives of their wives and families (wholly reliant on news media), and especially by the passivity of men within the home—most notably as Allison's brother sits on the couch, watching the collapse of one of the towers on TV, meagerly fidgeting with the remote control. Even McLoughlin's brother, a fellow PAPD officer, is diminished in the home, reduced to watching the news media in search of information about the attacks.

In this sense, the symbolic restoration of fathers to the American home is ambivalent, with the home gendered as pejoratively feminine: confined, constrained, and fearful. The home is a space in which knowledge is not only limited but feared. Throughout the film, women anxiously look out through the windows—and, sharing the women's perspective, so too does the audience—craving yet dreading news from without. When McLoughlin's brother first arrives at the McLoughlin home, Donna, afraid he is fulfilling his fraternal promise to deliver bad news, rushes out the front door. As if hoping to prevent (news of) the tragedy from breaching the home, she yells, "Don't you come in here! Don't you come in here and tell me he's dead!" The wives' anger about the persistent intrusions of television—which marks the reality of the attacks—into the domestic space also recalls the mediated experience of American homes on the day: "They keep showing it over and over and over!" Further testifying to the medium's ambivalence, television is at once a source of comfort and information, yet also oppressive and, paradoxically, partial.

Across a series of shared flashbacks, *World Trade Center* gently excoriates McLoughlin for leaving the home in a state of disrepair and neglect. Donna's desperate attempt to keep out the news and reality of the attacks draws attention to the unfinished state of the McLoughlin home. Unpainted interior walls, plastic sheeting in place of doors, and newspaper and electrical tape across the front door glass panes are temporary, insufficient endeavors to shield the home that also evidence its exposure. In the unfinished renovation job, the home recalls rhetorical representations of 9/11 as an attack on a nation unprepared—and the American home. The film further signals the perceived insufficiency of McLoughlin's nonuniformed identity by highlighting his incompetence with home maintenance and work tools. Yet, as much as it castigates McLoughlin, the film also signals deep anxieties about his prospective permanent absence if he dies *and* his figurative preattack absence, an *already*-absence reiterated in McLoughlin's fragmented final hallucination. In it, he plaintively asks Donna if he has been a good husband: "Did I love ya right . . . good enough?" In the absence of an immediate response, McLoughlin questions what is missing in their marriage, before Donna finally replies, "What with me and the kids, and you with the Department . . . I guess we kinda stopped looking at each other," her pause articulating the preattack disconnect between the two spaces. Despite acknowledging mutual responsibility, World Trade Center implies that McLoughlin's privileging of his uniformed role over that of husband-father left the home precarious and vulnerable, and uniformed masculinity was weakened not by the attacks but *before* them, particularly through male diminishment in the home. In contrast to the male-only space of search and rescue above, the hole is the only Ground Zero space women enter, and only figuratively, via flashbacks and the men's hallucinations. The wives are also only associated with their husbands' experience *after* they are trapped and *compelled* to negotiate compromised masculine identities. And although Donna and Allison want to go to Ground Zero, each is repeatedly deterred from heading to the site. In so conflating gender, and pejoratively aligning the female body with victim status and immobility, the home becomes an ambivalent space of return and restoration for the trapped men. This ambivalence is compounded, and the revaluation of a masculinity identified with the private home destabilized, in the film's subsequent need to idealize numerous returns to uniform—and again valorize public-protective masculinity.

The Return of the Uniform: Remilitarizing and Rehabilitating Masculinity

Immediately after the trapped men break down, *World Trade Center* introduces Dave Karnes, a Connecticut accountant and former marine, foregrounding his return to the uniform and lead role in their ultimate discovery. Karnes's marine uniform looms large in *World Trade Center*. Stuart Klawans, among others, considers Karnes to be the character on whom "the entire picture hinges." Yet why is Karnes's story a focus, especially given his limited role in the final recovery, over those who also put on uniforms and "took a far bigger risk" entering the highly unstable hole (Klawans)? By focusing on the men's survival, rather than their rescue and rescuers, and on Karnes, *World Trade Center* elevates the two officers' roles in their own survival and thereby their heroism.[36] And in Karnes, Stone fetishizes a return to the uniform to reassert American masculinity as militarized. The spectacle of the uniform and its display of masculine attributes, in Craik's words, combine in the performance of masculinity itself to seemingly recuperate uniformed masculinity. Uniforms, particularly military, play an ideological role, and one implicitly associated with gender. The highly gendered valorization of protective *uniformed* roles as representative of an ideal American masculinity explicitly associates the wearer—and remasculinization—with national identity. More than communicating belonging to a particular social institution, Stefano Tonchi asserts the military uniform connotes a sense of belonging to a specific idea and (idea of) nation (155). The military uniform helps the wearer adhere to associated values, expectations, and meanings. It equally reassures others, alleviating uncertainty in communicating commonly understood ideas of collective strength, authority, discipline, and order. The sense of reciprocal belonging, duty, and unity likewise connotes the abnegation of the self in service of the nation.

The trapped men seemingly recuperate their wounded identities by negotiating an alternative masculinity that eschews the uniform and celebrates their (symbolic) return to the home, however ambivalent. Despite this, *World Trade Center*'s final recourse remains to have more males put on uniforms, subsequently privileging multiple returns to prior uniformed roles as a return to one's "true" self. In so doing, the film denotes the redemptive characteristics of *performing* a protective role for American males. This idealization of uniformed protective masculinity is retold when the film introduces former marine Karnes, who dons a uniform to gain access to the World Trade Center site and search for survivors. The uniform revives what is inherent but dormant, but it also changes the wearer. The manner of this return to the uniform, privileging an earlier-and-now-redundant masculinity *after* it has been renegotiated, undermines *World Trade Center*'s attempts to broaden conventional masculinity through McLoughlin and Jimeno. Only in uniform are males redeemed *as* whole men.

Karnes's return to the uniform superficially resolves anxieties about normative masculinity, reinstituting an image of authority and control destabilized by the attacks and figured in entrapment. Karnes is also indicative of a prior cinematic

Figure 1.7. Karnes is demonstrably "out of place" in an everyday civilian setting.

trend in which Hollywood science fiction–disaster films in the 1990s focus on one's capacity to contribute to the "disaster response" rather than diagnose its genesis or assign broader responsibility (Kakoudaki).[37] Introduced as he watches President Bush's postattack press conference on television, Karnes's initial declaration to office colleagues, "I don't know if you guys know it yet, but this country is at war," is also the first confident statement of knowledge since the attacks. Karnes's declaration immediately counters and alleviates McLoughlin's preceding screams of "I don't know!" Moreover, Karnes's introduction recalls the representation of an outsized western hero when placed inside a domestic space, such as Ethan Edwards (John Wayne) in *The Searchers* (Ford 1956). As figure 1.7 demonstrates, Karnes not only towers over others but presses at the edges of the confined office space, demonstrably "out of place" within an everyday workplace setting. Karnes immediately visits his church and declares to his pastor that God is calling him on a new "mission."

Karnes most straightforwardly conforms to conventional notions of the hero in *World Trade Center*, especially given the film's repeated valorization of uniformed masculinity. A model of ideal masculinity—in his capacity to take command and wrest back control—his actions are typically transgressive, using the uniform first to gain access to the site and then to continue the search after it is officially postponed for the night. Dressing as a marine earns Karnes access to a Ground Zero site prohibited to those without a uniform; a national guardsman lets Karnes pass unimpeded as he tells other civilians they cannot enter. It is only by returning to the uniform and (re)claiming its associated attributes and authority that Karnes is able to participate in the rescue. Akin to Roderick McGillis's description of B-movie cowboys, Karnes fulfills popular mythic notions of the man who takes charge and shoulders responsibility, the man without whom society can neither be secured nor its success be achieved. In his return to the uniform, Karnes becomes not only vital but also necessary to the protection and sustenance of the (civilian) world of work, home, and family. As Patrick Calefato argues, the uniform symbolizes the separation of familiar and alien. In this sense, Karnes's uniform—and the omnipresence of other protective uniforms—introduces familiarity into the alien landscape of the ruins of the Twin Towers.

Karnes's return to uniform signals that America has transitioned to a time of war, although the presence of the military uniform in an American city is unsettling. Karnes's immediate declaration that America is at war, his remilitarization through return to the uniform, and his presence in military uniform at the site signify Ground Zero as a battlefield. Recalling Stone's earlier Vietnam films, *World Trade Center* also becomes a sort of war movie when Karnes joins with another former marine searching the site—another who has suddenly returned to the uniform. The centrality of Karnes *as* soldier initiates the parallel restitution of threatened normative masculinity and ruptured national identity. The military uniform connotes reciprocal belonging, duty, and unity, but it especially communicates a sense of belonging to a specific idea and (idea of) nation.[38] *World Trade Center* here reasserts masculinity *as* uniformed, and the uniform as representative of the nation. Remilitarized by president *and* God, Karnes gets a buzz cut and redons his uniform. In donning his old marine uniform, Karnes's "true" identity is associated with wearing a uniform and his performance *in* uniform. Karnes represents a return to a "muscular," militaristic American nationalism associated with the male in (military) uniform. In *World Trade Center*, reiterating Jean Baudrillard's assertion, uniforms exemplify and seal the "ideological cohesion of a nation" (qtd. in Calefato 201), the quality supposedly shared by all its male characters.[39] Reinstalling the alignment of normative masculinity with the uniform, Karnes's new "mission" likewise enacts national redemption in the return of/to the supposedly reassuring *performance* of uniformed masculinity. Karnes's final, assertive walking on top of the rubble of Ground Zero, the earlier site of emasculation, confirms it as (now) a war zone—and therefore the attacks as an act of war—rather than a space of search and rescue, by implicitly connecting them with future foreign battlefields. In a final telephone conversation after the men's recovery, Karnes, standing on the wreckage of the former towers, informs his boss that his return to work is uncertain: "They're gonna need some good men out there to avenge this." This also symbolizes the reassertion of uniformed masculinity and reasserts American certitude and dominance: Americans will now bring the attack back to those who attacked them.

Karnes's symbolic return to uniform remakes (*and* reestablishes) a destabilized societal order. The disaster is used to reorganize or refigure destabilized hierarchies and thereby revive a particular configuration of society. It equally signals Hollywood's and America's "addiction to fables of redemptive uplift," in Rosenbaum's words. Karnes's return to the uniform is a return or revival of his "true" identity, yet the uniform is again wholly transformative. Karnes readily (re)defines himself *through* his uniform, *becoming* what he dresses as. When emergency services officer Scott Strauss (Stephen Dorff) asks his name, Karnes first replies, "Staff Sergeant Karnes." Subsequently asked if he can use something shorter, Karnes drily responds, "Staff Sergeant." The uniform transforms its wearer from seemingly overcivilized accountant to hypermasculine marine and moves him from the margins of the narrative to its center. The attacks present an opportunity to return to an unconstrained performance of normative military masculinity. Karnes finds fulfillment in his new mission, in wearing the uniform and performing uniformed masculinity, which covers his civilian identity.

Another symbolic return to uniform is perhaps even more revealing. As the final recovery effort gets under way, Strauss asks if anyone among the assembled rescue workers is a paramedic. "Used to be": a male voice is heard farther down the wreckage, its owner indistinguishable in the dark and among the rubble. Strauss scoffs, but the man clambers up, informing him that he is capable, but his registration lapsed after he had "a few bad years." It is only when former paramedic Chuck Sereika (Frank Whaley) figuratively "puts on" his former uniform, recouping the associated attributes and duties of the role, that he can participate in the rescue. Sereika's story also signals the redemptive qualities of the (return to) uniform and a return to heroism from victimization. It is also only through "putting on" the uniform that Sereika is restored, or more properly rehabilitated; Sereika only becomes his best self when he again *becomes* paramedic.

During the trapped men's disinterment, *World Trade Center* emphasizes (male) redemption as collective via a compendium of uniforms—firefighters, police, FBI agents, paramedics, soldiers and, emergency services—another means of annulling difference. Extending beyond the frame, the unbroken chain of uniformed men, toiling as impromptu rescue workers, who pass the recovered men from one hand to the next down the wreckage of Ground Zero, are united *and* one. As ciphers for the united national response, the exclusion of females from the site and role of rescue to permit this remasculinization of the nation is again notable. Sereika's response when Strauss tells fellow rescuers to leave the hole because it may collapse confirms his motivating desire to redeem himself through undertaking the rescue: "I've been in and out of rehab for years. Finally figured out the only thing I've ever been good at is helping people. We're doing this together." Sereika's confessional tone, however improbable in the context of a rescue, renders the uniform also symbolically rehabilitative, emphasizing not only the rescuers' shared fate but the redemptive possibilities offered in *and* through the performance of uniformed masculinity. Sereika's transformation appears complete after the trapped men's rescue when an out-of-state police officer inquires what he is doing there. As the officer implicitly questions Sereika's right to be at the site, Sereika hesitates before confidently self-identifying: "Paramedic." The officer's resounding—and cringeworthy—affirmation, "Thatta boy," reinforces the alignment of ideal masculinity with a protective uniform and testifies to its redemptive qualities. The rescue rehabilitates what the uniform represents (American national identity), as much as who (its male wearers) and what it covers (their perceived insufficiencies). The restitution of the uniform reverses (and conceals) the impotence and helplessness otherwise embodied by the trapped men, and the men confined to the home and incapable of "performing."

25th Hour: Ambivalent Masculinity and Ground Zero

This ambivalence of male character in films that directly address 9/11, even if only obliquely, is equally evident in Spike Lee's *25th Hour* (2002). The film, which follows the convicted heroin dealer's final day of freedom before he is required to begin his sentence, associates Monty (Edward Norton) with the victims of 9/11 and the towers themselves—thereby linking masculine and national identity. Before reuniting with Monty on his final night before prison, his friends Jacob (Philip Seymour Hoffman) and Slaughtery (Barry Pepper)—whose apartment overlooks Ground Zero—discuss Monty's plight while looking down over the site. They express their own guilt, anger, and helplessness—suggesting "something of what New Yorkers feel about the 9/11 attack" (Taubin)—but Slaughtery also proposes that, having profited amorally from the despair of others, Monty is now reaping what he has sown. Taking place with Ground Zero in the background, Jacob and Slaughtery's conversation provocatively links Monty's experience and character to the attacks, complicating notions of victimhood and accountability (fig. 1.8). Similarly, the emasculation signaled in the collapse of the towers echoes the prison-bound Monty's fear of violent physical and psychological emasculation in prison. The Twin Towers, an ambivalent symbol of American power and commerce, may equally have invited punishment, an implicit association reinforced as the camera zooms in on Ground Zero to conclude the scene. One key change Lee makes from David Benioff's source novel—published before 9/11—is to resituate events in 2002. In so doing, *25th Hour* celebrates New York's (and America's) vitality *through* or *because of* difference. Monty unleashes a litany of declarations of "fuck you" in front of a mirror to New York's diverse populace, shown in cutaways, unleashing his anger—also impotent—toward each and every one of the city's diverse ethnicities, races, types, professions, and classes, and also finally at himself. In contrast to *World Trade Center*, while invoking shared experience, *25th Hour* also acknowledges and finally embraces the city's cultural and ethnic differences as difference.

Figure 1.8. Jacob and Slaughtery discuss Monty's punishment while overlooking Ground Zero.

Remasculinizing the Nation: Weirdness and Male Masquerade

World Trade Center's recuperation of the trapped men as fathers, by uniformed males as symbols of returned authority, restores masculinity to an ideal position. In the restoration of the father to the home—however ambivalently represented—paternal influence is restored where its presence had waned. Yet though Chuck Sereika does have to prove himself—to himself as much as other first responders—the privileging *again* of the uniformed persona in *World Trade Center* is equally troubling. The film's only recourse when uniformed masculinity is destabilized through entrapment and immobility is to redress this insufficiency *through* dress, to have other men don uniforms. Karnes's and Sereika's return to the uniform again highlights an unsettling schism or discrepancy between uniform and wearer. The uniform confers its associated attributes and qualities on the wearer, yet it also cloaks (and seeks to redress) the perceived insufficiency of the nonuniformed male. Karnes's return to the uniform reestablishes a normative American masculinity predicated on the uniform. This uniformed return also symbolically restores the (idea of the) nation as unified and resilient. Yet the emergence of military masculinity in New York City and the strangeness of Karnes's embodiment unsettle the return of uniformed masculinity. The privileging of its return also undermines McLoughlin's and Jimeno's (painful and pain-filled) redefinition of masculinity for one that *eschews* the uniform. James Kendrick's characterization of Karnes as "the quintessential American fighting man" and "a ready metaphor for the undaunted American spirit in the face of catastrophe" is too narrow (523, 526). A straightforward appraisal of the redemptive qualities of Karnes's putting on the uniform in the rescue and restoration of masculinity (and nation) ignores the utter ambivalence of both Karnes's representation *and* critical reception, as well as Stone's emphasis on the rescue as collective. Karnes is the first character to recognize America is at war, and he heroically locates the trapped men. However, after Karnes's messianic pronouncement about God "shielding us from what we are not yet ready to see," a firefighter—the most valorized first responder after 9/11—who is also participating in the search visibly rolls his eyes and drolly comments: "Nutbag!"

As portrayed in the film, Karnes engendered wildly diverse critical and audience responses. These ranged from appraising Karnes as heroic, divinely inspired, and emblematic of a renewed American muscularity to being characterized as a poorly rendered, unmotivated, robotic zealot. Audiences too seemingly registered this strangeness, and after test audiences believed his character to be fictional, Stone had to insert biographical details of Karnes's reenlistment and tours in Iraq in a postscript. While a minority of commentators note the character's ambivalence, most critics presume Stone's intentions—both to redeem his own reputation and to honor the attack's victims—to be contrary to those in his previous war films.[40] Yet Karnes's ambivalent characterization, the weirdness and self-consciousness of Karnes's remilitarization reiterated in Michael Shannon's casting and performance, is arguably more significant than this. Karnes's character is deeply unsettling; his character is *too* noticeable (for advocates and critics alike). Michael Shannon's portrayal—and Karnes's actions—draws attention to his character *as* character and *as* performed, troubling notions of performance in conventional Hollywood form and contrasting starkly with Nicolas Cage in the film. Stone signals the character's ambivalence in casting Shannon, whose background in theater has shaped an outsized, eye-catching performance style, reiterated in his repeated interest in extreme characters.[41] While any "dressing up" is somewhat self-conscious, Karnes's robotic religiosity particularly draws attention to his character *as* self-conscious—and thus his masculine-uniformed identity as constructed rather than "natural."

World Trade Center's seemingly straightforward privileging of the uniform paradoxically disquiets normative masculinity and its uniformed rehabilitation. Jennifer Craik observes that uniforms intended to express upright and positive attributes can equally become symbols of insufficiency ("Cultural Politics of the Uniform" 143). Both Karnes, in his role as accountant, and Sereika, through his implied alcoholism or drug abuse, admit not only the discrepancy between male and uniformed identity but the perceived insufficiency of their nonuniformed identity. Putting on the uniform seeks to erase such insufficiencies but merely conceals them, and each man's rehabilitation remains disconcertingly predicated on notions of conscious performance and masquerade. Uniforms in *World Trade Center* highlight gender's constructedness and how its performance is constituted by and through the uniform. Both Karnes and Sereika masquerade, a type of subversive performance or impersonation that exposes all gender as performed or constructed, in their protective roles. In locating the trapped men and remasculinizing Ground Zero, Karnes reasserts a masculinity embodied in *and* enacted through the uniform and the performance of a protective role. More than simply restoring uniformed masculinity, Karnes's embodiment is *self-consciously* hypermasculine, exaggerating and mutating the characteristics earlier associated with protective uniformed masculinity.

World Trade Center presents Karnes's and Sereika's returns to uniform as returns to their best or truest selves; they are inauthentic and incomplete out of the uniform. This expressly attempts to once again render uniformed masculinity as reassuring and able. But this reassertion is unsettling and unconvincing—for the audience and other characters. Both returns to uniform and participation in the search at least partially rest on falsity. As a former marine and an unlicensed paramedic, each man must at this stage "play" his role to participate in the search and rescue. Karnes clearly and consciously impersonates a marine, not only putting on the uniform but quickly getting a marine-standard buzz cut, to obtain access to Ground Zero. The film implies that this resumption of prior roles marks a return to performing an innate role, irrespective of whether it is yet official, yet it is telling that Stone focuses only on such dormant examples of uniformed male performance.

While superficially reassuring and restorative, their conscious and conspicuous masquerade to some degree reveals normative masculinity—and all masculinities—as performed rather than natural, something conventional and hegemonic masculinities are loath to do. As Judith Butler famously observes, the masquerade puts the "reality" of gender into crisis and reveals gender as changeable and revisable (*Gender Trouble* xxiv). Karnes's masquerade especially disturbs the restoration of uniformed masculinity because it is *only* through masquerade that normative (uniformed) masculinity is reinvigorated in *World Trade Center*.[42] These self-conscious notions of performance and masquerade disrupt Stone's emphasis on "authenticity"—including in aligning actor with real-life officer in the epilogue. Karnes ultimately reinstates a hypermasculinity that, adapting MacKinnon, inevitably and irrevocably disturbs the idea of masculinity it seeks to restore. Recalling Butler, masquerade "conceals this loss, but preserves (and negates) [it] through its concealment" (*Gender Trouble* 67). Recasting Karnes, the restitution of the uniform via Karnes shields us from "what we are not yet ready to see," that is, the failings and insufficiencies of normative masculinity in the attacks. Karnes returns what was overwhelmed (i.e., the protective uniform); his performance shields *yet reveals*, ultimately illuminating both the masquerade *and* what was (or *is*) lacking. In putting on the uniform, Karnes and Sereika force a recognition of masculinity *as* performed, problematizing the notion that each man's return is to a true self or the expression of an innate identity. While Karnes restores or produces order and acts as a palliative for the sense of failure and loss expressed by McLoughlin—"What good did we do?"—he is also an emblematic reminder of that failure and loss. Karnes is, as McGillis describes B-western masculinities, "a fantasy . . . an elegiac substitution for that which we cannot have" (4–5). Karnes's performance of uniformed masculinity (and nation) inevitably unnerves rather than reassures, because it reveals it *as* performance and so disturbs the return of certainty his performance supposedly enacts. In a way, Stone seems suspicious of such holistic, conventional notions of masculinity, let alone its (and the nation's) remilitarization. Karnes is again akin to the western hero, the individual on whom society relies, but who remains "out of place" and cannot be incorporated. He largely disappears at film's end, neither part of the rescue nor present in the epilogue of communal celebration.

Ideas of the return, redemption, and recuperation of masculine identity, both as father and through return to the uniform, are unsettled because they are achieved via male masquerade. Karnes's and Sereika's respective remilitarization and rehabilitation of (uniformed) masculinity spotlight the insufficiency each seeks to redeem or cover over. *World Trade Center*'s equation of (successful, complete) masculinity with the reinstituted performance of uniformed protective roles finally undermines the trapped men's *painful* struggle to redefine or construct an alternative masculinity that valorizes survival but eschews the uniform. The film broadens the number of available meaningful masculinities in the hole. Yet in subsequently advocating a return to the uniform, *World Trade Center* again privileges this expression of masculinity—privileges what McLoughlin and Jimeno were, *but no longer are*. After all, neither trapped man ever returns to the police force. *World Trade Center*'s ultimate response to the attacks' exposure of the insufficiency of the uniform lies not, then, in the establishment of an alternative masculinity but in having more men "dress up" to perform "protective" roles. *World Trade Center* incoherently, even hysterically, articulates conflicting "rhetorics of crisis" (Robinson).[43] In seeking both to reimagine an alternative masculinity *and* to remasculinize by healing the originary wound (to the uniform), the film persuasively achieves neither.

"That's When I Felt the Emptiness": Absence, Ambivalence, and Threat

These (male) insufficiencies and ambivalences are amplified by cumulative moments of unfathomable loss and absence after McLoughlin's and Jimeno's rescue that dwarf the film's closing; rather than optimistic and hopeful, *World Trade Center* finally resists closure. Even the trapped men's recovery cannot shield the audience from the persisting absences, including that of victim bodies, which shadow and overwhelm.[44] These many absences—the film unable (or unwilling) to fully represent the loss—complicate *World Trade Center*'s seeming conventionality and further undermine its male characters' redemption and the competing, already-strange recuperation of normative masculinity. On the morning of September 12, after the two men are reunited with their families, *World Trade Center* shifts focus to those who could not be rescued. Immediately after being told about the men's well-being, Strauss is informed, "We're still missing fourteen [colleagues]." His despair returns as he helplessly casts his eyes across the rubble: "There could be thousands of people out there. Where the hell are they?" The helplessness and impotence reversed in the men's rescue powerfully resurfaces, their recuperation overwhelmed by the magnitude of loss and the definitive insufficiency of any response.

Subsequent shots of various modes of public transport recall the film's introductory shots of McLoughlin's volunteer team, men who would all perish in the collapse. Each transport type, previously filled with New Yorkers, is now empty. Showcasing the city's persistence—its "resilience and continuity" (Pheasant-Kelly, "Abjection, Trauma, Catharsis" 12)—the empty public transports are finally inadequate, deeply unsettling signifiers of persistence. The transports are a haunting reminder of the devastating loss of the three deceased officers and the absence of all New Yorkers who caught the train, ferry, or subway on the previous morning, the lower camera positions on September 12, which emphasize the unfilled seats, reiterating the horrifying absence of commuters (figs. 1.9–1.10). The inclusion in an early establishing scene of actual PAPD lockers used by officers who lost their lives—which "remained untouched,

Figure 1.9. Pezzulo discusses the Yankees on a packed subway train on the morning of 9/11.

Figure 1.10. An empty subway car on the morning of September 12, including an unread newspaper.

and . . . [were hung with] memorialized 'legacy' photos" ("*World Trade Center* Production Notes")—not only accentuates this loss but foreshadows it, creating a foundational absence within the story world that shadows the entire film.[45] These absences are irredeemably underscored as Allison and her family solemnly survey the countless missing-person notices placed in the hospital, engulfing their reverie over Jimeno's recovery. In spite of the successful rescue, the film necessarily and repeatedly laments those who would remain forever unrecovered: a gap *World Trade Center* cannot—and likely does not want to—close, ultimately reflecting the gravity of the attacks. From seeking to contain the horror by focusing on the "small" human experience of the trapped men and their families over the architectural and historic, these moments return scale to the attacks—*and* the film. They extend the human element beyond the two men's story and grant a face to those absented by the attacks.[46] However necessary to acknowledge 9/11's wider consequences, the power of these absences in *World Trade Center* accumulates and eventually eclipses the presumed optimism of the epilogue. Stone's own recollections of 9/11's victims recognize this: "They'd never be coming home. That's when it struck me the hardest. That's when I felt the emptiness" (qtd. in Gentry 49).

Yet it is another unresolved, even more disquieting, absence that definitively destabilizes the superficial neatness of *World Trade Center*'s ending. Beyond Karnes's veiled reference to a "them" who will be confronted "out there"—a reference that opens up rather than closes off the narrative—*World Trade Center* assiduously looks away from its terror-Others. The attacks here serve to restore uniformed masculinity and recenter phallocentric power, evinced most clearly in Karnes's reassertion of remilitarized masculinity in walking self-assuredly over the top of the earlier site of emasculation after the men's recovery. The conscious absenting of the perpetrator terror-Other, the attacks only represented by the shadow of a plane and dull thud of the impact, is incoherently suggestive of an attack-event without an attacker-cause. However, as relational, the reassertion of normative (uniformed) masculinity is finally undermined in the yawning absence of specifically who attacked on 9/11, the unspecified and unnamed terror-Other. Stone's unwillingness (or incapacity) to identify the terror threat or the perpetrators is characterized by Michael Lewis as a "deliberate incuriosity" (43). Yet this may represent the film's lasting significance, one that signals the impossibility of persuasively reimagining or redefining normative (uniformed) masculinity against an absence or void. Masculinities are performed and defined in relation to and interaction with others, including Other and alternative masculinities; they neither exist, nor can be reconstructed, in isolation. Normative uniformed masculinity cannot be redefined against the discomfiting absence of the terror-Other, who by its very absence fundamentally troubles the recuperation of American masculinity in *World Trade Center*. The challenge violently announced by the perpetrator-Others on 9/11 cannot simply be erased by absenting them.

Despite seeming to deliver a simple, straightforward Hollywood narrative about courage, survival, and male (and through the uniform: national) redemption, *World Trade Center*—almost in spite of itself and perhaps unavoidably—ultimately reflects the ambivalent and unsettling reality of the attacks and their impact on conventional notions of American masculinity. *World Trade*

Center's formal and narrative attempts to promote redefinition, rehabilitation, and closure—for its male characters *and* the nation, all represented by the uniform—especially founder when the film frees the trapped men from the hole and itself from its contained "small" story. When the film (also, finally) conveys the wider horror of the attacks, it resists closure, appropriately mirroring the film's wider social context. Inevitably, the scale of the unrecoverable loss and its unfathomable absences overshadows *World Trade Center*'s epilogue of individual persistence, national revival, and masculine recuperation. In its unsuccessful striving for the coherence of classical narration, *World Trade Center* can neither fully contain the horror it represents nor represent the horror it contains. The film establishes the frightening absence and unknowability of the terror-Other and ongoing anxieties about the capacity to rehabilitate unstable and threatened conventional masculinities in the encounter with terror. *World Trade Center*'s apparent conventionality shields the audience from "what we are not yet ready to see," but what is concealed ambivalently and unsettlingly resurfaces and persists—and this is perhaps the film's real revelation.

2

"I DON'T KNOW WHY THIS IS HAPPENING"
Shamed Everymen and America's Own Unknowable Monsters

Giant monster movies, which portray how humanity has overreached or nature cannot be controlled, also routinely (re)present an opportunity to reinvigorate society. Much as in apocalypse-disaster films, this often requires purging guilt through (male) sacrifice, before renewing society via heterosexual union or familial reunion. In following five twenty-something New Yorkers after an attack by a large, unidentified monster, *Cloverfield* presents a highly mediated, ground-level experience of living *through* terror, using a quest narrative to redeem previously unheroic everyman masculinity. The film details the intimate experience of a perhaps apocalyptic terror event, signaled by opening Department of Defense titles that declare the following video was recovered from "the area formerly known as Central Park."[1] Comprising only this "discovered" amateur video footage—celebrating Rob's (Michael Stahl-David) going-away party before his departure to Japan for work—*Cloverfield* adheres to a pseudodocumentary, realist aesthetic and thus also to its inherent partiality and limitedness. The video also includes footage shot on an earlier day of Rob and Beth's fledgling romance, bookending and interspersed throughout recording the monster's attack—with the narrative intermittently cutting back to this footage, functioning as flashbacks contiguously unfolding on the video as the monster's attack ostensibly records over it. From the beginning, the power of looking through the camera and filming others is associated with a desire to surveil, control, and capture for male characters. Yet the handheld personal camera, which explores the limits and inadequacy of representation, also communicates the instability, vulnerability, and insufficiency of the urban American male.

The terror event nevertheless seems to offer the urban everyman an opportunity to reverse prior "unmanning" as spurned lover. Unable to counter the monstrous threat professionally, unusual in a giant monster movie, the everyman's response to large-scale terror must be displaced onto a heroic quest. After the attack begins during the party, Rob's brother, Jason (Mike Vogel), is killed when the monster destroys the Brooklyn Bridge. The group's escape blocked, Rob fixates on a quest to rescue Beth (Odette Annable), who now lies injured and trapped in her father's high-rise apartment. The monster's attack not only offers a platform for male redemption but also promotes sociocultural renewal through the heterosexual couple.[2] Rob's redemption is seemingly realized when his and Beth's final declarations of love, sheltered in a bridge tunnel in Central Park, figure him finally as quest hero. Indeed, director Matt Reeves attests that the film's meaning derives from Rob's making amends as quest hero and saying, "I love you" (*Cloverfield* DVD commentary). However, redemption for Rob is partial, temporary, and ambivalent—narratively undermined by, at best, the qualified success of his quest. This first redemptive kiss is disrupted by the reappearance of the monster. Ultimately, Rob's redemption and societal renewal are fatally compromised when he and Beth fail to escape Manhattan, trapped in the obliteration of the island by carpet bombing as the military initiates a "Hammer Down" protocol in the apparently vain hope of annihilating the monster.[3] It is certainly not unusual for the hero's redemptive actions to require such male sacrificial death, as in Charlton Heston's characters in *Earthquake* (Robson 1974) and *The Omega Man* (Sagal 1971). Yet for the object of the hero's redemption to also die (in vain) is atypical. Reeves's assertion that the ending is "life-affirming" *in spite of* their demise suggests a profound pessimism, acknowledging the limits of the everyman response to the eruption of terror. Rob wins a measure of redemption in simply coming back for Beth, but far from rescuing her, Rob's quest primarily seeks to "play at" rather than fulfill the hero's role. *Cloverfield* also centrally explores notions of containment, specifically the struggle to contain the monster and the horror of its attack, if not visually within the frame, then generically and narratively. The giant monster exceeds the everyman's capacity to "know" and (visually) "capture" it, exacerbated by the inherent limitedness associated with the handheld camera. The remasculinization quest Rob undertakes after the advent of terror is doomed to fail because of the disruptive giant monster's persistent elusiveness and unknowability for characters (its undiminished strangeness), the characteristics of a handheld camera consistently aligned with male characters, and the equally disruptive role of the film's seemingly maligned females.

The end of *Cloverfield* confirms there is *no* safe space for the characters—and no secure seat of spectatorship for the audience. The giant monster, the film's terror-Other, and the apocalyptic military response fatally close off the possibility of safe haven; as Rob acknowledges at film's end: "There's nowhere to go." Far from renewal and reaffirmation through redeemed masculinity and prospective heterosexual union, *Cloverfield* offers only obliteration and the ambiguous prospects of the horrific persistence of the terror-Other. While the Department of Defense titles signal that society survives—and we watch the film, after all—everyday life has been terminally disrupted. *Cloverfield*'s state of permanently embracing fear, restricted vision and limited knowledge, and inscrutable monster as "stranger" signal a limited imagination not only of masculine redemption post-9/11 but of the prospects of survival at all.[4] In the end, absent knowing what the unknowable, incomprehensible monster-as-stranger is or why its attack is happening, everyman masculinity remains unredeemed. Moreover, displacing national-institutional fears of masculine inadequacy onto the everyman hero's body, *Cloverfield* finally identifies him as the truly "monstrous" figure that requires annihilation and abolishment.

Cloverfield, New York, and the Remediated Experience of 9/11

Hollywood's unadulterated pleasure in destructive spectacle was criticized after 9/11, as the assumed hollowness of such spectacles suddenly felt saturated with meaning.[5] Social commentators and scholars speculated that spectacular imagery of New York's destruction would cease post-9/11. In line with its historic openness as an immigration site, the city is an island target and entry point for destruction by enraged movie monsters and threats invariably coming from or involving water.[6] Nevertheless, a number of Hollywood films, including *The Day after Tomorrow* (Emmerich 2004), *War of the Worlds* (Spielberg 2005), *Cloverfield*, and *The Day the Earth Stood Still* (Derrickson 2008), soon revisited the city's imagined destruction, extending New York's unabated symbolic status within Sontag's "imagination of disaster."

Cloverfield's clear and discomfiting evocation of iconic 9/11 imagery also elicited an ambivalent critical response. Initial critical attention focused almost exclusively on the film's imagery, which exploited well-known amateur footage to re-create the terror of the ground-level experience of the attacks. *Cloverfield* overtly evokes the amateur street-level footage that constituted much of the most iconic coverage of 9/11's early destruction and panic. This reprised earlier critical debates that Hollywood would, in Stephanie Zacharek's appraisal, repackage 9/11 as entertainment for profit ("*Cloverfield*"). While she claims there is no reason horror films should not mirror real-life fears, she criticizes the filmmakers for needlessly "cheapening . . . real-life tragedy" for commercial reasons.[7] In the case of *Cloverfield*, popular critical opinion seemed especially discomfited because it was a supposedly low-genre horror film that was referring explicitly to 9/11. Olly Richards, on the other hand, represents another, less common vein of popular criticism that praised how *Cloverfield* re-created the experience, emotionally and aesthetically (or technically), of 9/11, via "the sort of frantic [amateur] footage we associate with unfathomable terror." Most clearly, early in the monster's attack, a skyscraper collapses in on itself, shot from the same street-level angle as amateur footage of the collapse of Tower Two. As the building collapses, a dust and debris cloud (again) heads toward the camera—a handheld camera operated by one character—sending panicked citizens running toward and past it. The handheld camera even mimics oft-used footage of the consequent hurried escape into a store as the dust cloud completely envelopes the street outside and turns all black. When the main characters emerge from the store, they discover the people outside covered in gray ash, wandering like ghosts, as paper flutters down from the sky.[8]

Most scholars likewise focus primarily on how the film used viral marketing for promotion, including encouraging fan-produced videos, and how it affectively restaged the subjective experience of 9/11 and reenacted the mediation of iconic and frightening footage of the attacks via an amateur camera aesthetic.[9] In this vein, scholarship also focused on how the film technically reenacted the experience of contemporary terrorism, both in its style (Bordwell, "A Behemoth from the Dead Zone") and in its use of sound (Coyle).[10] The scholarly literature largely echoes Steffen Hantke's observation that *Cloverfield* "not only depicts but affectively reenacts, re-creates, and reproduces the massive devastation" of 9/11 ("Return of the Giant Creature" 237), with Monahan discussing how the film attempts to re-create the sensory assault of 9/11's mediation to stimulate and shock audiences who witnessed it.[11] It is not just the imagery, but how it is visually presented, that recalls 9/11. *Cloverfield* comprehensively reconstructs the *imagined* experience of 9/11, an aesthetic conflation of the predominant mediated, televisual experience and the personal, ground-level experience represented in those televisual images via amateur handheld video footage. In evoking amateur ground-level footage, *Cloverfield* induces the fear associated with such a limited, unknowing position. Indeed, the film's aesthetic is especially jarring, which prompted numerous apocryphal tales about the adverse bodily effects of its "shaky cam" on cinema audiences. This not only places the audience in the chaos of the moment but also persistently recalls audience attention to the camera. Critics and scholars also focus on the film's generic hybridity, most obviously its blend of science fiction, disaster, and horror, merging the "recovered footage" film in vogue at the time and the giant monster movie most common to 1950s Cold War American cinema.[12]

Giant Monsters and Invasion Movies: Contemporary Fears and Anxieties

Giant monsters and science fiction creatures occupy a rich cinematic and generic history. They are routinely considered to reflect contemporary sociopolitical fears and anxieties, especially in periods of perceived national crisis, such as their oft-cited relation to Cold War anxieties. Steffen Hantke observes a post-9/11 resurgence in Cold War–era science fiction invasion films, particularly in relation to remakes, like *War of the Worlds* and *The Invasion* (Hirschbiegel 2007). Hantke also observes that contemporary critical consensus recognizes a wide range of ideological variation across films. This complexity and ambivalence are often precluded from critical considerations of post-9/11 monster and invasion films. Perhaps unsurprisingly, 9/11 and the war on terror were succeeded by the revitalization-yet-reimagination of such figures of terror. Giant monster movies typically delight in spectacle, especially of their gigantic creatures and the havoc they wreak, allowing audiences both to displace *and* to confront contemporary fears and anxieties.[13] Matt Reeves acknowledges, in characterizing Rob's quest, that *Cloverfield* represents a "way of dealing with the anxieties of our time" (*Cloverfield* DVD commentary). These films articulate and ultimately evacuate their creations to contain the fears and anxieties they arouse. While *Cloverfield* textually acknowledges its indebtedness to, and intertextual association with, famed Hollywood monster movies and monsters, it perhaps most readily compares to *Gojira* (Honda 1954).[14] As the emergence of Gojira frighteningly articulated Japanese anxieties in the wake of its experiences of firebombing and atomic weapons late in World War II, *Cloverfield*'s amateur handheld camera aesthetic imagines the subjective and mediated experience of terrorism.[15] Yet the *Cloverfield* monster is starkly different from its direct forebears.

The giant monsters in *Gojira* and *Godzilla* (Emmerich 1998) are neither malevolent nor irrational, however destructive. They are recognized as our creations, in a sense, and can be described, analyzed, and understood—and so nullified or countered. However, the *Cloverfield* monster's threat is, or at least is perceived as such, by its victims. Admittedly a camera within the film's story world, the handheld personal camera doubles as the camera-that-films and is the only perspective offered, with the exception of the Department of Defense titles. This malevolence also characterizes monstrous and alien threats in *War of the Worlds* and *Quarantine* (Dowdle 2008) through to *A Quiet Place* (Krasinski 2018). In its deliberate yet indiscriminate targeting of civilians, the *Cloverfield* monster is quite clearly a terror agent, if not strictly by recognized scholarly definitions—its lacks discernible political goals, for example—then certainly by popular discursive standards. Incomprehensible and without apparent motivation, as Hantke observes, the monster "displays a sense of enmity so uncharacteristic" ("Return of the Giant Creature" 244). Steen Christiansen argues that the *Cloverfield* monster, more than merely a Freudian return of the repressed, is the "perfect personification" of how Western culture regards the terrorist, "a myth of evil" that "attacks the symbolic landscape . . . from a position of secrecy." Akin to modern terror, the monster seems to come out of nowhere, and its attack is without apparent motivation. The uncharacteristic multiplicity of this terror-Other is equally pertinent. The giant monster carries dog-sized, spiderlike parasites that render the terror more intimate and personal, bringing it to ground level. This also links the monster-parasite relationship to the structure of the modern terror organization, with a symbolic host giving succor and a platform to smaller organisms, like terror cells. In line with creator J. J. Abrams's aspiration, *Cloverfield* is a monster movie for post-9/11 America, with a monster that is clearly "[America's] own."

Realist Horror and the Pseudodocumentary Aesthetic

Science fiction creatures and monstrous bodies are also historically and thematically tied to horror film.[16] Yet *Cloverfield*'s interest in the victim-experience of broadly sketched characters picked off one by one by an unrelenting monster also recalls the slasher, long academically associated with issues of gender identification and gender anxiety. *Cloverfield* indulges the desire to punish the young—and encourages shifting audience allegiances, taking pleasure in how the monster-killer progressively eliminates the film's less-than-interesting character types—vacuous, banal, and self-obsessed. In *Cloverfield*, the features of the American slasher film, in which character affluence and whiteness (read: blandness, or lack of differentiation) are historically characteristic, intriguingly intersect with features of modern terror. The selective elimination of victims, typically a consequence of some moral transgression or perceived slight against the monster, is paradoxically random and indiscriminate but also feels highly specific and targeted.[17]

Stylistically, *Cloverfield* exemplifies the cinematic resurgence—thoroughly exhausted (and often *exhausting*) by the early 2010s—of realist horror that employs the recovered-footage conceit, a pseudodocumentary form, an amateur or personal subjective camera, and a film-within-a-film, including *Paranormal Activity*, *Diary of the Dead*, and *Quarantine*.[18] David Bordwell observes that *Cloverfield* employs what is termed "restricted narration," where a "film confines the audience's range of knowledge," often to a single character's or group's perspective ("A Behemoth from the Dead Zone"). Bordwell outlines the advantages of this perspective, particularly for a lower-budget film, including the capacity to "delay full revelation of the creature," "build up uncertainty and suspense," and encourage audience involvement through their persistent attachment to the characters' experience and peril. As Bordwell argues, the handheld technique "yields a severely restricted range of knowledge," likewise promoting gaps in audience knowledge. While not uncommon in horror or science fiction, it stands in stark contrast to the omniscient perspective characteristic of giant monster movies.

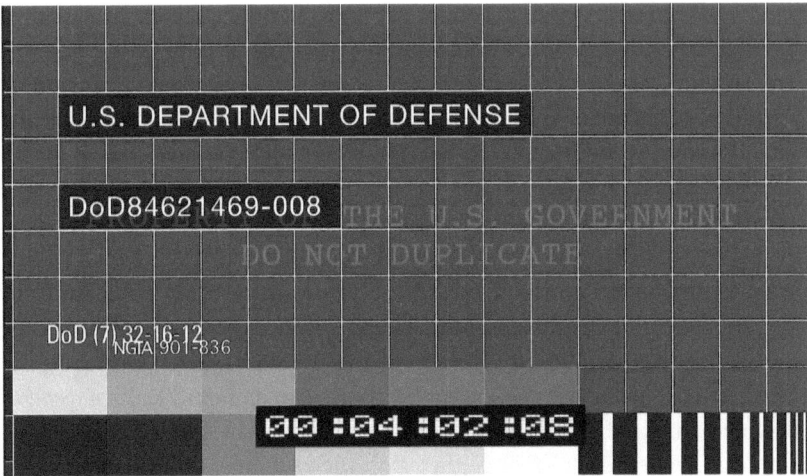

Figure 2.1. A Department of Defense notification "authenticates" the video footage to follow.

The conceit of the amateur video camera also strives to establish the video document's authenticity, with the discovered-footage device raising the prospect of the depicted events as real or having happened.[19] This aesthetic approach employs the banality of the everyday to increase terror and dread. The absence of a score or nondiegetic music also implies the video footage is unadorned—and, in a sense, that we are *not* watching a "movie." The film's opening Department of Defense notification (fig. 2.1) similarly authenticates the succeeding video, akin to the "based on real events" opening title conceit, with accompanying ominous voice-over, employed since *The Texas Chain Saw Massacre* (Hooper 1974). Yet, as Clover notes, this now characteristic generic device long ago devolved in its capacity to shock audiences. The aesthetic convention now situates the film generically, rather than being an effective strategy to frighten, and might relate more to broader cinematic trends, technological developments, and budgetary concerns. It has become so commonplace that audiences recognize it as a device and experience it as an effect with intended affect. The device perhaps now functions oppositely for audiences, serving to contain rather than enhance the threat of terror.

The Emergent Hero: Privileging Everyman Masculinity

The "emergent hero" is a staple of giant monster and science fiction–disaster movies. For example, in *Them!*, the police officer (James Whitmore) who first witnesses the giant radioactive ants' devastation becomes an integral part of the battle to defeat the monsters. The (imminent) disaster or attack thrusts a previously minor, marginalized, or misunderstood character, an eccentric scientist or a humble police sergeant, into the role of hero. The emergent hero becomes tasked with leading the response to unprecedented, potentially catastrophic challenges to society and possesses skills or knowledge of specific value in learning about and countering the monstrous or apocalyptic threat. Although elevated to hero status by circumstance, the emergent hero was inherently heroic; the catastrophe merely calls on or provokes his heroism. Invariably detailing a successfully coordinated, collective response, such films primarily thematize authority, power, and professional competence. In Cold War–era films, this culminates in "reaffirming the integrity and efficiency" of institutional power (Hantke, "Return of the Giant Creature" 240). Despina Kakoudaki contends that 1990s science fiction–disaster films like *Armageddon* (Bay 1998), which she considers melodramas, represent a shift in generic focus onto "disaster response." That is, they shift their emphasis from assigning or identifying responsibility onto the capacity to contribute to the collective effort to identify the threat's genesis, find a solution, and resolve it.[20]

Yet, as also a horror film, *Cloverfield* repositions the emergent hero *as* an everyman, atypically attempting to configure everyman masculinity as heroic. Andrew Tudor identifies horror film's historic investment in the victim function and trials of the everyperson, who faces the monster isolated from authorities. Yet Karen Renner and Lori Crowe separately observe that *Cloverfield* is part of a contemporary focus in Hollywood science fiction–fantasy on "average" or "ordinary" protagonists, in films like *War of the Worlds* and *2012* (Emmerich 2009). In contrast to 1950s films like *When Worlds Collide* and *The Beast from 20,000 Fathoms*, this narrative focus shifts from protagonists officially tasked with saving humanity, averting catastrophe, or defeating the aliens to protagonists who can at most save themselves and their immediate families.[21] Such everymen are unable to draw on specific professional skills or knowledge to resolve the threat, nor do they possess privileged access to (or a role in) the governmental-institutional response. These everymen are overwhelmed by extraordinary circumstances, *less than ordinary* rather than representative. The monster exceeds the comprehension of the everymen, indicated in Rob's final testimony: "Something attacked the city. I don't know what it is." In this sense, *Cloverfield*'s concentration on an everyman protagonist, as well as its adherence to the handheld camera, additionally foregrounds restricted vision and limited knowledge. This links the film to other "subjective" films and examples of restricted narration in film noir, such as *Lady in the Lake* (Montgomery 1947) and *Dark Passage* (Daves 1947). The everyman figure is common to film noir, especially associated with private eyes who struggle (often in vain) to overcome their position of unknowing. However, unlike the optical point-of-view shots in those films, *Cloverfield*'s first-person points of view are mediated, with characters instead using a recording technology to retell the story events. The shift in narrative attention also spotlights—and perhaps reflects—military-governmental failure or incapacity to understand and effectively counter the monstrous threat. Catastrophe makes authority available to the hero.

War of the Worlds and Remasculinizing the Everyman Father-Protagonist

Recent films with an everyman father-protagonist, including *War of the Worlds*, *The Road* (Hillcoat 2009), *The Mist* (Darabont 2007), and *2012*, primarily detail his desperate attempts to restore or maintain his paternal status in the absence of protective institutions.[22] Paternal redemption is an acknowledged staple of science fiction disaster and apocalyptic films, with the apocalyptic crisis offering a space in which deficiencies of fatherhood are supposedly resolved. This extends even to more conventional disaster-apocalypse movies like *The Day after Tomorrow*, in which redemptive emphasis largely lies in the perceived need to redeem paternal failings as a father (and husband) as much as, if not more than, professional disaster response and saving society. In *War of the Worlds*, a remake of H. G. Wells's novel and a 1953 film, for example, the military is evidently ineffectual against the terror threat, with institutional authority overwhelmed and ostensibly absent from early in the attack. Persistently unable to "establish a sense of order and protection," the military is even only restored offscreen (Gunn 6). Although explicitly located in a post-9/11 world, with the hero's daughter asking if terrorists are responsible for the attacks, the film numerously recasts 9/11 imagery of collapsing buildings, a downed airplane, and rows of missing-person photographs.[23] It also evokes fears that arose in 9/11's immediate aftermath, with the Martian attack arising out of the American (sub)urban street, the alien threat incubating undetected, like a sleeper cell, from inside—"They're already here." In the film, Ray (Tom Cruise) is a deadbeat working-class dad from New Jersey. Divorced and estranged from his wife and children, Ray neither holds the respect of his teenage son nor even recalls his daughter's peanut allergy. His ex-wife's new husband has even symbolically replaces Ray as "father." The film focuses on the everyman father's response to terror as Ray attempts to deliver his children to their mother and the home after aliens invade Earth. Although this response is distinctly nonprofessional, he in part redeems his earlier insufficiencies as father by repeatedly protecting his daughter through transgressive violence. James Gunn argues that the audience transfers authority and responsibility onto the everyman-father as the only individual possessing the power to protect. Institutional absence creates a power vacuum in which Ray is able to reestablish his own paternal authority (or reassume one he had eschewed). The terror threat enables oft-maligned, even failed, emergent everyman heroes to redeem previous personal failings. The everyman protagonist inevitably needs the disaster as much as, if not more than, his family needs him when the disaster-apocalypse strikes.

The recuperation of the working-class everyman father in *War of the Worlds* is, however, ambivalent. Ray delivers his daughter safely to the family home, and his son, who had earlier run away to the military, miraculously survives. The family is reunited and the home reconstituted, with fathers (actual and institutional) invoked in their sustenance and preservation. However, it is as if *War of the Worlds* employs the improbable triumph of a father, "plagued with evidence of his unmanly ineptitude" from the film's outset, to erase America's "memory of a deep and defining defeat" (Faludi 10). The son's unexplained and implausible return—he literally emerges out of nowhere—and newfound respect for his previously disdained father, are particularly jarring. Nevertheless, Ray restores a status quo that ultimately excludes him on the basis of class, but which his labor and struggles have served to support. The final, irrevocable redundancy of this working-class father is stark. Like Ethan Edwards (John Wayne) in *The Searchers*, whose obsessive drive to avenge the killing of his brother's family and recover his kidnapped niece slowly but surely erodes his humanity, Ray has had to become monstrous to restore the home, having used all violent means to protect his daughter from fellow citizen and alien alike. His violence, though, finally precludes his presence within the home. As father, Ray is redeemed but not restored to the family or the home. Still replaced by his ex-wife's new husband, Ray cannot enter the familial home, for he is no longer part of it or the postconflict future.

Remasculinizing the Everyman-Hero: Needing a "Sleeping Beauty"

Cloverfield is similarly primarily occupied with Rob's vain attempt to rebuild everyman masculinity. Characteristic of horror, *Cloverfield* offers the individual, terrified experience of the everyman, rather than the military-governmental response. Rob is not even the initial emergent everyman hero more typical of monster and science fiction–disaster movies. When the attacks occur, his brother, Jason, displays multiple characteristics of the emergent hero. Decisive, confident, and proactive, Jason quickly establishes the group's plan to escape the city via the Brooklyn Bridge, with Rob falling meekly in behind. Rob is by no means heroic in the immediate wake of the monster's attack, but panicked, confused, and fearful. He is persistently marginalized within the frame, occupying off-center screen space and repeatedly positioned with female characters. When the monster's tail comes crashing down on Jason on the bridge, *Cloverfield* provocatively proposes that the ideal everyman hero is not only not privileged in the encounter with modern terror but targeted, eliminated, and effectively redundant.[24]

After Jason's death and the destruction of the Brooklyn Bridge, the remaining group congregates, their escape route seemingly devastated. Rob continues to be marginalized within the frame. He stands helplessly, physically incapable of consoling the distraught Lily. His weakly outstretched hand hangs limply, as if he cannot bridge the gulf in (male) competence between him and Jason, a gulf figured in the body of Jason's fiancée. It is only upon retrieving a voice message from Beth, who lies injured in her father's high-rise apartment, that Rob *is discovered by* his quest. Frightened, overwhelmed, and helpless, Hud's continued custodianship of the camera—another less-than-ordinary everyman—thrusts Rob into *playing* (at) hero in *Cloverfield*. He moves from off-center and marginalized to occupy the narrative and cinematographic focus. Incapable of directly countering the monster, Rob's response is displaced onto a quest to rescue Beth. Through the quest narrative, and in contrast to a conventional science fiction–disaster hero, the film privileges Rob's displaced response over direct engagement with the threat. Accompanying him on his ultimately futile quest are Jason's bereaved girlfriend Lily (Jessica Lucas), her cynical friend Marlena (Lizzy Caplan), and Rob's best friend, Hud (T. J. Miller), who films much of the group's experience of the monster's attack. Marlena is killed by dog-sized parasites that "feed off" the monster, and Hud is later killed by the monster, although it appears that Lily is safely evacuated on a military helicopter.

Deron Overpeck comes closest to exploring *Cloverfield* in relation to masculinity but claims that using terror as an opportunity to embark on a redemptive quest, as the everymen in *War of the Worlds* and *Cloverfield* do, is more emblematic of the nation's narcissistic response to 9/11. This perspective overlooks the trope in apocalypse and science fiction–disaster films of tying the emergent hero's rise to personal redemption, most notable in 1970s disaster films like *Earthquake*. The quest narrative means that the monster's attack affords an opportunity for Rob to redeem perceived failings and overcome personal slights. More significantly, it signals how the hero's quest is refigured, with the ostensible everymen heroes of *War of the Worlds* and *2012* similarly focused on small quests in the face of massive threat, redeeming familial status privileged over disaster response. *Cloverfield* offers a pessimistic representation of the bare necessity of such a local, individual response to terror, acknowledging not so much a lack of interest in the wider horror as how it exceeds the capacity of the everyman. Isolated and overwhelmed, with the government and military unable to offer protection, the everyman may redeem himself in the eyes of family and friends, but he is shockingly ill equipped to understand or effectively combat the monstrous threat. The monster's invasion is catalytic rather than central. Hantke recognizes this in describing the monster's function to "draw attention to the subjective experience of the havoc it creates, to feelings of victimization, helplessness, and loss of individual and collective agency" ("Return of the Giant Creature" 244). While the giant monster's attack is as much an opportunity for the hero, Rob's rescue quest does imply the limits of the everyman's heroism to redress contemporary societal anxieties, viewing the prospects of saving humanity and defeating the monster pessimistically.

The film uses Rob's quest to partially contain the horror of the giant monster's attack, imposing a master narrative of sorts on the otherwise overwhelming and chaotic experience of terror to deflect its troubling excessiveness. *Cloverfield* also seeks to deflect the giant monster's threat by valorizing a heteronormative relationship and reestablishing conventional gender roles in relation to (im)mobility. Rob is initially passive and immobile, particularly in the wake of Jason's death, but the monster's attack leaves Beth prostrate and helpless. Beth's immobility initiates Rob's rescue quest, the only response available to the everyman to counter his redundancy in the face of overwhelming terror. Rob needs the monster's attack as much as Beth requires rescue after she is incapacitated. In this respect, mirroring post-9/11 public discourse about the nation, Rob must become *more* masculine to reverse his passive victimhood.[25] Through the rescue quest, the everyman is afforded a path to remasculinization. The prostrate "Sleeping Beauty" affords him a heroic role to perform in calling on him to come to her aid. The monster's attack facilitates remasculinizing Rob *as* hero but also requires female passivity and helplessness, rendering Beth an immobile victim to elevate Rob into the role of male rescuer. *Cloverfield* centrally explores notions of containment, specifically the struggle to contain the monster and the horror of its attack, if not visually within the frame, then generically and narratively. First, in its remasculinization quest, *Cloverfield* endeavors to impose a comprehensible narrative response and generic structure onto an otherwise *too large, too excessive* experience, to contain the terror depicted. Second, in his quest, Rob as everyman undertakes a displaced response to a terror event and monster that he is otherwise incapable of directly countering.

Formal and Generic Containment: Spectacle and the Handheld Camera

Everyday life and "seeing" in *Cloverfield* are highly mediated, via handheld video cameras, mobile phone cameras, and television news media. Rob and the other partygoers turn immediately to the television news media after an earthshaking shudder and blackout mark the monster's "entrance." Television establishes the veracity of the threat for characters, recalling 9/11's construction as an event intimately associated with its mediated coverage. In a sense, the attacks are made real *through* television, with people glued to televisions as the news media both confirm the actuality of the attacks and construct a narrative through which to make sense of them. Persistently documenting events and one's life via media technologies *makes* them real. For characters in *Cloverfield*, the handheld camera cements the reality of events (as having happened) and confirms one's existence (an index of being) and presence (having-been-there). In *Cloverfield*, the camera is needed to not only show what happened but prove that (and how) it happened. When Hud is asked why he is compelled to continue filming—an observation also made by Reyes—he replies that people will "want to know . . . how it all went down." In this sense, the camera's capacity to make it "real" supports Rob's attempted (re)assertion of masculinity, both encouraging his rescue quest *and* that Hud film it.

The handheld video camera conflates *being* with *having-been-there* and connects people to the events they witness. This is, however, underscored as ambivalent, with camera phones recording the banal—Rob's surprise-party speech—with equivalent enthusiasm as the extraordinary. Early in the attack, before the monster's existence is clearly indicated, Hud's camera films the decapitated head of the Statue of Liberty hurtling toward them on the street. Christiansen rightly claims this confirms a symbolic "attack on American values as much as on American soil," designating the monster as a terrorist. However, this underplays the statue's long-standing symbolic ambivalence in cinema, particularly in relation to notions of "America lost" or identifying who is responsible for liberty's sundering.[26] Frequently deployed in science fiction and disaster films, the statue has symbolized the end of certain ideas of America, including exceptionalism, liberty, and freedom, but is not necessarily tied to (terror) attacks. Mostly, though, this overlooks how *Cloverfield* pejoratively portrays the response of the young urban populace to this supposed attack on freedom. For example, when the decapitated head of Lady Liberty comes to rest, it is surrounded and eagerly photographed and videoed by young urbanites, their backs turned to the source of its decapitation, unprepared and blind to the threat.

The handheld camera and its operator claim greater access to events *and* capacity for objectivity, evident in Hud's repeated declarations at the party, "Look out, documenting." This superficially supports James Kendrick's claim that the documentary or home movie aesthetic, "rough, shaky, immediate," is both a vehicle for the "real" and a source of terror for the audience that cuts through boundaries between audience and screen—suggestive of *presentation* rather than *representation*. The video camera is nonetheless the only privileged object in the film; it must survive even if no other character does. The ubiquitous presence of the camera and persistent use of direct address uneasily instantiate a culture of the ongoing, self-conscious performance of identity (a being-for-others, which incorporates the camera) *and* the camera's function as testimony (of having-been). Rob's and Beth's final direct-to-camera testimonies in the tunnel, as the sirens warning of the impending "Hammer Down" begin wailing, recognize the capacity for the electronic record to both survive them *and* extend their life—"Just tell them who you are." Similarly, Rob's declaration of the names of those in the group killed by the monster implies that the video testifies to both being and loss; it documents, grounds, and memorializes, including Rob's redemptive quest. Yet the inherent limits of the handheld camera also create uncertainty about the documentary record; the film both valorizes *and* mistrusts video images. While characters' immediate response is to document events on camera, nagging doubts remain about the veracity of what is shown—how much is captured and how much missed—and its relative permanence, with the capacity to record over (and erase) video undermining its assumed capacity to document.[27]

Cloverfield also uses genre and formal style to contain the extreme terror it articulates. Cinematic conventions, such as the introductory production company logos, and generic devices, such as the Department of Defense stamp—and the persistence of institutions indicated by each—ostensibly envelop and contain the film's terror. The Department of Defense title implies that although everyday life is terminally disrupted—neither the characters nor Central Park survives the attack—military institutions, and thereby some form of society, survive.[28] While the proximity and limitedness of the handheld amateur camera approximates real disaster—it "creates frighteningly open-ended realms of meaning," as the audience "cannot know what happens next, to whom [or] why" (Kakoudaki 146)—its aesthetic deployment within genre conventions in part contains and reassures. Yet *Cloverfield*'s handheld camera aesthetic—its stylistic authenticity—is formally constructed and concealed in various ways. The film's cinematographers offer the mannered appearance of amateur camerawork, using a single camera and multiple takes rather than masters, reverse shots, close-ups, and coverage shots. The video characters' shoot is seemingly unedited and off-the-cuff, with cuts or edit points artfully concealed in whip/swish pans and crash zooms. As a result, *Cloverfield* has much longer-length shots than other contemporary Hollywood films (Bordwell, "A Behemoth from the Dead Zone"). The film's constructed authenticity includes actors' shooting of footage, particularly of events before the attack.[29] Steve Pile claims that in "spectacularizing the horror," *Cloverfield* "veils the traumas" of 9/11 (302–3). However, it may be that the concealment and blurring of spectacle via the representational limits of the handheld camera function to contain the terror of 9/11. *Cloverfield* seemingly does not afford a master gaze or frame; this is its organized feature, giving the *appearance* of instability, discontinuity, and unsteadiness. The attacks of 9/11 were so anxiety inducing for viewers because, although the mediated construction of "9/11" comprised a superabundance of images from a multiplicity of perspectives, its co-option within a news media narrative left it without a master (or Hollywood) perspective. The event of 9/11 is both unrepresentable (including in cinema) because it is too "massive" *and* overrepresented. *Cloverfield* therefore occupies the space in between, between over- and under-abundance. Despite the limitedness the amateur camera connotes, *Cloverfield* contains anxiety through a single perspective, a master frame of sorts, however inadequate. Yet *Cloverfield*'s generic hybridity, divergences from genre conventions, challenging females, and violently disruptive monster inevitably confound such containment strategies.

Giant monster movies enthrall audiences *as and through* spectacle, allowing a privileged, all-encompassing perspective and maximum visual pleasure of the monster and its destruction. However, unlike the self-reflexive genre pastiches and parodies of premillennial adaptations of classic 1950s science fiction films, *Cloverfield* mimics the partial perspective associated with real disaster-terror, its amateur mediation explicitly evoking the fear-filled, disorienting individual experience of 9/11. The omniscient perspective provides a safe aesthetic distance from which to revel in the spectacle of destruction. The film's adherence to the perspective of the amateur video camera disrupts the typical audience position in monster movies. *Cloverfield* is more interested in the victim experience than in its gigantic creature, with the intensity not even temporarily relieved by the occasional provision of the monster's point of view. This is a consequence of the film's stylistic aesthetic—and the raw, horrified, limited personal experience of terror.[30] This aesthetic connects to the *Cloverfield* audience's earlier experience of 9/11 in their youth—presuming a predominantly late-teen and early adult demographic—reenacting how the attacks "disrupted seats of spectatorship" (Muntean). The "discovered" video itself arguably similarly establishes the veracity of the threat, but the multiple story lines the video presents—the opening love story and the party—are all literally disrupted. Rob's and his friends' collective response is characterized by panic, inaction, and impotence. Being "caught in the middle" of events, as Rob later testifies, suggests that immediate proximity to terror—spatial and temporal—limits the capacity to grasp its meaning. Rob speculates that anyone who later watches the video will undoubtedly know more about the monster. Horror for the audience of *Cloverfield* lies not only in the monster's transgression and threat to society but in being anchored to the characters' restricted, ground-level experience of terror. The film's confinement to the personal or subjective camera frighteningly collapses the distance between character and audience. Positioned with the victim-characters, the film's persistent adherence to the subjective camera (and sound) traps character and audience alike within the spectacle of terror.[31] In *Cloverfield*, the true horror lies in being caught inside and being overwhelmed by the spectacle of terror. More than this, the success of Rob's heroic quest is unsettled by the incomprehensibility of the giant monster and the characteristic attributes of the handheld camera.

Empowering and Undermining the Male (Look) through the Camera

The handheld camera in *Cloverfield* repeatedly facilitates male desire to obtain a sense of power and control through its look. Rob first uses the camera to film his and Beth's fledgling love story. Jason then takes up the camera, filming preparations six weeks later for Rob's going-away party, before thrusting it on Hud, who films the party and later his everyman perspective of the monster's attack and Rob's quest to rescue Beth. It is telling that the video—and the film—begins with the camera in Rob's hands, filming Beth's apartment, but mostly the sleeping Beth. These earlier moments—which precede the monster's attack temporally but act as bookends narratively—function as "mementoes of innocence and youth," as Rebecca Coyle claims (223), but also express acts of (male) power. This power is, however, disavowed throughout by each cameraman. For example, throughout the going-away party, Hud repeatedly invokes the invisibility of the camera and its operator: "I'm just documenting. I'm not here." In this sense, the male look seeks to conceal itself behind the camera, and

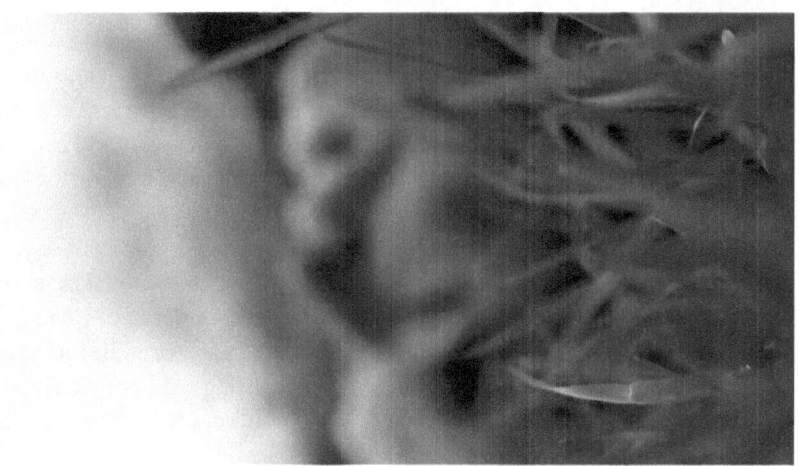

Figures 2.2–2.3. The camera's autofocus oscillates between Hud and the background, sundering the intimate alignment between male operator and camera.

to naturalize the union of man and camera. Yet the camera equally allows Hud to insert himself into the action and gain greater access than usual. And once the attack begins, it establishes distance from what would otherwise overwhelm.[32]

The camera allows each everyman to claim a mastery otherwise absent in his life, a power repeatedly exercised to disempower and objectify females. Hud particularly embraces the role of camera operator to compensate for his own marginality and incompetence by documenting events. However, *Cloverfield* unsettles the assumed power the camera—and looking—affords male subjects. Initially, the camcorder in *Cloverfield* is wholly aligned with male perspectives, shot choices, and narrative focus. While not sutured to its male characters, the camera's look is structured through male perceptions. The film's intimate and persistent alignment of male consciousness with the camera is never more evident than late in the film, after the monster downs the helicopter as the surviving characters attempt to evacuate Manhattan. While it is important not to automatically equate *optical* point of view with *character* point of view, which also encompasses Hud's ongoing to-camera narration, Hud's statement "If this is the last thing you see, it means I died" implies the male look and the camera's "eye" are one. If he dies, the recording ends. When the monster downs the helicopter, the momentary loss of camera sound aurally signifies Hud's temporarily dazed state. And when the monster soon thereafter kills the cameraman, the camera becomes unmoored from Hud's look—a poignant example of the fallen-camera convention, according to Bordwell ("A Behemoth from the Dead Zone"). The camera's autofocus oscillates repeatedly and uncertainly from Hud to the background, unable to register or fix on either (figs. 2.2–2.3). These repeated focal shifts do more than signal the camera's focal indecision. They signal Hud's death—he no longer *registers* for the camera—and imply the camera too can longer see without its male operator. The persistent alignment reiterates the unity and interdependence of male operator and camera, one (visually) sundered by the monster, but first contested by females who decide to *look back*.

Male shot choices before the monster's attack consistently convey the power of looking and the camera as its agent. Each male character who takes up the camera first uses it to watch a female whom he sexually desires *without her knowledge*. Each uses the camera to fragment the female form, lingering on an exposed leg, scanning over a sleeping body, or seeking out a potential mate. In Beth's father's apartment, Rob's camera aerially surveys New York from the window of the high-rise apartment (fig. 2.4).

Immediately after his aerial survey, Rob's camera slowly passes over Beth's naked, sleeping body, surveying and objectifying her as he has the landscape below (fig. 2.5). The seeming rationale for Rob's desire (or need) to film his presence in Beth's bed is to evidence his sexual success—to make it real. This moment also explicitly signals Rob's desired mastery and control. Associated with bearing the (camera's) look, he seeks not only to empower himself but to disempower and possess what—or who—is made-object. In first filming her sleeping, mirroring her later prostrate unconsciousness, Rob prefigures Beth in his own imagination as a "Sleeping Beauty."

Likewise, Hud swiftly uses custodianship of the camera at the going-away party—and assumption of a supposed right to look—to talk to Marlena, a friend of Lily's whom he covets. Indeed, he uses the camera to seek her out

Figure 2.4. Rob's camera surveys New York from the window of Beth's father's high-rise apartment.

Figure 2.5. Rob uses the camera to similarly survey Beth's sleeping form.

upon her arrival, the camera literally permitting him to zoom in on her. He subsequently uses it to distantly and invisibly surveil her, and when he finally builds the courage to move toward her, it is as if his camera specifically targets her, seeking to constrain her within its frame (figs. 2.6–2.7).

Although the camera's look is intimately aligned with its male operators, and shot choices initially objectify and fragment the female form, the everyman's dominion of the power to look is repeatedly and almost immediately challenged. *Cloverfield* foregrounds the limits of looking through and with

Figure 2.6. Hud later uses the camera to distantly observe Marlena without her knowledge.

Figure 2.7. As Hud moves toward Marlena, it is as if he and the camera target and seek to constrain her within the frame.

the camera in the effective erasure of Rob's first video and female characters' explicit rejection, even overturning, of their to-be-looked-at status. For example, despite Hud's pretensions to mastery, Marlena pointedly refuses to be the passive object of his look after he and his camera zero in on her at the party; her direct look at the camera causes him to avert his surveilling gaze. Additionally, the initial construction of a controlling gaze is persistently countered by characters' direct address of the camera (and thereby the male operator). This further denaturalizes the camera and demystifies its presumed power, again akin to "first-person" films noir like *Lady in the Lake* and *Dark Passage*. While the camera-film merges the character-operator with the camera, such addresses equally remind the audience—and the partygoers—of the existence-presence of the camera and the look of the male.

Rather than the omniscient perspective typically dominant in the giant monster movie, the restricted perspective and subjective experience offered by the handheld video camera are defined as much by what it does or cannot see. Carol Clover, in her seminal book *Men, Women, and Chain Saws*, notes that the subjective camera, by also "calling attention to what it cannot see . . . gives rise to the sense not of mastery but of vulnerability" (187). In *Cloverfield*, the male camera operator's look is partial, decontextualized, and often incoherent. This is especially evident in frequent jump cuts, characteristic of personal video, throughout the film, which disorient temporality and space. Hud's committed attachment to the role of camera operator after the monster's attack seeks to document what would otherwise merely overwhelm in its abstract excess. Yet the characteristics of the handheld camera formally undermine the presumed power of looking through and with the camera. Hud's handheld camera persistently "misses the action." For example, the first time the group is caught in cross fire between the military and the monster, Hud's camera, fixed on the group, largely misses the spectacular confrontation. While not uncommon in horror, this is certainly atypical of giant monster and science fiction–disaster movies, where the entwined spectacles of monster and destruction are central. In this sense, the film undercuts Hud's repeated but precarious claims to authority and agency: "I'm documenting."

Rob's illusion of mastery is also almost immediately ruptured when Beth momentarily takes control of the camera on the couple's first morning in bed. Already undermining his claims to control of and through the camera-look, Beth's action "unmans" Rob, sundering the initial conflation of gender and sex via the camera. Rob's unease is stark when Beth turns the camera *on* him: he squirms uncomfortably in front of the camera, made-object of the female look through the camera (fig. 2.8). Rob's emasculation is redoubled when Beth playfully mocks the boyish spectacle of his body, pointedly mocking his hairless chest. This active female look fetishizes and even "feminizes" Rob, a precursor of the horror later signaled by being similarly made-object and targeted by the giant terror-Other. Rob's unconvincing assumption of the role of quest hero is marked as compensatory and masquerade from the film's opening, the camera evincing rather than reversing Rob's male emasculation and protective inadequacy. This male masquerade is even apparent in the "salaryman" suit Rob will wear throughout the attack, a uniform especially ill fitted to the role of protagonist-hero.[33] Compounded by his youthful looks, the suit confirms

Figure 2.8. Rob squirms uncomfortably when the camera is turned on him and he is made object.

that Rob can only play at rather than perform everyman heroism. When Rob is temporarily the object of the female look (and the camera), he is clearly evasive, uncomfortable, and vulnerable. It is as if he, she, and it see through his performative inadequacy as a hero. Rob's initial assumption of the camera cannot conceal or compensate for his self-conscious "unmanliness" when the camera communicates a female perspective.

While slasher horror identification was historically assumed to be sadistic and masculine, Carol Clover identified the subgenre's privileging of the feminine, masochistic, but ultimately triumphant victim-perspective. Considered to speak "deeply and obsessively to male anxieties and desires," this requires the "masculinization" of the final girl, particularly through "unmanning" the killer (61). Yet *Cloverfield*'s narrative focus is primarily invested in Rob's response to terror, rather than the survival of its final girl, Lily, who is seemingly the group's only survivor, safely evacuated by helicopter. This male focus evokes comparisons with the Vietnam-era "city-country" horror cycle of the 1970s, and films like *Deliverance* (Boorman 1972) and *The Hills Have Eyes* (Craven 1977), which demonize modernity's emasculation of the urban male and detail his supposed remasculinization in violent confrontation with the "country" male or nature. Representing equally overcivilized urban males, *Cloverfield* arguably likewise blames their predicament on prior "unmanning," recalling conservative arguments proffered after 9/11.[34] Accordingly, some form of remasculinization is required to reestablish threatened or destabilized male identity. And Rob's deep discomfit at scene's end—and the video camera's subsequent switch and advance to the day of the attack—only confirms that the need to secure fragile masculinity is, rather than a response to terror, signaled prior to its advent.

Displacing the Shame of 9/11: Shaming the Young Urban Male

The interrogation of young urban male shame in the critically underappreciated home invasion horror film *The Strangers* similarly articulates persistent cultural anxieties energized post-9/11 about American male inadequacy to fulfill normative gender role expectations. Bryan Bertino's accomplished if derivative first feature, consciously indebted to 1970s slashers and psychological horror, can fruitfully be read along traditional horror theoretical lines such as urban-rural conflict and external threats to the home.[35] However, the film most interestingly exemplifies post-9/11 horror's renewed interest not only in representations of violent transgressions of home and family but in explorations of male responsibility and protective capacity, in films such as *30 Days of Night* (Slade 2007), *Last House on the Left* (Iliadis 2009), *Vacancy* (Antal 2007), and the first *Saw* films (Wan 2004; Bousman 2005). *The Strangers* is seemingly a tidy conservative allegory for the attacks of 9/11, in which an empowered female's rejection of the bonds of matrimony emasculates the American male, not only weakening the familial home but inviting its breach by masked assailants—the film's agents of terror.

An opening montage, overlaid by a panicked, ambiguous 911 call—after a playful opening title that conspicuously evokes *The Texas Chain Saw Massacre*—foreshadows the bloody outcome of these "brutal events" while crucially withholding identification of either victim or perpetrator. As the film subsequently introduces its protagonists, the uncertainty about what has (or will) take place is compounded by the unrelieved silence between James (Scott Speedman) and Kristen (Liv Tyler), driving home from a wedding reception. His downcast head and her tears are only explained, after James has crossed the hearth of his family's summer home without her, as they awkwardly survey the champagne, candles, and rose petals James had readied earlier. There will be no nuptials for this couple.

An early flashback to that evening's declined proposal pointedly appears to represent a sort of *shared* flashback: either constructed from both their perspectives—it reproduces both first-person cameras—or James's *perception* of how he sees himself and how he thinks he is seen by Kristen. Regardless, James clearly manifests characteristics of shame, here and throughout the film, in his perception of how Kristen looks on him: assiduously averting his eyes from her gaze—as the camera approximates her point of view—his eyes and

Figure 2.9. Spurned as "husband," James disconsolately eats ice cream directly from the tub, the declined engagement ring in front of him.

head cast downward. In contrast to embarrassment and guilt, each centered on a specific behavior or action, shame is more fundamental. We feel shame not only for what we have (or have not) done but for who we are; shame cuts to the core. Shame is reflexive and social, "requiring that we look at ourselves and at the way others view us" (Morgan 14). Rather than how others actually see us, "we are ashamed *about ourselves* but *before others*" (Morgan 49, emphasis in original). Shame is tied to our relations with others; shame only becomes shame in the face of another, is only constituted in and through their look on us. The flashback suggests that James's shame is located in—and even caused by—Kristen's perceived judgment, but in truth, he responds, in Michael Morgan's words, to his "own accusation" (20–21). James is unworthy in his own eyes, in *his* projection of how she might see him.

Likewise spurned in love, James is explicitly feminized, depicted disconsolately eating ice cream directly from the tub, the declined engagement ring in front of him in the frame a lingering reminder of his deemed unsuitability for the role of husband (fig. 2.9). After bathing, Kristen returns to the dress she wore to the wedding, which offers a twinned intimation of marriage *and* death: "I only get to wear it once." The film also presents further indication of James's inability to assume the role of husband; his subsequent attempt to consummate a union is thwarted by a knock at the door, marking the onset of the home invasion. James's shame is located not in his rejection by Kristen but in something more fundamental: his incapacity to convincingly perform maleness.

James is *already* shamed, a shame soon embodied as protective failure as the masked threesome's invasion of the home escalates. His response to the monstrous threat, manifested by the home invaders, is undermined by the heavy absence of a powerful father figure. One scene in particular locates his shame as also in (James's perception of) the eyes of the Father. As the home invasion escalates, Kristen, almost needing to remind James of the performative requirements of the role, tells James they need a gun. Eventually finding his father's shotgun, they search for shells in the bedroom. As James fumbles with the gun and shells, he admits, again avoiding meeting Kristen's gaze, "I don't know how to use this thing.... I'm not even sure how to load it." Kristen responds worriedly: "But you said you used to hunt with your dad." Again lowering his head and still avoiding Kristen's gaze, James's mumbled reply trails away as the shame of protective inadequacy is revealed before the suitably horrified Kristen: "No, I never did. It was just something I said." In shame it is not the transgression so much as having that transgression, that perceived deficiency, revealed before another that is the issue. Shame is not so much about being a failed self as about "being an *exposed* failed self" (Morgan 49). His previously declared assurance of male protective capacity is false, an untruth now painfully bared; Kristen will even load the gun for him before he can shoot it.

Shame carries with it the desire to conceal or nullify itself "by negating what gives rise to it" (Morgan 29). However, typically considered too overwhelming, shame is often displaced. Likewise, James's subsequent attempts to end the home invasion culminate in shooting not one of the attackers but his best friend, Mike (Glenn Howerton). As Morgan observes, although shame may begin with a specific failure, it never ends with that failure; one feels shame not only for what one has (or has not) done but for who one is. Mike is significantly also another who exposes his shame, having come at James's request to remove him from the sight/site of his shame, and also having helped him earlier set out the champagne and rose petals. What is supposed to conceal shame is merely, according to Jacobs, "another kind of evasion," "call[ing] attention to what [it is] meant to hide." James's attempt to eradicate his pervasive sense of shame through redemptive violence merely serves to call attention to the very shame of protective incapacity he wishes to conceal. James is soon after captured by the male home invader—satisfying the desire to be punished—leaving Kristen alone, seemingly in the tradition of the final girl.

The young urban male's shame similarly *precedes* the onset of terror in *Cloverfield*. Rob too is *already* shamed, located in his persistent unmanning *in front of* others and the camera. Rob's shame is located in his projection of how Beth (and the camera) perceives him and tangentially associated with an absent father figure. After quarreling with Beth at his party, she leaves with another man. Rob turns his back to the camera when he returns to the apartment, his shame amplified by its (and its male operator's) witnessing of his humiliation.[36] Rob's incapacity to directly respond to the threat implies that it is overcivilized American males who are unable to counter the threat of modern terror. This conveniently displaces wider cultural anxieties about the institutional-national failures of 9/11 onto young urban males; it is they whom the film (and its monster) targets. Rob likewise exhibits the physical symptoms of shame throughout, most clearly evinced in his repeated avoidance of Beth's gaze (casting down or averting his eyes). Rob also attempts to conceal this perceived inadequacy from the penetrating look of the camera (which under Hud's custodianship is effectively another male's), frequently turning his whole body, and especially his face, away. Beth's apartment is identified as her father's, which significantly doubles as the location and goal of Rob's redemption. Rob's quest is seemingly as much about *getting back* to the prelapsarian site of his sexual conquest in the father's apartment—that space and time after bedding Beth, but before the camera is turned back on him—as it is to rescue her. It is *because of* his perceived inadequacy that Rob films. He films the apartment and Beth to vainly acquire rather than evidence power and mastery.

The manifestation of the monster, the actuality of which is also associated with its (at least partial) filming, coincides with Rob's reiterated humiliation when Beth leaves the party with a new lover. Thus, as well as assigning blame for emasculating the American male onto a female, the shamed young male is perhaps even implicated in the monster's eruption. The monster's attack is "called up" or created, like so many monsters, to punish the transgressive female and violently reverse Rob's shame, now figured as monstrous rage. Such representations of internal tensions as external threats are not uncommon in American film. For example, the monstrous personification of evil in *Cape Fear* (Scorsese 1991), Max Cady (Robert De Niro), seemingly conjured by the young daughter (Juliette Lewis), is arguably also called up by the father (Nick Nolte) to reunite the family and reestablish the home (with the father as head). In *Cloverfield*, Beth "unmans" Rob first when she turns the camera on him, objectifying and mocking him, *and* subsequently when she replaces him with another man. The latter act potentially precipitates the monster's attack, which results in Beth's suffering and motivates Rob's remasculinization quest.

Inviting Terror: Blurring Inside and Outside Spaces

Monsters in horror film conventionally blur, challenge, and redefine boundaries between public and private. However, in *Cloverfield*, just as the young everyman is already shamed, so the boundary between city and home is already porous. The proliferation and mobility of personal media and communication technologies make the home(land) vulnerable through dissolving boundaries. The everyday mediation of experience blurs notions of private and public, and inside and outside, and marks the troubling permeability of domestic spaces. The *Cloverfield* monster's attack is first brought into the home—and becomes real for characters—via television. Yet the horrific blurring of public and private space is precipitated from the film's beginning as the handheld camera dizzyingly moves between inside-domestic and outside-public spaces, demonstrating how media and communication technologies not only mediatize experience but collapse traditional spatial distinctions. Repeated jump cuts disorientingly move the audience from one space to another. For example, the film opens with Rob filming in Beth's apartment before a jump cut to Jason filming (about six weeks later) in the streets below. Another jump cut returns the audience to Rob's apartment and preparations for the going-away party. The multiple, fragmented, overlapping stories persistently connect public and private spaces. However, they also destabilize and dissolve the protective boundaries between. Marcia England, exploring breaches of the feminized body and home in horror, observes that in horror such porousness is disconcerting, as the home becomes a conduit for the horror (360). The blurring of public space and private home breaks down the myth that there is a distinction between each; the home is no longer insulated but horrifyingly porous—and thereby open to breach. This may even expedite the monster's unexpected entrance. While the monster confirms the horrific permeability of city/state *and* the home via its breach—especially apparent in how its movement collapses the sheer immensity of the city—the way characters use the camera to blur these boundaries renders modern American society *always already* porous and vulnerable. Beth's father's apartment building, on which a neighboring building has fallen, exemplifies this. It becomes a "frightening space," ripped apart by the monster and now exposed to the outside, the home permeable and frighteningly vulnerable to further attack.

Much like the monster, *Cloverfield* also blurs public and private distinctions via the mutability of the video itself, which is simultaneously home video, documentary evidence, and feature film, and intended variously for personal consumption, military evidence, and cinematic exhibition. For example, the video's—and the film's—final shot captures an *earlier and public* "home video" moment. After their apparent death in the military bombardment, the video again switches back to the couple's first day together, on a merry-go-round at Coney Island. Seemingly a private memento of blossoming love, the unidentified object seen hurtling into the ocean in the distance before the lovestruck couple turn the camera back on themselves—yet another cinematic marine threat to New York—renders the video as simultaneously military-government documentary evidence and a reworked monster origin trope.[37] This duality of viewing position is echoed throughout in Hud's self-consciously evolving role as camera operator. Only reluctantly assuming responsibility for filming the surprise party, his role immediately shifts after the attack, from documenting the private-banal to documenting the public-spectacular for a wider (potential) audience: "People are gonna want to know . . . how it all went down." Relatedly, Kimberly Jackson notes that "there is a sense that turning on the camera sets the events in motion," as if the filming creates the monster (55). She also rightly argues that, in the final frozen image of a smiling Beth, "preserving that last image is what the entire film has been about, rescuing not the 'real' Beth but the image of her" (82). Considering this to mark the revitalization of the image she observes as a direct consequence of 9/11, she attests that "the monstrous image is unable to vanquish" this "idealized, irretrievable past" in the end (73). The moment certainly seems to privilege the blinkered individual experience over wider public tragedy. This final-but-earlier moment concludes and idealizes their love story but also contains the seed of the couple's inevitable doom. The camera, but not its self-regarding protagonists, captures the fleeting image of the unidentified object hurtling into the ocean. Whether depicting the monster's arrival in a pod or a fallen satellite that rouses it from the depths, this moment of seemingly unalloyed joy and apparent redemption—he gets her back in the end, narratively speaking—also encompasses the genesis of the monster and the kernel of demise and destruction.[38] *Cloverfield* thereby indicts such insularity, which both foreshadows and exposes these Americans' fatal myopia. The film's conclusion, rather than a self-absorbed deflection, positions their (and America's, pre-9/11) narcissism as containing the source of their (and the city's or nation's) destruction. Their narcissism, especially the narcissism of the male redemptive quest, is thus not a response to terror because, provocatively, male (and national) vulnerabilities precede, even invite, terror.

The monster's attack on New York City, and the consequent presence of the military, also figures the city as battlefield. After narrowly escaping an attack by the parasites, the group leaves the subway tunnels to ascertain their precise location. They enter an abandoned department store, with mannequins functioning as ciphers for otherwise absent victim-bodies. The store is suddenly flooded with blinding light as the military enters, coming out of the light.[39] In *Cloverfield*, however, male-identified military and government institutions are portrayed ambivalently. The monster's attack not only overwhelms their capabilities but also possibly poisons their attitudes toward civilians. The marines immediately treat Rob's group as potential threats, and when Marlena, infected by a parasite bite, starts to bleed from her eyes, she is immediately quarantined. Her subsequent explosion, her insides spraying across the hospital curtain in silhouette—again marks the punishment and violent excision of a female who decides to look back. Her body veiled from the camera's look, the group are unsure whether she explodes because of her infection or was shot by military personnel—an ambiguity that Matt Reeves embraces, considering either equally terrifying (*Cloverfield* DVD commentary). The government-military view of citizens troublingly signals how the attack blurs distinctions—or at least their capability to determine them—between victim and threat, but also establishes a patterned preparedness to sacrifice citizens as collateral damage in the encounter with terror. This is antithetical to the pointed unwillingness of representatives of state power in Cold War–era "creature features" to harm civilians.[40] In *Cloverfield*, this is in large part a result of their incapacity to understand the monster and their consequent inability to defeat it. The military disconcertingly acknowledges no understanding of the monster or how to combat it. As Hud declares in horror: "Did you see that [soldier's] face.... They have no idea [what it is]!"

Rather than participating in the securitization of the city and society, the military in *Cloverfield* not only fail to eliminate the monster but perversely terminate Rob's and Beth's prospective heterosexual (re)union. The opening Department of Defense title now assumes a starkly different hue. Even the final military attempt to save New York *by destroying it* is seemingly unsuccessful, with the monster seemingly surviving the bombardment: a voice on a radio declaims, "It's alive," at the end of the credits. The final "Hammer Down" carpet bombing of Manhattan and the monster is yet another spectacle that the everyman-held camera misses—and the film withholds. As a consequence of the film's stylistic adherence to the amateur camera *and* the everyman perspective, there is no cathartic payoff for the audience, withholding the pleasure that attends watching cinematic destruction from a safe, omniscient vantage point. As much as the limits of the handheld camera and unnerving blurring of public and private, the monster's seeming invulnerability—and the futility of the remasculinization quest—lies in the insufficiency of the professional-military response and the doomed couple's (and America's) self-centeredness.

The Monster as Stranger: Unknowable and Unassimilable

Rob's attempt to recuperate his everyman masculinity through the rescue of a prostrate female is fatally undermined by the *Cloverfield* monster's eruption into the narrative. The already destabilized male power of looking through the camera is avowedly shattered as the monster magnifies white male vulnerability. *Cloverfield* exemplifies a persistent tension between concealing and revealing the source of terror, its giant monster, at the levels of production, distribution, and narrative but seems ultimately more interested in concealment. The film's production was highly secretive—concealing production plans from cast, crew, and the online film community. It revealed snippets of extratextual information on the internet to pique fan interest and strategically released trailers that concealed both title *and* monster. *Cloverfield* is also a film whose monster is consistently concealed—symptomatic of both the sense of invisibility associated with modern terrorism and urban anonymity. The monster evades representation and exceeds the capacity of male characters to visually capture it within their camcorder frame. Most disturbingly, it *remains* elusive, as the film's unfailing adherence to this limited perspective precludes the identification of an origin story or any rationale for its attack typical of a giant monster movie.

Scholars largely argue that the unnamed monster's intertextual relation to 1950s movie monsters and creatures contains and reassures, despite the monster's figuration with contemporary terrorism. Daniel North rightly observes that the film "simulat[es] the impression that the monster is a chaotic agent not under the control of the filmmakers" (76), yet calls for further elucidation of the fundamental and persistent "mystery" of the monster's meaning (91). Only Hantke, who nonetheless decries the film's unwillingness to explore the larger causes and consequences of 9/11, recognizes that the monster's "incomprehensibility . . . constitutes its major allegorical function" ("Return of the Giant Creature" 244). Yet perhaps it is this very unwillingness, figured equally in the film's unfailing attachment to the amateur camera aesthetic *and* the monster's (consequent) unknowability, that represents *Cloverfield*'s allegorical significance. This is not to suggest that the monster exceeds the control of the filmmakers, but rather that its incomprehensibility frighteningly reflects the seeming incomprehensibility of modern terror, which does exceed control.

It is not unusual for the monstrous threat to evade or resist visual representation in horror film. Films like *Curse of the Demon* (Tourneur 1957) and *Cat People* (Tourneur 1942) pronounce a basic idea of the inadequacy or limits of visual representation. And discovered-footage horror films are routinely populated by unrepresented and unrepresentable threats or monsters that persistently elude framing, always located beyond the edge of the frame. Also, as a consequence of typically lower budgets, such films cannot afford—either economically or epistemologically, assuming "evil" is unrepresentable—to offer convincing representations of their monsters. This, as well as demonstrating the limits of representation, increases the associated fear and dread; what cannot be seen frightens. In *Cloverfield*, the incapacity to "capture" the monster is first a formal consequence of how the monster's attack is experienced and mediated. Tied to the limited perspectives of the handheld camera, which offers only first-person fragments from the victim's perspective, the inherent partiality and restricted vision of the camera cannot contain the monster. In this sense, North contends the *Cloverfield* monster is "a truly 9/11 beast" (90).

However, the monster's excessiveness and resistance to representation remain unresolved and unrelieved at film's end.[41] It is *not* beyond vision but remains *unknowable* to character and camera. And because it cannot be "known" by Hud's amateur camera, it cannot be assimilated, understood, or eliminated.

One sense in which the *Cloverfield* monster is perhaps knowable rests in its intertextual kinship to other cinematic monsters. Steen Christiansen contends that, with monsters reductively characterized as evil and inhuman, rather than representing "transgressive and dangerous Otherness," movie monsters represent "distinctively American responses to social fears" (7–8). That is, rather than being Other, they are an integral part of American culture because they are intimately linked with earlier genre monsters. Thus Christiansen claims that the allegorical terrorist-monster's potentially frightening difference is annulled *through* the cumulative cinematic history of constructions of monstrosity. In so doing, post-9/11 American cinema deploys monsters to manage and annihilate difference. However, he mistakenly suggests that *Cloverfield*'s "structural dependence on the history of monster films" similarly renders its monster "hauntingly familiar" (7). Indeed, Christiansen nevertheless recognizes that the monster also significantly differs from earlier monsters and in relation to monster film history, finally acknowledging the strangeness of the film's incomprehensible monster, one that "neither can nor should be understood" (1). Claiming that the representation of the *Cloverfield* monster is reductive and reassuring is possible only if we overlook the film's many key generic divergences, such as the amateur video camera and failure to (visually) capture or (militarily) eliminate the monster.

Noël Carroll argues that while horror is centrally concerned with the encounter of the known and the unknown, a chief project lies in making the unknown—and thereby frightening—at least in some sense *known*.[42] While monsters are characteristically excessive and unknowable, horror films conventionally figure a return to some form of normalcy through the evacuation—however temporary—of a monster whose transgressions are ultimately punished. Furthermore, in giant monster movies, the monstrous threat and its genesis are typically revealed to the audience. In *Gojira*, for example, the monster and its origin are knowable, both through omniscient (or unrestricted) narration and through the knowledge work of its traumatized and disfigured scientist-protagonist.[43] And much like slasher films, *Godzilla* numerously engages the monster's perspective. The monster is also known to the camera/film and audience through empathy-inducing monster point-of-view shots and subsequent—perhaps consequent—declarations of empathy from the scientist Nick Tatopoulos (Matthew Broderick): "He's not some enemy. He's just an animal." Although the monster is characteristically excessive and unrepresentable, particularly where restricted vision and limited knowledge are characteristic, science fiction and horror invariably provide a motivating story or expository information about the monster-threat. Even discovered-footage films invariably offer contextual information, however fragmented or partial, on the nature of the threat and its onset—even if only as retrospective exposition for the audience.

Yet the manner in which the *Cloverfield* monster is not only unknown *but remains so* is most significant. Confined to the limited handheld camera and unsteady victim-perspective of its everymen, the monster's genesis and motivation remain beyond the purview of the everyman. The film offers us neither monster point-of-view shots nor an origin or motivating story. The stark absence of information about what it is and where it comes from is discomfiting and signals how it disrupts and confounds. In *Cloverfield*, not only is the monster's motivation unknown and its perspective unavailable, but neither is there a return to normalcy nor an evacuation of the threat. As Jackson similarly identifies, in contrast to "offering the fullness of presence, these monstrous images" represent an "excessive presence," including for the audience (56). The monster is not only visually but epistemologically unavailable to the camera, the everyman victim-characters, and the audience, none able to resolve its fundamental, excessive Otherness.

In detailing the initial construction of a "surveillance gaze," Emanuelle Wessels ultimately acknowledges that the monstrous figure is excessive and difference is not abolished, its "pliable and flexible, chaotically fluid" body allowing it to "avoid apprehension or containment" (117). Despite claiming that difference, embodied in the monster, "is fantasized as something that can be visually identified, marked, and 'caught' on camera" (111), Wessels finally acknowledges that the hopelessness of Rob's quest to protect is mirrored in Hud's "essentially ineffectual" quest to document the monster's attack, and "those who got too close, and faced alterity directly, were eradicated" (138). *Cloverfield* explores how the handheld camera is unable to record, know, and recognize difference. The camera operator certainly intends to contain the monster—and indeed so does the film's narrative and genre structure—through documenting it via the visual record. However, this goal is ultimately frustrated, both by the monster's surviving alterity and by the limitedness inherent to the handheld camera; the video record is partial, fragmented, and uncertain, and white American (male) affluence is destroyed.

Another sense in which the *Cloverfield* monster is perhaps knowable is in its evocation of contemporary discourse on terrorism. In this respect, Steen Christiansen asserts the monster is the "perfect" Western cultural personification of the terrorist, "a myth of evil," and thus "conventionally coded," "recognizable and familiar" rather than frightening. Christiansen dismisses

Cloverfield's representation of monstrous threat because it "only reveals how American terror discourse is constructed." This implies the disconcerting and profound *unknowability* of the monster within the contemporary discursive construction of terror. In rendering its Otherness inextinguishable, *Cloverfield*'s monster exceeds Hud's camera's capacity to visually capture, know, and master it and thereby precludes any alleviation of the fears and anxieties it represents. As much as the limits of the everyman, his handheld camera, and the immediate proximity to terror, it is this gaping, monstrous unknown at the heart of the film that makes *Cloverfield* truly horrific. And absent knowing "what" the unknowable, incomprehensible monster-as-stranger is or why its attack is happening—not unusual in horror, but certainly so in giant monster movies—everyman masculinity cannot be redeemed.

For Jeffrey Cohen, the monster always escapes, always resurfacing in another cultural and temporal context. Yet the unabolished Otherness of the *Cloverfield* monster extends this notion, marked as a "stranger" and defying (state) attempts to define and label it—and thus assimilate and make it known. According to the sociologist and philosopher Zygmunt Bauman's characterization, the stranger—a consequence of modernity—arrives uninvited, "casting me on the receiving side of his initiative, making me into the object of action" (149). *Cloverfield* represents not only how the city contains the subversive, destructive element within but how the anonymity of the urban context conceals the monstrous threat. A notable feature of films like *The Naked City* (Dassin 1948), this anonymity gives the *Cloverfield* monster the panoptic power to act "invisibly" despite its size, a quality of the city exacerbated by the film's attachment to the restricted perspective of the amateur handheld camera. This invisibility taps into fears that modern terror wears no face and survives—even thrives—invisibly within. The modern terror threat arises similarly from within, but also from without: it cannot be spatially defined or bounded; it is dispersed, everywhere (and nowhere). The stranger "is a constant threat to the world order" and "the bearer and embodiment of incongruity" (149–50). Like the stranger, the *Cloverfield* monster disturbs the world's spatial ordering, bringing *inside* "the kind of difference and otherness that are . . . tolerated only at a distance" (150). Indeed, such distancing arguably becomes symbolically impossible given the discursive construction of the post-9/11 terror threat as stateless. The *Cloverfield* monster's ultimate threat resides not so much in its size and power as in its indeterminacy, unassimilability, and proximity-but-foreignness.

The *Cloverfield* monster is in some sense not unlike the Cold War–era (or even World War II) "enemy within." It similarly signifies the permanent, everyday menace of (potential) threat, in which, as the German cultural critic Siegfried Kracauer famously declares, it is unclear "when or where the . . . horror will arrive" (106). *The Thing*'s (Carpenter 1982) similarly uncertain ending suggests the *Cloverfield* monster is neither unprecedented nor its threat a new paradigm. Yet while Marlena's infection, for example, particularly invokes parallels with Cold War "narratives of infection," like *Invasion of the Body Snatchers* and *The Thing*—both remade since 9/11—it also distinguishes each epoch's varying expressions of enmity. While modern terrorism similarly attacks from positions of secrecy and thus insinuates itself silently into society, it also desires to erupt into spectacular visibility. Unlike in *Cloverfield*, "enemy within" films work to identify and draw out the monster, even if its threat remains unresolved. And as enemy rather than stranger, the Cold War enemy within can be ideologically (and geographically) distanced, bounded with the defined, external enemy. The *Cloverfield* monster, and the threat of modern terror, cannot be similarly "kept at a secure distance, ... [nor] on the other side of the battle line" (Bauman 149). Like the stranger—and the 9/11 attack(er)s—the *Cloverfield* monster's breach unsettles physical and epistemological borders. It comes from within and from nowhere, undetected until it (and its story line) violently and suddenly *breaks into* the party (and its narrative)—too close while remaining distant and unknowable.

Cloverfield too signals the fatal danger of looking at the monster-stranger, persistently communicating the folly of taking up the camera to redress male insufficiency. After the helicopter crashes, Hud momentarily leaves the camera. Yet, still needing to document his actuality, he runs back for it and once more voluntarily assumes its victim perspective. Looking up, his first unimpeded look at the monster, hovering menacingly directly above and over, immediately precedes—and perhaps mandates—his death. As if contemplating the camera, the monster looks directly at (and as if through) it to its operator—and the audience—before biting Hud in two. Recalling Marlena's earlier direct challenge of Hud's camera, which unsettles assertions of male power associated with (looking with) the camera, immediate proximity to and an unobstructed look on the monster-stranger are fatal for the everyman. As Jackson observes: "The predatory aspects initially attributed to the subject of the gaze, the male operators of the camera, now belong to the monster" (78). The everyman characters' inability to know the terror-Other inevitably frustrates Rob's redemptive act. In *Cloverfield*, while Rob's remasculinization quest is eviscerated in its only partial, fleeting success, the monstrous threat is not—and anxieties about fundamental, inexorable alterity disconcertingly persist.

Throughout, *Cloverfield*'s handheld camera aesthetic explores the limits and inadequacy of representation. It also communicates the instability, vulnerability, and insufficiency of the young urban male by destabilizing (the power of) looking. Confined to the limited and unsteady victim-perspective and absent monster point-of-view shots, which foreground restricted vision and limited knowledge, the monster remains frighteningly unknowable to the male protagonists—and the audience. *Cloverfield* unleashes an excessive monster-stranger, whose undiminished Otherness confirms masculinity as unstable and doomed—reinforced and exacerbated by the limitedness of the personal camera. The monster articulates how the elusive terror-threat troubles genre, narrative, and politico-military strategies to contain (its) terror. The redemptive quest itself cannot redress anxieties and uncertainties associated with its troubled masculinities. Assuming gender as relational, Rob's remasculinization through the quest (and Hud's as documentarian) flails helplessly, unable to be convincingly redefined or reasserted against the *unknowability* of its monster. In the end, *Cloverfield* suggests that absent knowing what it is or "why this is happening," as Beth asks immediately before her death, the unknowable monster-as-stranger *remains* "America's own monster" and leaves the everyman's masculine inadequacy unredeemed and unrecuperated.

In *Cloverfield*, after the monster forever thwarts any chance of escape by downing the group's helicopter and killing Hud, Rob again takes possession of the camera. This reassumption of the camera in one sense affirms his remasculinization, given that he has not "possessed" it since being repeatedly emasculated before the monster's attack. However, it—and Rob's tenuous status as hero—is formally undermined by his assumption of the instability, limitedness, and restricted perspective associated with the handheld camera. *Cloverfield*'s first-person perspective is victim identified and male; helplessness and fear are clearly situated in the male body and perspective. Carol Clover famously contends that the horror gaze is often victim identified, with its "first and central aim" being "to play to masochistic fears and desires in its audiences—fears and desires . . . repeatedly figured as 'feminine'" (229). Rather than the fetishistic gaze initially configured in Beth's apartment and at the party, in *Cloverfield* the camera is locked into the masochistic victim-perspective. This fatally undermines notions of the supposed coherence and stability associated with the controlling male look through the camera. *Cloverfield*'s male (mediated) victim-perspective mirrors the first-person "killer-cam" or "I-camera." According to Clover, this unstable, unfocused, and limited perspective calls attention to the vulnerability and inevitable demise of the perspective holder (the slasher killer) who, marked as monstrous, will be (at least temporarily) defeated or evacuated from the narrative. Nor is this atypical of the realist horror film, with *The Blair Witch Project* and *Paranormal Activity* conventionally extending the vulnerable, unsteady, and doomed "I-camera" to protagonists. Rob's and Hud's (following on from Jason's) repeated assumption of the ill-fated perspective of the handheld camera foreshadows the ultimate fate, compounded by their demonstrated inadequacies, of these everymen. In displacing national-institutional shame about the 9/11 attacks and associated fears of national-masculine inadequacy onto Rob's body, perhaps it is Rob who is finally identified as *Cloverfield*'s "true" monster. In the end, it is the figure who most transgresses against American myths of masculinity who must be punished: the shameful, monstrous, and less-than-ordinary everyman.

Conclusion: Effacing the Shamed "Monster"

The home invaders in *The Strangers*, who wear masks throughout the attack, exemplify this notion of the monster-as-stranger. The film's victims—and the audience—know nothing of their attackers' motive, and so they are deemed to be without one, without rationale, indiscriminate. The next morning, when Kristen asks why they were targeted, she is offered only the cryptic and banal reply: "Because you were home." These strangers come, or rather erupt, both from within *and* from nowhere. Even when they unmask in the final moments as they prepare to kill the besieged couple, their faces remain withheld from the audience.[44] Signaling the unrelieved persistence of strangeness and unknowability, seeing the face of the incomprehensible monster-stranger is again to invite one's own death. In a symbolic wedding cum massacre, James and Kristen—returned to her pseudo-wedding dress—are reunited by "the strangers," who function as witness-attackers in the macabre wedding ceremony (fig. 2.10). Much as Beth's final declaration of love functions in *Cloverfield*, so Kristen seemingly redeems the previously spurned James after their capture by declaring her love and wearing his engagement ring, which she had earlier refused but later tried on and been unable to take off (fig. 2.11). This elevates James finally to romantic hero and "husband." As in *Cloverfield*, it seems the home invasion–terror attack is necessary for James's remasculinization through violence (however ineffectual) and the (temporary) reconstitution of society through symbolic (re)union.

The film seeks to obliterate the shame to which it bears witness by annihilating what—or who—is most shameful: James, the failed male protagonist. James is a surrogate for the nation-audience's twinned desire to have its fears eradicated and shame punished. Shame brings with it the desire to negate or conceal the shame of witnessing, for there is shame too in realizing that the shame that is witnessed cannot be undone (Morgan). As Alan Jacobs rightly observes, the exposure of shame "cannot . . . be undone; what is revealed remains, in memory and image," even after attempts to reconceal it through deflection or violence—strategies likewise evident in discursive and political responses

Figure 2.10. The macabre wedding ceremony cum massacre.

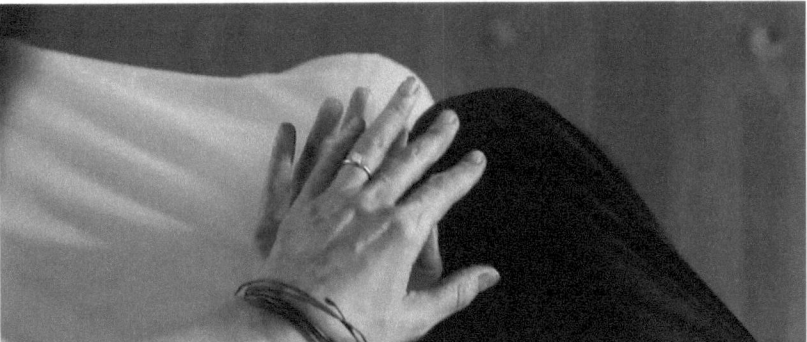

Figure 2.11. James finally becomes "husband," with Beth returned to her wedding clothes and wearing his ring.

Figure 2.12. James dies not as husband but as symbolically feminized: bound, acted on, and penetrable.

to 9/11. *The Strangers* exposes but does not redeem James's—and the (male) audience's—shame for allowing terror to cross the home's (and America's) hearth. Critics considered the final scene gratuitous, even exploitative—and James's death *is* uneasy—primarily because it significantly departs from horror's tendency to, as Carol Clover observes, kill male victims swiftly (51). James's killing is deeply unsettling in its very banality; his death is *spectacularized* if not spectacular. The camera lingers on his face and body, on his abject terror, and gives the audience—and James—"time to contemplate [his] imminent destruction" (Clover 51). A fate previously reserved for female victims, this has become a prominent feature of recent horror. James helplessly awaits the repeated plunging of the knife into his torso, dying not as "husband" but as again symbolically feminized—bound, acted on, and penetrable (fig. 2.12). Perhaps, rather than the home's transgressors, it is James, the shamed and shameful overcivilized urban male, who poses the true threat to the home—the "monster" whose project of remasculinization unravels and who must then be annihilated and abolished.

3
"I CAN STILL FIX THIS"
Restoring Protective Masculinity and/but Becoming a Monstrous Savior

A flashback early in *I Am Legend* (Lawrence 2007) recounts the military physicist Robert Neville's failed attempt to evacuate his family before the military cuts off Manhattan as a viral plague overwhelms the city. The first time we see him as a father, he is wearing a military uniform, as soldier-father. Neville's protective masculinity, another conflation of "public/private sphere paternalism" allied with post-9/11 ideals of masculinity (Godfrey and Hamad 164), sheathes his paternal role in his military identity. Yet while foregrounding paternal identity as uniformed, it is subsumed within the professional. *I Am Legend* stars Will Smith as Neville, the apparent sole human survivor of a viral plague that annihilates much of humanity and turns the remainder into mindlessly violent vampire-zombies, a hybrid of sorts of the vampire and zombie. Set three years after the viral apocalypse in an eerily empty New York City, the film depicts the struggle for survival and search for a cure by its "final man"—the fabled last man on Earth.[1] As Neville battles isolation, psychic disintegration, and survivor's guilt as much as he battles the terror-Other, a series of flashbacks cumulatively reveals the traumatic death of his wife and daughter early in the outbreak. *I Am Legend* depicts not so much the experience of a terror event but the memory of it and anxieties of thereafter living with a persistent threat of terror (and the realities of loss). In so doing, the film figures its apocalypse more as horror than disaster. In many respects, *I Am Legend* suggests the real horror rests in being the "survivor": isolated, besieged, and guilty.[2]

Tying Neville's heroism to his perceived paternal responsibilities, this professional identity is not only military—although this is privileged—but also scientific. In Neville's dual protective capacity, he fails to either safely evacuate his family or find a cure to save society. With his public and private positions of authority lost, Claire Sisco King observes that Neville is most damaged

Figure 3.1. Neville's reflection in the china cabinet indicates the motivation behind his regimen and his separation from his family.

by "ruptures in his performance of hegemonic masculinity" (150). Paternal and professional guilt is equally tied to his uniformed identity, given that he spearheaded the failed government response (as a preapocalypse TV news report and *Time* magazine cover confirm). A second flashback depicting his continued attempt to evacuate his family confirms that his continued efforts to find a cure postapocalypse are motivated by his family—and their loss. Neville's hybridized paternal-professional identity is destabilized because of multiple protective failures, through which his professional capacities and paternal identity are questioned.

The instabilities of Neville's fragmented military, scientific, and paternal identities are readily apparent. Neville thoroughly doubts his protective capacity, shattered professionally by his failed lead in averting apocalyptic plague and paternally by his daughter's death. Neville's exercise routine is implicitly linked to his familial motivation, displaced onto an obsessive search for a cure. Neville's exercising figure is reflected in a China cabinet over photographs of his family as the camera tracks right across the glass cabinet. On one side are photos of his wife and daughter, with his reflection on the other side, separated by the wood frame (fig. 3.1). Their deaths not yet depicted, this gives paternal purpose to his regimen but also suggests his dislocation from wife and child, the family fragmented.³

This first scene at Neville's now empty home confirms the symbolic linking of his professional protective role with his status as father. Most significantly, Neville's fridge displays the preoutbreak *Time* magazine cover in which a uniformed Neville is touted as "Savior: Soldier, Scientist." Figuring his multiple professional identities as divine, the subheading foregrounds his military identity, lauding the "Lt. Colonel's battle" against the virus. However, an appended question mark,

Figure 3.2. The appended question mark signals Neville's doubts about the headline's veracity.

partially over his face, registers Neville's—and invites the audience's—doubts about the capacity of institutional masculinity, the value of celebrity, and the alignment of militarized masculinity and the state (fig. 3.2). The electrical tape attaching the magazine to the fridge additionally implies Neville added the cover only after he became confined to the home and after his failures to evacuate his family and halt the outbreak.[4] Through this display, Neville questions not only his professional capacity, marking his perceived failure as soldier (and scientist), but his very professional identity. Revealingly, the magazine cover specifically obscures Neville in the family photo beneath, the military uniform representing a "putting on" that first shields but then effectively erases him as father and confirms paternal guilt as graver than professional failure.

Science Fiction Apocalypses and Post-9/11 America

I Am Legend is the third filmic adaptation of Richard Matheson's famed science fiction–horror novella, first published in 1954. Matheson's novel addresses post–World War II atomic fears, changes in urban populations, race relations, and white anxieties and was regularly adapted for the screen throughout the 1960s and early 1970s.[5] Although each film version variously marries science fiction and horror to explore anxieties of modernity, race, and gender, the films are invariably more concerned with the lonely experience of their "final man," isolated and preyed on in a threatening world, than with their monsters. Only loosely based on the source novel, *I Am Legend* most avowedly reworks *The Omega Man* (Sagal 1971), which transforms Neville into a military scientist and literal Christ figure.[6] Sagal's film stars Charlton Heston as military scientist and polymath bachelor, Robert Neville, three years after a global viral atomic plague wipes out much of the world's population. Neville is a survivalist holdout in Los Angeles against the Family, a cult of albino-like infected survivors violently opposed to Neville's defiantly unchanged, even intensified, consumer lifestyle. Neville conducts daily searches for its members, to experiment on (to replicate his own immunity) but mostly to exterminate them, but is nightly besieged by the group, led by newsreader cum zealot Matthias (Anthony Zerbe). *The Omega Man* explores Cold War atomic fears, but the film's focus arguably centers more on perceived domestic threats to white male hegemony in late-1960s America. The film represents a somewhat incoherent and confused/ing parody of the racial, gender, and sexual politics of late-1960s America and the subsequent unsettling of (white) male power, foregrounding and effacing, embracing and mocking.[7] Although the film is also about urban decay more generally, Adilifu Nama associates the rhetoric of the Family not only with the civil rights movement and unrest of the late sixties but with black militancy. Neville also finally passes on a cure derived from his blood, ensuring the rejuvenation of humanity and symbolically recentering white institutional masculinity through Christlike self-sacrifice.

Popular science fiction and horror cinema are routinely, and especially, considered to address current sociopolitical anxieties and concerns, particularly in periods of crisis and turmoil.[8] Claire Sisco King argues persuasively that *I Am Legend*, like supposedly more serious films such as *United 93*, (re)deploys the rhetoric, iconography, and imagery of 9/11 to "revise, rewrite and remember history" and facilitate recovery (128). Indeed, she asserts that *I Am Legend* is a post-9/11 "sacrificial allegory"—and part of a wave of "sacrificial films" in the years after 9/11—by virtue of being an "empty" blockbuster, in displacing the traumas of the attacks to make sense of them (163). According to King (129), remakes like *I Am Legend* and *The Omega Man* doubly displace 9/11 to "replay" anxieties purportedly disrupted by 9/11 and Vietnam "about America's identity as an allegedly masculine nation-state." *I Am Legend* encourages "moving on" not only through narrative but also through an already-familiar story, that is, "to move forward with a return to the past" (130)—both evidence of destabilization *and* a way to respond to it.

I Am Legend is numbered among a significant resurgence in Hollywood postapocalyptic films post-9/11, one that Karen Renner attributes to multiple terror, environmental, and economic events and Lindsey Mantoan to the condition of constant war, and its roots in ideological, economic, and religious difference, that succeeds the attacks.[9] Such claims downplay or ignore the evocation of millennial anxieties in apocalyptic blockbusters from the mid-1990s to post-9/11 likewise associated with issues of national identity, gender, and remasculinization. Yet while premillennial blockbusters were preoccupied with impending apocalypse, more recent science fiction and horror films tend toward postapocalyptic worlds set after largely unexplained or unknown catastrophe and a sustained period of devastation, including *The Road* (Hillcoat 2009), *The Book of Eli* (Hughes and Hughes 2010), *It Comes at Night* (Shults 2017), and *A Quiet Place* (Krasinski 2018). Rather than Sontag's famed "imagination of disaster," Mick Broderick, writing about premillennial postnuclear cinematic armageddon and survivalist heroes, argues that postapocalyptic science fiction–disaster cinema predominantly affords an imagining beyond disaster to survival. *I Am Legend* offers a narrativization of survival as much as a depiction of apocalyptic disaster only revealed in (fragmented, partial) flashbacks.

In postapocalypse narratives, the apocalypse typically initiates some form of rebirth and renewal, however localized, partial, or tentative, after the annihilation of a supposedly corrupt world order, with the cataclysm a form of punishment, retribution, or judgment against humanity. In classical and biblical examples, apocalypse thus not only presents a time of tribulation but also instigates the revelation or unveiling of dormant-though-desirable human qualities, for example, and a final victory. As Alec Charles recognizes, apocalyptic films "delineate a purged world ripe for reconstruction" (3). Contemporary secular cinematic apocalypses diverge in important ways from their biblical antecedents, predominantly offering visions and warnings of the spectacular annihilation of a broken world order (Weaver 14–15).[10] Although Hollywood evocations of apocalypse resemble their biblical and classical predecessors, they operate "within more of a moral than a religious context" (Renner 207). While the film makes multiple Christian allusions, they represent an ambiguous mix of biblical and secular notions, including the permanent presence of Christmas decorations. Hollywood often nostalgically represents a return to and reinstallation of an *imagined past* through an imagining of catastrophe, particularly through (refigured) gender roles and the return of the Father. Adilifu Nama, who persuasively critiques Hollywood's strict policing of racial difference in science fiction, contends that only an apocalyptic context allows the imagining of racial change, ambivalently cueing social change while associating black power and visibility with (oncoming) apocalypse. Either science fiction apocalypse movies link Cold War paranoia about radioactive contamination and racial contamination through "the association of the implosion of racial boundaries with dystopian and apocalyptic visions of the future," or more recently, a black man becomes president as a comet heads toward Earth, such as Morgan Freeman in *Deep Impact* (Leder 1998) (Nama 7).

James Berger says apocalyptic events "function as definitive historical divides." For those who experience them, they are "ruptures, pivots, fulcrums separating what came before from what came after." Such apocalyptic events, he says, require a new language, as "previous historical narratives are shattered" and "new understandings of the world are generated" (5). Somewhat alternatively, Connor Pitetti contends postapocalyptic narratives complicate neatly organized accounts of epochal rupture and absolute division by outlining how represented survivals and continuities blur distinctions of before and after. In these respects, Jeremy Burns, writing on how *I Am Legend* draws on the cultural memory of 9/11, argues that the "memory of lived disaster runs beneath images of imagined disaster" (31). Despite the revolving attachment of various directors and stars throughout the 1990s, a contemporary remake of *I Am Legend* seemingly only acquired renewed raison d'être after the attacks of 9/11.[11] *I Am Legend* most evokes 9/11 and its aftermath by relocating events from Los Angeles and in repeated rhetorical designations and echoes of New York as Ground Zero, which spotlights the city as site of disaster and horror.[12] The film evokes the cultural climate in the weeks succeeding the attacks, with scenes of panic depicted in flashbacks and a subsequent profound sense of loss. In Neville's flashback to events early in the outbreak, he attempts to evacuate his wife and daughter from Manhattan. A presidential radio address echoes President Bush's characterization of the threat post-9/11: "And make no mistake, my fellow Americans, we are at war for our very survival." As well as the scenes of destruction and rhetoric after 9/11, the film explicitly recalls the aftermath of Hurricane Katrina. An abandoned building into which Neville's dog runs in pursuit of a deer—in stark contrast to a lower Manhattan apartment that Neville earlier enters—is marked not only by graffiti but by stenciled symbols that bear horrifyingly detailed information about survivors and dead on each home. Although the overall critical response was mixed, critics routinely praised the film's re-creation of a postapocalypse New York.[13] The daily radio broadcast Neville makes from the lower Manhattan seaport where his wife and daughter died conjoins the notion of survivors with New York—animating cultural memories of the city as a site of traumatic loss. Neville's setup at the seaport, facing the water at a table with an open laptop, invokes New York's history as a key immigration point, a point reinforced when Anna—a boat refugee early in the outbreak—later emerges at the site. And according to King, Neville's need to not only announce his capacity to provide for other survivors but repeat it—he notes this ability thrice during his daily broadcast—similarly indicates masculine anxiety and further demonstrates the trauma as feminizing (152). Neville's daily broadcasts—as much a plea for a response as an offer of asylum in his plaintive use of "Please"—also, then, communicate anxiety about his inability to persuasively perform normative masculinity.

I Am Legend articulates professional and paternal guilt through traumatic repetition and an accompanying desire to return to the time *before* apocalypse to both prevent and (symbolically) erase it. In Neville's flashback to events early in the outbreak, arguing with his wife about his professional responsibility to stay, Neville swiftly transitions from the use of "we" to describe collective efforts: "This is Ground Zero. This is my site. I'm not gonna let this happen. I can still fix this." In so doing, Neville ties the site of disaster to protective paternal-institutional responsibility and, in military uniform, constitutes it as a battlefield. He also links it with masculine responses to disaster—gendering Ground Zero—with "ownership" implied also via a responsibility *toward and for place*. This idea of male dominion of urban space is similarly implied in *The Omega Man* in Neville's obstinate declaration about his reasons for refusing to vacate either his apartment or the blighted postapocalyptic city: "That's where I live. It's where I used to live. It's where I'm gonna live," an attachment to place that also prophetically foreshadows his final fate. This also foreshadows the deleterious effects of an attachment with place that prohibits emotional distance from the site of loss and a consequent inability to leave. In many respects, the deleterious effects of Neville's psychological obsession with place and his consequent inability to leave Ground Zero are registered in his inability to establish emotional distance from the site of disaster and loss—recalling first responders' profound attachment to a site that contained the bodies of comrades and victims for whom they felt connected and responsible.

As a remake, star vehicle for Smith, postapocalyptic-disaster film, and evocation of the wake of 9/11, *I Am Legend* has stimulated extensive scholarship focused on the film's conservative-capitalist tropes, its redemption of sacrificial militarized masculinity, and its annihilation of difference in the restitution of white patriarchy. Claire Sisco King discusses *I Am Legend* as a "sacrificial allegory," in association with *The Omega Man*, while Sean Brayton and Janani Subramanian primarily read the film through discourses of race and trauma. Adilifu Nama's important exploration of "blackness" in science fiction cinema considers *I Am Legend* in relation to its filmic precursors and Smith's screen persona. Yet the overwhelming critical perspective asserts the film's conservative ideology, with Kirk Boyle's analysis contrasting the film's neoconservative capitalist ideology with *Children of Men* (Cuarón 2006). By film's end, *I Am Legend* seemingly restores normative notions of masculinity by privileging militarized masculinity, individualism, and a Christological worldview. It further valorizes protective professional-fathers, assuages guilt through redemptive male sacrifice, and recovers institutional masculinities as foundational in America's postapocalyptic reinvigoration. Neville ultimately sacrifices himself to protect a cure he passes on to two fellow survivors, a younger Latin woman,

Anna (Alice Braga), and an "adopted" white boy, Ethan (Charlie Tahan), heading toward a rumored survivors' colony, before using a grenade to martyr himself and kill the attacking monsters. Only Steffen Hantke, who discusses the film in relation to Cold War discourses, wonders whether *I Am Legend* may eventually be recognized for its "complexity in the margins" ("Historicizing the Bush Years" 183). In this chapter, I use more sustained analyses of *The Omega Man* and *The World, the Flesh and the Devil*—a heretofore only cursorily examined touchstone postapocalyptic film—to move beyond identifying *I Am Legend*'s incoherence and instead assert its greater complexity and significance. In so doing, I recast presumptions about the film's supposed articulation of Neville's sacrificial heroism and remasculinization through violence: the "legend" of its "final man."

Gendered Apocalypse, Feminized Final Man: Disrupted Fantasies of Control

I Am Legend's narrative structure and generic tropes seek to contain the catastrophe and the hero's perceived failure and subsequently facilitate his redemption. Yet apocalypse narratives often offer traditional representations of race, gender, authority, and (consequent) male redemption. Indeed, Laura Copier, writing about 1990s Hollywood apocalypse films, claims that classical and popular apocalyptic discourses privilege male redemption associated with masculine ideals of self-mastery and power and characterized by a "malignant representation of women" (42–43). Copier further asserts Hollywood apocalypse narratives link professional women with apocalypse to "resolve a crisis in the gender system" through "enact[ing] the subordination of women" (44). *I Am Legend* explicitly genders the apocalypse by associating it with a female scientist *and* indicating its feminizing impact on the final man protagonist. In an opening television interview, Dr. Alice Krippin (who, despite being played by Emma Thompson, is uncredited) self-contentedly announces her scientific team's cure for cancer via viral mutation. Krippin tellingly—albeit certainly not elegantly—likens the virus to a very fast car being driven by a very bad man, with the cure representing his replacement by a cop. In this sense, Krippin identifies the cure as modifying or reengineering undesirable male behavior. As figures 3.3 and 3.4 indicate, a sharp cut to an empty, radically depopulated metropolis neatly links the female scientist with bringing forth the apocalypse.

Later, Neville obsessively rewatches morning television news video from before the viral apocalypse, forever seeking to return to the time before his professional-paternal failures as if in hope of stopping them from occurring. In the report, a male newsreader describes "ongoing mutations" of the cancer

Figure 3.3. The female scientist is associated with the supposed cure for cancer.

Figure 3.4. A straight cut to a New York emptied of human life equally associates the same female scientist with the succeeding virus that precipitates the apocalypse.

cure, with Krippin now reduced to an inset photograph. Nöel Carroll identifies this convention in science fiction–horror to assign blame to science, with *I Am Legend* arguably depicting an instance of well-intentioned but catastrophic *female* scientific "overreaching." However, it is telling that the Krippin virus, rather than her supposed cure, is named after her; female scientist and apocalyptic virus become synonymous. The news report also positions Neville as a counter or antidote, attempting to reverse her errors, with Neville doubly defined against "Krippin," both female scientist and virus.

The apocalypse functions to cleanse the world and simplify life. Mathias Nilges argues that a key appeal of postapocalyptic film and television lies in their presentation of "simplified versions of life that stand opposed to the complexity of our present" (30). In *I Am Legend* this simplified world primarily means a post-Fordist consumer paradise seemingly without the problems of other people or labor. Postapocalyptic reinvigoration in *I Am Legend* is not so much about reinvoking traditional gender traits and behaviors as a revived masculine urban experience of solitary, unfettered consumption and recreation. From the introduction of postapocalypse Manhattan, *I Am Legend* offers an incongruous fantasy, a postapocalyptic car commercial, of a speeding sports car whose progress is unchecked by traffic. The decayed, polluted postapocalyptic city is initially represented as a male fantasy playground for Neville.

The urban racing fantasy is suddenly transformed as a herd of deer crosses his path and Neville gives chase. Seemingly completing the fantasy, the film figures its postapocalyptic "final driver" as also urban game hunter. In *I Am Legend*, nature's eclipse of the city offers the final man (and his canine companion, Sam) a renewed-though-nostalgic way of surviving the urban "jungle." *I Am Legend* first militarizes its postapocalyptic final man as urban game hunter, alone but for his dog. Sarah Gilligan notes a shift in twenty-first-century science fiction and action cinema whereby the construction and performance of masculine identities have been displaced from the body onto clothing and gadgets (177). Indeed, Neville's sports car and rifle are introduced on-screen *before* he is, his masculine identity and body explicitly defined by each. Neville's postapocalyptic life is that of a consumer rather than a producer. Nature's postapocalyptic eclipse has transformed Central Park from an apocalyptic site for mass graves (briefly implied in a shot of an old newspaper) to a postapocalyptic idyll, as a provider of food. Although Neville harvests corn in Central Park, we do not see him work to produce it (see also Boyle). And while Neville presumably planted the crop, the film decidedly depicts only his consumption, rather than the production or maintenance of his postapocalypse lifestyle. Neville also uses an aircraft carrier for golf and the Museum of Modern Art for fishing, as opposed to collecting paintings or otherwise preserving markers of human civilization through high culture. This final man consumes and replaces rather than produces and preserves.

Neville's roots as a postapocalyptic consumer lie in *The Omega Man*, in which another Robert Neville in a speeding sports car immediately invokes the persistence of capitalist ideology. *The Omega Man*'s Los Angeles is desolate and deserted, a wasteland that offers wry comment on popular perceptions of the city, as much as 1970s American urban decay more generally. As in *I Am Legend*, so this earlier Neville is intimately associated with the car and the gun as he careens unencumbered through the streets of Los Angeles in a red convertible. The openings of *The Omega Man* and *I Am Legend* depict their respective final man in complete control and mastery of his urban environment, his sports car speeding unimpeded through the urban streets. *The Omega Man* and *I Am Legend* initially depict the postapocalypse as a fantasy masculine consumer playground, joyously emptied of and free from other people. The two

Nevilles all but "own" the urban streets, invoking the seemingly uncomplicated and idyllic persistence of consumption behaviors and ideology, and dominion initially presented as natural and unchallenged. The postapocalyptic cityscape affords each final man unique opportunities and freedoms, providing the space to (re)establish male control and mastery.

This masculine fantasy of seeming control also connects the film to *The World, the Flesh and the Devil* (henceforth *TWTFTD*), a largely overlooked touchstone postapocalyptic film also predominantly set in New York. This absence does not afford Ralph Burton, a black miner who frees himself from a Pennsylvania mine collapse to find a world suddenly emptied after atomic conflict and poisoning, the freedom it seemingly offers the two Nevilles. *TWTFTD* is a postapocalyptic "social problem" film starring and produced by Harry Belafonte, an equally iconic though more activist black crossover star, made at the nascence of the civil rights era. Belafonte criticized the film's timidity in depicting its interracial romance, pejoratively associating it with the black-white "miscegenation film" cycle of the late 1950s (Courtney). However, *TWTFTD* intriguingly deploys Cold War atomic anxieties to examine preapocalypse (read: contemporary American) class, race, and gender relations, and especially the psychic effects of racial and sexual codes on black masculinity.

Although Burton believes himself to be alone, the deserted city is not empty for the film's working-class black protagonist, and the felt presence of others bears down on him. A skyscraper perspective that orients many of the early shots of Burton's arrival in New York—stereotypically cut off, Manhattan is only accessible by boat—as Burton runs through the empty urban streets announcing his presence, functions similarly. He continually looks up at the silent buildings above, clearly associated with white America; as he calls out to the (white) others he feels, hopes and fears surveil him: "I know you're there," "I can feel you watching me." Low-angle shots connote how the looming towers surround, bear over, and overwhelm Burton. Point-of-view shots, as Burton panickingly scans the skyscrapers, and skyscraper-eye shots, equally imply his (perceived) smallness. As Courtney observes, Burton's arrival signals "the enduring power of white regimes of vision and space to encode and enforce black subjection" (238). Even though he now appears to be New York's only living inhabitant, the city was and is not his domain. Although he is figuratively free of and from others, preapocalypse racial norms and social roles shape Burton's immediate experience of the postapocalypse and the abandoned city. Indeed, they are upheld by Burton himself as he sustains the civilization—representing the dominant ideological norms and attitudes held by white American society—that oppressed and excluded him, by repairing and rebuilding its infrastructure. Burton's systematic restoration of the city's dead infrastructure marks the black final man as a producer rather than a consumer and arguably affords him a sense of ownership and newfound sense of control. However, *TWTFTD* consciously counters racial fears associated with "white flight," as the black man occupies a city already abandoned and chooses a vacant apartment rather than taking one over. Across the three films, the postapocalyptic city is by turns haunting, opportune, and ideal for its final men. Each variously enacts the masculinist desire to control and manage urban space, with the dead postlapsarian cityscape enlivened and revived by the survivalist final man.

Despite their seeming paradisiacal mastery of their urban environments, the two Nevilles' reinvigorated displays of accessorized masculinity are similarly revealed to be unstable. Each Neville's carefree opening drive, a male fantasy of urban domination, is quickly troubled. In *The Omega Man*, Neville's sports car sharply rounds a corner when, coming to a sudden halt, he grabs a heretofore-unseen machine gun and wildly strafes a building above as a hooded figure passes behind the veiled windows. This disturbance is immediately echoed when he swerves and crashes after screeching around another corner, discovering his previously unimpeded movement through the uninhabited city blocked by a large truck. Neville's casual discarding and swift replacement of the sports car, contemptuously "buying" another from the skeleton of a car salesman, fleetingly reinvokes the postapocalyptic city as a male consumer playground, but the disruptions have cracked the illusion of control; neither is the final man alone, nor does he have unchallenged dominion over the urban streets.

A deeper unsettling of *I Am Legend*'s final man is articulated over succeeding scenes early in the film. Neville's dominion over urban space in *I Am Legend* is only fleeting, with the urban deer hunt violently interrupted by a lioness that takes his prospective kill from him. Neville does not kill the lioness after her male mate enters Neville's view, tellingly consigned to protecting their litter—his figurative subordination mirroring Neville's. This emasculation is echoed upon his return home. Speaking to Sam as if to a child, Neville is figuratively maternalized, preparing a meal for the dog while wearing an apron, before gently censuring Sam for not eating his vegetables.[14] Such representations of the male action star as *also-mother* are not unusual. The absenting and replacing of the mother are similarly evident in the postapocalyptic *The Road*, but also in Smith's *The Pursuit of Happyness*. As Copier observes, not only does this denote the contemporary fractured family and how the apocalypse threatens humanity *and* the family, but maternal absence ensures that threats can only be solved by the father (108). As sole survivor, Neville of course needs to assume both masculine and feminine roles, not just feminized but also "mother." Nevertheless, the preeminence of females pre- and postapocalypse, the coupling of virus and female scientist, and Neville's subsequent emasculation, preliminarily indicated by the lioness, suggest female culpability for feminizing the final man. The gendered apocalypse signals the discomfiting vulnerability of even the militarized male—a "final hunter" unable to master the postapocalyptic urban jungle, his masculine identity uncertainly buttressed by compensatory technologies of modernity.

Erasing Race and Privileging Class: Science Fiction and Smith's Star Image

Perhaps not surprising for a film putatively about the final man, critical reviews dwelled not only on Smith's performance but on his performance *as* star. For example, A. O. Scott asserts that Smith's performance "not only shows what it might feel like to be the last man on earth, but also demonstrates what it is to be a movie star" ("Man about Town").[15] Yet, as is typical both in science fiction and in relation to Smith's star image, race is ambivalently expressed in *I Am Legend*. Race is ostensibly invisible and inexpressible, and yet the postapocalypse represents an undeniable marker of black survival. Throughout Smith's career, the elision or displacement of racial difference tends to enshrine rather than destabilize white dominance. Indeed, the film arguably tries to erase ethnic difference among the survivors and (then) displace it onto the alien-monstrous Other. Janani Subramanian observes that Smith's films and star image "simultaneously mark his blackness while foreclosing its narrative significance" (44). In contrast to Belafonte's explicitly political racial star persona, for example, Smith's crossover success is routinely attributed to the ambivalence of his star image in relation to race and sexuality.[16]

It is also a critical commonplace to assert that the dispersal of race in science fiction predominantly lies in its displacement, in the racializing or Othering of the alien-monster as black. Despite the structured absence of black representation, Nama argues that it is "often present in science fiction films as narrative subtext or implicit allegorical subject" (2). This is typical in Smith's earlier science fiction films, whereby "blackness" is metaphorically transposed onto the alien Other in films like *Independence Day* (Emmerich 1996) and *Men in Black* (Sonnenfeld 1997). Subsequently "deraced and repositioned, it allows him an unfamiliar centrality and thus a universal acceptability"—"the race he is defending is everybody's" (Tolliver). Additionally, his blackness is inevitably subordinated in the service of saving the nation and (white) state power. While David Magill recognizes that multiple discourses of Smith's stardom exist for multiple audiences, Smith is nonetheless conventionally considered to possess a "safe" or nonthreatening blackness, and his characters are often used "to assuage anxieties about the Other" (129)—both acknowledging and defusing racial stereotypes.[17]

Scholars also complicate Smith's characterization as "safe." Willie Tolliver observes that Smith never disappears into a role; there is always an "uncontained aura" of his star personality that remains in or hovers over any performance. This point is especially evident in the persistence of critical conflations of Smith and his characters—and particularly pertinent in the popular criticism of *I Am Legend*. Smith's blackness is also undeniably visible, particularly so in mainstream science fiction cinema. Nama, who is most preoccupied with representations of difference (especially via the monster), finds that black characters, let alone black protagonists, are rare (2). In this sense, "Smith has forged a sea change in Hollywood's expression of heroic masculinity" in science fiction cinema, which "opens up multiple levels of dialogue around race, visibility, and identity" (Palmer 29). Smith's very presence, much less his prominence, in science fiction fantasies implies the visibility and survival of blackness in the future. Such prominence is given added significance when the black star/man is put in the atypical (and central) position of saving the world.[18]

A concentration on race underplays the significance of class in relation to Smith's star image. According to Tolliver, Smith is a (the) signifier of a new, hybridized postracial identity. Smith's star image speaks to multiple, disparate audiences and is composed of a series of contradictions and oppositional messages. Yet while his image interrogates and rewrites existing notions of black masculinity, he also consistently "projects a blackness that is voided of its content in order to create new characterizations, to complicate constructions of blackness and to appeal to global markets" (Tolliver). Offering an alternative perspective of Smith's oft-discussed transcendence of race, Tolliver asserts social and cultural mobility of identity is central to Smith's image, that is, "he moves the image of the black man into unclaimed and unexpected spaces."[19] Smith's hybridity marks the intersection of issues of race, class, and masculinity, but this means race must be sacrificed; Smith's postracial star identity "decentralizes and deracializes blackness." In *I Am Legend*, this perhaps signals the strange manner in which Smith/Neville is both racially contained *and* uncontainable. Smith/Neville's blackness is partially "contained" by being placed in (typically white) contexts and spaces that ultimately neutralize the perceived threat of blackness. While Janani Subramanian's claim that Neville's four-story Washington Park brownstone is an upper-middle-class signifier that dissociates him from "historical connection to the black community" is debatable, in disavowing blackness, the film does "diffuse the racial implications of white hordes (and white zombie-dogs) chasing a lone black man" (49–50). More than this, Smith/Neville's attempts to conceal his blackness in *I Am Legend* are unsettling. On his nightly return home, Neville bleaches (a literal whitening agent) the stairs at the entrance to mask his location, partially implying that to be black and successful in a sense requires he erase his blackness. This class emphasis is also integral to understanding how Smith's body is presented and how Neville sustains his identity and performs community postapocalypse.

The Spectacular Star Body

The focus on Smith's muscular star body makes race irrevocably visible but equally highlights issues of containment.[20] This ambivalence—a dual capacity to make visible *and* blur Smith's racial identity—is associated with Smith's star image *and* contemporary Hollywood's attitudes to race. Nama's work reflects this conflict when he characterizes Smith as championing "a more central, defiant, and charismatic version of black cool" in science fiction, yet he also describes Smith as "racially nonthreatening" (39). Lorrie Palmer argues that the notion Smith transcends race almost implies "that Smith's race is something that needs to be transcended," an aspect exacerbated by "continually evoking the concept of threat through its perceived *absence*" (34, emphasis in original). As compelling as Palmer's analysis of critical readings of Smith is, however, this persistent tension may also in part represent how Smith strategically positions himself, and so diminishes Smith's control of his persona.

I Am Legend again seeks to recuperate Neville's initial emasculation while hunting and in his feminization within the home; the film invites us to look at Smith/Neville's seminaked torso as an undiminished, but nonetheless objectified, marker of ideal masculinity. This tension between agency and passivity, a tension played out across Smith's black star body—simultaneously visible *and* invisible—is especially evident when *I Am Legend* spectacularizes Neville's body when he works out indoors as part of his daily regimen. The film-camera fragments Smith's muscular body, "offered up for the voyeuristic gaze, as an idealized image of (black) male beauty" (Gilligan 179). During his workout, Smith's star body—continuing his association with athletic physicality since *Ali* (Mann 2001)—is to-be-looked-at by others, even in a postapocalyptic world. In the consumption of the star image, *I Am Legend*'s focus on Smith's star body recalls *The Omega Man*. Heston/Neville's surveillance setup includes a closed-circuit camera he trains on his living room, and he repeatedly looks at and engages his own screen image, numerously seeking agreement from it, *as if distinct from himself*. Admittedly signaling his oncoming madness, Heston/Neville's body is often presented for his own edification, whereas Smith/Neville repeatedly avoids his own reflection. Yet in the film's spectacularizing of Smith's body, and the audience's gazing at it, Smith/Neville is seemingly feminized and racially objectified.

The manner in which *I Am Legend* shows Neville building his physique corroborates Yvonne Tasker's observation that muscles draw attention to "the work put into the male body" (*Spectacular Bodies* 119). Thus "whilst Smith's body initially appears fetishized, his representation is characterized by performance and fragmentation that renders the body and blackness a construction," rather than naturalized or essentialized (Gilligan 172). Gilligan further notes that discourses on Smith's star body since *Ali* have centered on its fluidity and transformations, fastidiously attending to the changes to his body from role to role—an idea reiterated in the *I Am Legend* production notes, for example. Gilligan further argues that Smith is not simply passive or to-be-looked-at because he is "shown in action" (181). The presentation of Smith/Neville's exercising star body thus seems to reassert an undermined masculine ideal centered on physical strength and capacity. However, while Smith's body *appears* dynamic—these are "moving pictures," after all—it remains only a moving *on the spot*. Neville, confined to the home and running indoors on a treadmill, literally runs nowhere, all the more remarkable in a world at this point presumably free of other people. The mobile camera underlines—and perhaps compensates for—his immobility. This again underlines the deep ambivalence that underpins Smith's star image and Neville's reality: constructed and uncontainable rather than "natural" and essentialized, but also immobile and (physically) constrained.

(In)security, Urban Space, and the Home

In the absence of a functioning state, the father typically assumes its symbolic (patriarchal) authority in science fiction–postapocalypse cinema. In *I Am Legend*, Neville does not merely become representative of the state but *replaces* it, an equation particularly appropriate given the conflation of paternal and professional-military identity.[21] The death of his family and the figurative breakdown of society—as bombs cut off the city's bridges and frantic citizens swiftly become a mob—occur simultaneously at the seaport. In explicitly linking father and state, this signals that *his* redemption lies in *its* restoration. As well as making space for the hero's redemption, the systemic failure or complete absence of the military, police, and government in post-9/11 disaster-apocalypse films is conventionally claimed to critique real-world governmental failures.[22] The presidential (voice uncredited) announcement of Manhattan's quarantine over the radio as Neville unsuccessfully tries to shepherd his family to safety, and the air force's subsequent bombing of New York bridges to seal off Manhattan, imply not only authority's distance (and effective absence), but even its culpability. James Hay and Mark Andrejevic argue that American neoliberalist Homeland

Security rhetoric in the wake of 9/11 described the threat to domestic daily life as diffuse and proliferated. In articulating "total" insecurity, this rhetoric advanced the necessity of open-ended provisions both against insecurity and to displace existential fear—including onto technologies for monitoring citizens—communicating their dual signification as potential threats *and* to police fellow citizens. Such rhetoric depoliticized, rather than indicted, governmental failure to prevent terror and shifted responsibility for security onto individuals who must secure the home against the ongoing, active threat of (all) Others. This supposed shift is perhaps more connected to long-standing ideas of American individualism—and long associated with particular types of movie hero—but arguably prompts a reinvigorated reassertion of personalized security against persistent threats to everyday life.

This rhetoric certainly sought to shift responsibility for security measures onto individuals to encourage personal security regimes tied to modes of consumption after 9/11. And *I Am Legend* depicts an individuated experience of postapocalyptic survival absent the state and expressed through consumption practices. In this sense, it "sells" rather than indicts insecurity, echoing rhetoric about the citizen-as-soldier and the home-as-fortress; each necessarily self-sufficient, *but also* persistently isolated and vulnerable in the face of dispersed, vaguely defined threats. Selling insecurity depends on, rather than dispels, the perception of persistent threat *and* persistent vulnerability—the home(land) both supposedly secured post-9/11 and forever weak. *I Am Legend* institutes this neoliberal ideal of the consumer-citizen as (also *and* first) soldier via its military scientist.[23] Neville as citizen-soldier is vigilant and disciplined, evident in his exercise regimen and reliance on alarms, regimentation, and order. Neville has transformed the family home into a securitized fortress, more masculine-identified laboratory, gym, and armory than the maternal domestic space first presented.

Neville's nightly attempts to hide his location and barricade himself within his securitized home articulate contemporary American anxieties about *all* Others, both foreign and domestic (including fellow citizens)—a condition intensified in the Trump era. No longer merely a consumer playground and a space to (re)claim a reinvigorated masculine identity, the postapocalyptic city in *I Am Legend* is a fearful, threatening space for Neville and irrevocably *not his*. Neville displays an enduring insecurity in public spaces—arguably symptomatic of the changed relationship to space in modern urban life—even in the fullness of day. The scholarship tends to assume and overstate Neville's mastery of the postapocalyptic world and his status as hunter as opposed to prey. Far from infiltrating hives or stalking, Neville only unwillingly enters a space where he thinks the vampire-zombies might reside, like the dilapidated building into which he hesitantly follows Sam. Far from a predator, Neville never actively hunts the vampire-zombies but rather hunts deer—and unsuccessfully at that. The vulnerability of even the securitized final man is reinforced by his indoor exercise regimen. In contrast, in *The Omega Man*, Heston/Neville defiantly exercises outdoors, running around the modern metropolis with map and gun, his jogging incorporated into his daily search-and-destroy missions for the Family's "nest." Smith's Neville has only tenuous dominion over urban space, with space outside the home controlled by a monstrous threat still only aurally established in the narrative. Even when Neville daily leaves his home, he warily surveys the surrounding city from his stoop, threat not only everywhere, but always. This naturalizes the notion that individuals must be responsible for their own security, the citizen a soldier and the home a fortress against the ongoing, active threat of (all) Others.

Confirming the hollowness of Neville's early assertions of mastery and control, his family brownstone is a place of retreat and hiding rather than open resistance. In the previous film versions, including *The Omega Man*, the home, although fragile and penetrable (as if wounded, like the hero), is at once exposed but defiantly announced, besieged but predominantly unthreatened. The monsters, whether vampiric or albino cult, are an irritant rather than threat, disdained rather than feared. On the other hand, Neville's home in *I Am Legend* is nightly vulnerable, and although to what remains vaguely outlined at this point, it seemingly represents a far greater threat to the home: he bleaches the entrance stairs on his evening return and institutes a comprehensive dusk lockdown, shuttering all windows in an attempt to secure self and home against the outside world and (all) Others.

While a state of enduring, dispersed, and proliferated threat to domestic life naturalizes constructions of the citizen-as-soldier and home-as-fortress, *I Am Legend* also admits the profound vulnerability of fortress *and* soldier. This is reinforced after lockdown as the camera (re)enacts Neville's physical and psychological retreat upstairs from the front door and the city beyond, huddling frightened in a bathtub with gun and dog. The camera here is compensatory, countering yet drawing attention to Neville's consistent immobility—in stark contrast to the movement and energy purportedly indicative of Smith's star image. The bathtub, earlier a symbol of cleansing and everyday family routine—it is bathed in late afternoon sunlight when Neville washes his dog—now connotes insecurity and stasis. The terrifying shrieks outside confirm that the postapocalyptic city is nightly controlled by an ongoing but yet unseen marauding threat, whose sustained invisibility within the modern metropolis taps into fears that modern terror survives, and even thrives, within; everywhere *and* nowhere. As well as advancing the unceasing necessity of ongoing (consumer) provisions both against insecurity and to displace existential fear, the sequence confirms Neville's emasculation. Neville cannot maintain the fiction of the fortified home as a safe space. Security in *I Am Legend* is seemingly only imaginable in completely destroying the home when the monsters come *inside* and, with it, all that is different and incomprehensible. The inadequacy of individualized security is fatally substantiated by the vampire-zombies' breach of the home at film's end. Neville's numerous defense mechanisms are quickly overwhelmed, shown to be *always already* inadequate. The home is irretrievably susceptible and penetrable, and only its concealment temporarily preserves the hollow spectacle of the individualized security ethos. Rather than advocating conservative social regimes of personal security responsibility linked to reified modes of consumption, *I Am Legend*'s imagination of disaster ultimately acknowledges the twinned insufficiencies of the neoliberal security ethos *and* its militarized final man, a false security torn asunder by the violent incursion of the terror-Other. First depicted as an urban game hunter, Neville is finally the hunted prey—starkly reversing his initial relationship with the postapocalypse urban landscape and more like the beleaguered black final man in *TWTFTD*.

Mannequins: Performing Consumption, Eliding Race

Rather than imagining the end of capitalism, Neville (and the film) consistently tries to sustain and reconstruct it. Seeking to reassert a sense of control over space and his daily routine, Neville's reconstruction of consumerist society, however, inevitably destabilizes and fundamentally unravels his remasculinizing efforts. Capitalist ideology—unlike humans—survives postapocalypse in spite of the viral plague, through ubiquitous billboards and the reconstruction of consumption practices, not to mention the film's copious product placements and Neville's somewhat remarkable postapocalyptic "brand loyalty." Such steadfast brand loyalty is mirrored in the postapocalyptic nuclear winter depicted in *The Book of Eli*, in which the gun similarly prefigures the introduction of the hunter-protagonist. Before he is even identified as Nobody (Denzel Washington), the reluctant hero lovingly handles, even deifies, an iPod and fast-food branded towelettes. Partly a reflection on contemporary life, these instances imply neoliberal capital's persistence and resilience, albeit not necessarily positively. While product placement and advertising naturalize capitalist ideology—further echoed in the consumerist spectacle of apocalypse offered by Hollywood cinema itself—*I Am Legend* signals its hollowness through Neville's psychological reliance on consumption practices. While the pleasures of the apocalypse witness the erasure of labor and production in *I Am Legend*, Neville's experience of isolation and consumption habits are each inevitably debilitating.

It seems only the overt and self-consciously constructed performance of normative masculinity through consumption remains. The ambivalence toward capitalist ideology and the instability of normative male identity is especially evident in how each must be reconstructed and can only be sustained through the *performance* or *reenactment* of consumption. Neville's performance of gender and consumption becomes key to sustaining social and capitalist structures and restoring destabilized notions of identity and gender. Yet while the DVD store is arguably a cultural destination, a culturally democratic marker of "civilization" that valorizes mainstream culture, the postapocalypse society that Neville nevertheless *chooses* to construct is markedly consumerist.[24] As a consumer, connoting a racelessness and classlessness of sorts, Neville consumes and replaces, rather than preserves through considered collection, as Burton does in *TWTFTD*. Christopher Anderson observes, writing about the nostalgic fondness for consumer goods in postapocalyptic Hollywood cinema, that to be human postapocalypse necessitates one form of a nostalgic attachment to consumer goods.

I Am Legend extends this attachment to goods to an attachment to consumption *practices*.[25] Smith's Neville peoples his postapocalyptic world, arranged throughout a DVD store he regularly visits, with mannequins—also ciphers for wholly absent victim-bodies. Confirming his insecurity rather than mastery, he even uses his dog to scout spaces he effectively constructs, like the DVD store. Mannequins become a necessary fantasy for him to cope with isolation and reinvoke, simulate, and reconstruct community through consumption practices. Neville uses store mannequins to sustain both individual identity *and* society, but each is ultimately destabilized through the (self-conscious) performance of consumption. Even his routine of returning the DVDs he borrows models "appropriate" consumption practice. It is Neville's performance of identity/consumption with the mannequins he arranges in the DVD store that most significantly decentralizes race, even when figured in the mannequins. Mannequins—commoditized, mass-produced, and inanimate—enable Neville to sustain consumer society and practices and foreground his active role in its sustenance. Of course, to safeguard the illusion of (consumerist) society requires Neville to disavow his role in its preservation. He regularly feigns surprise at the mannequins' presence to reenact everyday social encounters. These interactions do not only affirm the desire for community. Mannequins become a necessary fantasy for Neville to forestall madness and allow him to perform (gender) identity, yet they also elide race and sex and highlight control as illusory.[26]

This elision stands in stark contrast to *TWTFTD*, in which Burton's cautious claims on postapocalyptic (self and urban) mastery are swiftly unsettled by mannequins he too professes to control. Even though civilization—representing the dominant ideological norms and attitudes held by white American society—has ostensibly ended, racial and class prejudices haunt and constrain the black final man from his arrival in New York. This haunting is primarily articulated through Burton's own preservation of "old world" social roles and ideologies. Much as Neville arranges and interacts with mannequins to simulate and reinvoke society, when Burton starts collecting provisions, he gathers two white mannequins, a female and a male. Yet *TWTFTD* more explicitly explores the performance and persistence of class and race postapocalypse. For Burton, New York is a racialized cityscape, one that continues to impose on the body and psyche of the black man—a heavy unpresence—even after the end. This is first articulated in Burton's traumatic arrival in the city. As well as the city, the persistence of civilization is embodied in the mannequins he collects for companionship, used to communicate a fantasy of control over the postapocalyptic cityscape. The white mannequins symbolically (re)animate and preserve (white) society and an urban space marked by white privilege, racial prejudice, and the black man's exclusion and invisibility. Class, race, and sex issues foreshadowed in Burton's early interactions with the white mannequin couple are explicitly—if always indirectly—explored with a later white female survivor, a blond final woman. For Burton, civilization also prohibits the possibility of black-white interracial romance. The late arrival of a white male sexual rival thereafter seemingly shatters the pair's fledgling hope of romance. Mannequins communicate how Burton's class and race identity is discursively circumscribed by society even postapocalypse.[27] Ongoing racial dis-ease, with threat identified with whiteness, erupts into (symbolic) violence when Burton suddenly takes to anger toward the white male mannequin, Snodgrass: "What's so funny? I'm lonely and you're laughing.... You look at me, but you don't see me." The camera here looks over the mannequin's shoulder, approximating its point of view to communicate Burton's continued feelings of black invisibility. His voice trails off, before he picks up Snodgrass and throws the white male mannequin off his balcony, "and you've laughed at me once too often!"[28]

Unlike Burton's conflict with and "murder" of Snodgrass, Neville constructs a postracial world where consumption is privileged over race; even though he only interacts with white mannequins, he is ostensibly blind to their racial difference. When Neville first arrives at the DVD store, he first greets Fred (a mannequin whose later repositioning will confirm Neville's loss of control), then a picture-perfect nuclear family. Sexuality is similarly elided in his encounter with a female mannequin. Sexual desire is persistently dulled with each film version of Matheson's novella, transferred from Neville's sexual obsession with female vampires (bodies no longer alive) in the novel onto mannequins (bodies *never* alive) in *The Omega Man* and *I Am Legend*—becoming more commodity fetishism than sexual desire.[29] The objectification and fetishization of these inanimate bodies is especially evident when Neville spies a new, sexy (white) female mannequin perusing the adult section of the DVD store. Despite signaling his sublimated desires and her supposed availability, it is telling that the idea of sex resides only in a mannequin body: a lifeless, pliant ideal of objectified womanhood. Postapocalyptic survival and social renewal in *I Am Legend* seemingly require the reenactment of consumption practices with mannequin bodies that reify consumption and commodify desire. Yet in propounding a consumerist response to apocalyptic disaster and dispersed threat, *I Am Legend* also articulates its insufficiencies, because society is *only* conceivable through the ultimately *debilitating* reiteration of consumption practices. While mannequins affirm the desire for community and forestall insanity, they finally confirm and cement isolation and madness. The mannequin bodies also highlight control as illusory and precipitate Neville's final loss of control.

Repetition as Disorder and Losing Control: The Costs of Performance

Neville's consumer-citizen habits, rather than safeguarding normality, signal—even encourage—an unhealthy psychology and a feared loss of control that further inhibits efforts to remasculinize postapocalypse. Director Francis Lawrence describes Neville as displaying the regimentation of both a soldier and a solitary man ("*I Am Legend* Production Notes" 5). Neville's obsessive regimentation, routine, and repetition are celebrated initially and are key to retaining his sanity. However, over succeeding visits to the DVD store, the repetition and regimentation become (evident as) a disorder, typically a response to a lack of control. An earlier example of almost compulsive repetition hints at grave doubts over Neville's behaviors. When Neville takes a jar of pasta sauce from his kitchen cupboard, he immediately replaces it with another, placed in exactly same position as the previous one. All uniform and all uniformly replaced, his stacking recalls the iconography of the supermarket. This stockpiling of canned goods highlights Neville's disciplined routine but is also an early sign of a repetition compulsion indicative of trauma, evident even when he compulsively turns his dinnerware before eating. Repetition facilitates Neville's paradoxical desires to retreat into and stay in the time *before* apocalypse, to exercise his guilt *and* to expunge it. Signaling how his *now* is shaped by his *before*, as his flashbacks likewise indicate, Neville replays events to earn a de facto "do-over." Neville engages in a series of repetitions throughout the film, including repeating his daily broadcast from the seaport—the site of personal and institutional trauma, where his family was killed and civilization collapsed. He also daily watches and rewatches videos of preapocalypse morning and news television. More than merely expository, these reinvoke a sense of lost normality and routine. Neville's watching also represents a futile attempt to prevent or undo the very onset of the plague.

Flashbacks also represent horrific return and repetition that become associated with gaps in and losses of time. The fissures signal not only what *cannot* be remembered (like the family's moment of death) but also Neville's diminishing hold on sanity. Alarms wake him from flashbacks (through memory-nightmares), a common trope but also indicative of lost time, and the horrific blurring of waking hours and nightmares. Similarly, his preapocalypse declaration, "This is Ground Zero. This is my site. I'm not gonna let this happen. I can still fix this," is not only met with incredulity by his wife but disturbingly later repeated verbatim to another survivor, Anna. These moments present further evidence of unhealthy repetition and Neville's seeming unwillingness to accept the apocalypse has *already* happened.

Mannequins foreground his role in society's sustenance and compensate for earlier losses of control; Neville cannot stop the virus and watches helplessly as desperate citizens send a military helicopter spinning wildly toward a fatal collision with the Coast Guard helicopter carrying his family. Yet they also manifest a profound lack of control. Neville exhibits numerous symptoms of post-traumatic stress disorder in his obsession with routine/discipline, feelings of threat and hypervigilance, and persistent traumatic flashbacks and hallucinations. The deleterious effects of repetition are most tellingly signaled in the dangers of disappearing into performance, with Neville eventually unable to decipher what is real from what he has (consciously) constructed. Reexposing the absence of control signaled in his traumatic flashbacks, Neville loses control even of "his" mannequins. The reconstruction and simulation of society through mannequins and consumption practices lead to psychic breakdown, one intensified by Neville's persistent disavowal of dominion over the mannequins. His breakdown is implied when, in a shot approximating Neville's psychological perspective, he sees the mannequin Fred, out of context, shifted away from the DVD store, slowly *turn his head* to look at Neville. In stark contrast to the earlier exercising ideal, Neville is now visibly graying and physically diminished. Neville's anger toward Fred is swift and furious—"If you're real, you'd better tell me right now!"—and he fearfully surveys the skyscrapers surrounding him, shooting wildly up at them before riddling the mannequin with bullets. This scene recalls not only Burton's anger against Snodgrass in *TWTFTD* but his anxious, fear-filled arrival in the deserted metropolis. Each man's irrational mannequin "murder" is a final admission of his lack of control over the postapocalyptic city *and* himself. The stark cost of Neville's psychic reliance on consumption practices to simulate sociality may indicate a broader cultural ambivalence toward consumption and mass-produced objects, both reinforcing a deep affection for consumer practices and reflecting anxieties about their ultimately catastrophic effects. Neville's mannequins, who initially buttress his damaged identity, inevitably mark his final psychological breakdown.

Immediately after "killing" Fred, Neville is ensnared in a trap. Although the trap perfectly mirrors his earlier capture of a female vampire-zombie, Neville is unable (or rather unwilling) to evade it, disbelievingly watching it slowly unfold before him. The moment holds equally disturbing implications, about either a fatally self-destructive Self or a radically underestimated terror-Other. The elaborate, mirrored trap implies, as if he set it himself, his desire to end his solitary struggle (and his guilt).[30] Neville seemingly struggles throughout against the persistent temptation to put an end to his lonely ordeal. Earlier, he wakes in the morning from a flashback-nightmare, in which his daughter screams when a plague sufferer crashes into their vehicle during their attempted evacuation. A pistol foregrounded by his bed, clearly inadequate self-defense against a horde of fast-moving vampire-zombies, most likely permits suicide to escape painful death—or memories. Neville's self-destructive complicity is further suggested in a near-suicidal, after-dark act of revenge at the seaport in which two survivors, Anna and Ethan, arrive to rescue him. Again returning to the site of paternal-professional failure, he even deploys another mannequin as a cipher. Taken together, these instances evidence an insistent male desire in post-9/11 film not only to suffer but to *be made to* suffer and be punished for perceived failings.

Neville narrowly escapes from the trap after being knocked unconscious and further injured in releasing himself—stabbed in the leg with his own knife—with the protective intervention of Sam. However, Neville's psychic disintegration is restated across ensuing moments in which reenactments of consumption behaviors that had previously sustained him are revealed as constructed. As Judith Butler identifies, performative citations of gender normativity become especially unstable and untenable when exposed as performance. First, Neville returns to the DVD store to finally talk to the sexy mannequin—"Please say hello to me"—but the repeated presentation of Neville's psychological perspective finally places the mannequin in focus *for* him, confirming her lifelessness and his loneliness. His breakdown is then reinforced in his compulsive, blank recitation of *all* the dialogue parts from a scene from *Shrek* (Adamson 2001), likewise reinforcing how Neville is haunted by perceived paternal failure. Attempting to build empathy with Ethan, after Anna returns him home, Neville delivers a creepy, "zombielike" recitation of multiple character parts. Definitive evidence of the deleterious effects of isolation, the moment also represents the schizophrenic effects of solitary consumption, performance, and repetition.[31] Neville's exhibited social withdrawal and detachment from others and his restricted affect following on the heels of impulsive, self-destructive behavior and loss of belief further evidence his post-traumatic stress disorder. Neville is unable to engage in real conversation, beyond the one-sided ones he shares with Sam and the mannequins, exposing the constructedness of his performance of masculinity and sustenance of identity. He is also visibly shamed by his own name—another symptom of post-traumatic stress disorder—and averts his eyes from Anna when she later asks if he is "*the* Robert Neville," a shame thus linked to his professional identity. Neville's conspicuous and tenuous performance of normative masculinity eventually ruptures when revealed as (self-) consciously constructed rather than natural.

The Indeterminate Terror-Other as Monstrous Mirror

The prominence of an Alpha Male vampire-zombie throughout the film just as troublingly differentiates him as an identifiable leader and clear antagonist, despite Neville's dismissal of such an idea. If the implication about a fatally self-destructive Self is dismissed, the equally disturbing alternative is a radically underestimated terror-Other. The only terror-Other that Neville battles one-on-one, the Alpha Male leads the assaults on Neville, possibly moves the mannequins and sets up the trap, and then unleashes vampire-zombie attack dogs after Neville's entrapment. *I Am Legend* installs a binary structure absent in other iterations, further signaling its post-9/11 resonance: the vampire-zombies as wholly Other, rather than an emergent, alternative humanity. Never presenting the vampire-zombies as "us," always as Other, the film largely withholds their perspective and experience. Unlike in earlier film versions, Neville has no prelapsarian association—whether neighborly or dialectical—with any *now*-terror-Other. Thus the Alpha Male's possible agency and leadership become unsettling, given that neither the narrative nor Neville (appears willing to) genuinely engage with the terror-Other. Despite multiple hints that the Alpha Male could—and even should—be interpreted differently, his implicit significance is unmotivated and incoherent.

The hybrid vampire-zombies in *I Am Legend* have attracted wildly divergent and contradictory critical interpretations, variously defined as black, white, or terrorists, and even on occasion as more than one. Sean Brayton, for example, interprets the terror-Other through the prism of Hurricane Katrina and as a proxy for the abandoned black underclass—the vampire-zombies huddle in darkness in the dilapidated building Sam enters—before reverting to his predominant reading that they represent white terror, as in *I, Robot* (Proyas 2004).[32] Others extend the association of the vampire-zombies with terror, schematically likening them to Arab/Muslim terrorists. Matching the post-9/11 characterization and construction of modern terror, *I Am Legend*'s terror-Others are an irrational, violent, and existential threat without ideological purpose in their indiscriminate, irrational targeting of the civilian populace.[33] Concealed in and by the city, they invoke the mendacious invisibility of modern terrorism. Beyond reason, these terror-Others ignore Neville's final entreaties that he can save them. As he reaches for a grenade with the vampire-zombies bearing down on him, he concludes: "They're not gonna stop." In this sense, *I Am Legend* continues the characterization of enemies in action cinema as anonymous, interchangeable, and "killable."

The indeterminacy of the terror-Other largely lies in *I Am Legend*'s failure to satisfyingly render them aesthetically, prompting widespread critical confusion about what exactly they are, labeled variously as vampires, zombies, or both.[34] This ontological uncertainty is amplified because the monsters are computer-generated creations.[35] This has two equally dehumanizing consequences. Brayton contends: "It is their difference that accentuates (and legitimizes) their dispossession. [They] . . . personify not only mayhem but also marginality . . . [and] are an abject entity of the state" (72). Likewise, their sameness, at least as constructed through CGI, further defines the creatures as categorically Other (Hantke, "Historicizing the Bush Years"). Their uniformity renders them "all the same," and so anonymous. This not only makes it easier to render them abject, inhuman, and monstrous but also permits Neville's experimentation; unlike his mannequins, Neville does not even grant them a name.

The indeterminacy of the vampire-zombies can partially be explained by the proliferation of zombies and vampires in contemporary American film and television: a tabula rasa on which to project countless cultural anxieties. However, *I Am Legend* not only permits multiple oppositional interpretations but sketches the terror-Other as portentously indeterminate. In *I Am Legend*, the motivation of the terror-Others is unknowable for the protagonist. Their indeterminacy, as well as being a consequence of incoherent characterization after a hastily reshot ending, lies in the narrative's privileging of Neville's limited, distorted perspective. After Neville, using his blood as lure, captures the female terror-Other, the Alpha Male briefly puts his head into direct sunlight in an attempt to retrieve her. He screams in rage *and* hurt, momentarily withstanding the sun's immediate burn before retreating into the dark. Although the Alpha Male's actions clearly indicate a social commitment to his captured mate, when Neville later describes the incident, he woefully misreads the Alpha Male's behavior. Rather than seeing it as evidence of social bonds, fidelity, and adaptive behavior, Neville instead declares that the Alpha Male's actions confirm that "social de-evolution is complete. Typical human behavior is now entirely absent."[36] Neville's willful mischaracterization obscures any coherent rationale or agency for the Alpha Male. Yet the interstitial indeterminacy of the terror-Others perhaps unwittingly denotes their key symbolic significance, emblematic not only of a refusal to engage the Other but of the consequences of not doing so for the failed paternal-professional final man.

On the other hand, the lead Other in *The Omega Man*, Matthias (Anthony Zerbe), is Neville's clear ideological antagonist. An early flashback montage of the outbreak is symbolically shared between the two adversaries, beginning with Neville and ending with Matthias, a former newsreader. Establishing their dialectical relationship, Matthias's association with countercultural rhetoric is violently opposed to Neville's individualism but is also in some sense legitimized in giving the hybrid form a "voice." Adilifu Nama argues that *The Omega Man* exemplifies representations of masculinity in 1960s Hollywood science fiction, with "real-world racial paranoia over black militancy's spread to urban centers" augmenting widespread perceptions that white masculinity and institutions were under constant threat during the period (51). Neville's stubborn resistance to the Family's attempts to expel him from the city mobilizes contradictory discourses of whiteness, figured throughout as both deadening and heroic, diseased and curative. Neville is considered heroic, dangerous, and complicit in equal measure. Indeed, the young African American survivor he cures, Richie (Eric Laneuville), recognizes that the final man shares Matthias's monstrosity, with both men equally and intimately attached to hatred, violence, and the infected postapocalyptic city. Richie presciently identifies that neither Neville nor Matthias has a place in the new world: "You're hostile, you just don't belong." More than this, Neville and Matthias are mutually constitutive, a point confirmed in Neville's hesitance to destroy his enemy even after discovering his hiding place. To eradicate Matthias would be to lose the adversary who defines Neville's own existence.

Seeing Monsters, Becoming Monstrous

Despite Neville's erroneous assessment of his behaviors, the Alpha Male in *I Am Legend* is also ultimately if opaquely elevated as a mutually constitutive adversary. As in *The Omega Man*, each becomes defined through the struggle against the other, culminating in their symbolic final violent coming together. The Alpha Male's unrelenting attempts to recover his captured mate imply that he too is driven by a desire and need to recover family. Most unsettlingly, though, he also arguably becomes Neville's monstrous mirror. While the film does not show Neville hunt the vampire-zombies, his wall of photographs of dead test subjects does reveal his systemic violence against the terror-Other. And after he buries Sam, who is fatally wounded in rescuing him, Neville's actions literally move into the darkness in his suicidal act of vengeance, associating him with the monstrosity of an Alpha Male simultaneously moving into the daylight.

In his brutal medicalization of the body of the Other in search of a cure, Neville is arguably *already* monstrous. When he first tests a vaccine compound on the captured female, photographs of the death masks of countless terror-Others are shown on his lab wall—anonymous, undifferentiated, and reminiscent of Holocaust victims.[37] The photographs are out of focus from Neville's point of view; he can no longer see them. And while he refers to human trials, Neville never engages the terror-Other as if (once) human and denies them personal pronouns. The "professional distance" typically afforded to science fiction–disaster protagonists becomes itself monstrous in *I Am Legend*. In this sense, the absence of "typical human behavior" he diagnoses in the Alpha Male is equally apparent in Neville's emotionless, clinical testing on formerly human subjects. These monstrous threats mark a turn inward, articulating fears about, and the desire to discipline, the *perceived* terror-Other *within*. Reminiscent of America's characterization and treatment of "enemy combatants," Neville dehumanizes the vampire-zombies to conduct his experiments. In so doing, Neville becomes inured to his actions, alienated from himself and likewise dehumanized.

The first time we see the death masks *in focus* is when Anna looks at them when she visits Neville's lab, the film-camera momentarily assuming her point of view. According them their humanity and her pity, Anna is the first to finally proffer a name to the Darkseekers and calls the captured female subject "her" (while Neville persists with "it").[38] Anna's perspective—and voice—upsets the unquestioned dominance of Neville's presumptions about the Darkseekers. Her subsequent observation of Neville as he continues his work refigures his role in experimenting on (and killing) them with neither comprehension nor remorse. The film's brief assumption of Anna's point of view affirms that Neville's ideological debate is not with the terror-Other or even Krippin but with Anna—a dialectical argument between faith and science, religion and secularism, community and solitude. Until Anna briefly disrupts the alignment of the film-camera with his point of view, Neville refuses to understand the

Figure 3.5. In looking at the captured female Darkseeker, Anna briefly assumes the camera's perspective.

Figure 3.6. Neville's "wall of death" subsequently comes into focus for the first time.

Figure 3.7. Neville moves out of focus as Anna attends to the consequences of his attempts to find a cure.

terror threat. The Darkseekers' threat to the redemption of Neville's masculine identity thus resides not only in their indeterminacy but in his unwillingness (*and* the film's inability) to genuinely engage and represent them. This unwillingness to "see" the Other likewise blurs Neville's identity as he becomes *out of focus* in Anna's view, a transition that foreshadows his ultimate monstrosity (figs. 3.5–3.7). From her arrival, Anna is immediately and repeatedly associated with religious iconography, even calling Neville back into the light. When Anna first rescues Neville, she emerges *out of* the blinding white light of her vehicle lights. Perhaps most significantly, as he slips into unconsciousness, he focuses on the crucifix dangling from her truck's mirror, ambiguously foreshadowing his delivery unto sacrificial death.

"I Can Save Everyone": Resurrecting Fatherhood via a Militarized Christ

After Neville's nighttime rescue, the film returns fatherhood from the margins. As he fades in and out of consciousness, he again returns to his final moments with his family immediately before their death. After he reawakens, Neville hallucinates the return of his family in his kitchen, a canted angle immediately suggesting a distorted perspective. Offering Neville's psychological perspective, the film first shows his wife and daughter, returned to the home. A subsequent shot from his optical point of view breaks this delusion, however, and Neville discovers the unknown woman and boy (figs. 3.8–3.9). By associating these new arrivals with his wife and daughter, his hallucination initiates Anna and Ethan into an ad hoc multiracial family. They also offer the opportunity to redeem previous paternal failure as a sort of "holy mother and child," all too obviously having come from Maryland and traveling toward a rural survivor's colony that Anna has envisioned at Bethel, Vermont.[39]

Immediately after presenting Anna's horrified perspective of the consequences of Neville's experimentation, *I Am Legend* cautiously restores his status as a father. After awkwardly adjusting to the existence of this "second family," Neville gently places the sleeping Ethan onto his daughter's bed, under Anna's watchful eye. This act finally acknowledges the loss of Neville's daughter, and in the return of the child to the bedroom, the "holy child" and the deceased daughter revive the familial home and firmly repair Neville as father, a point all too obviously made when Bob Marley's "Redemption Song" plays over the final credits after human survival is announced to be "his legacy."[40]

I Am Legend is routinely considered to restore militarized masculinity, with Neville's self-sacrifice to save humanity, represented by a fledgling survivors' colony envisioned by Anna, seemingly resurrecting the symbolic father as

Figure 3.8. Neville initially "sees" the return of his deceased wife and daughter to the home.

Figure 3.9. The presence of Anna and Ethan in the home offers Neville the opportunity to redeem his prior paternal failure.

also savior. That is, through a typically self-sacrificial hero, the ending of *I Am Legend* outwardly "revalorizes sacrificial economies of violence, masculinist heroism, and rejection of the Other" (King 155).[41] When Neville looks at the photo of his wife and daughter as he reaches for the grenade he will use to kill the descending Darkseekers and protect Anna, Ethan, and the cure, he seemingly (re)unites his hybrid paternal-professional identity.[42] With live grenade in hand, Neville quite literally meets the Alpha Male (Dash Mihok) head-on, unsettlingly elevating the Alpha Male as his adversary and destroying the home. Sean Brayton observes that the film here fails "to disrupt the unholy alliance between the military-state apparatus and masculinity" and memorializes a militarized masculinity in sacrificial death (73). By rendering Neville as Christ figure, *I Am Legend* ostensibly restores normative notions of masculinity by privileging militarized masculinity, individualism, and a Christological worldview and recovers institutional masculinities as foundational in the reinvigoration of "America." Yet all film versions render Neville a Christ figure, although this figuration is clearest in *The Omega Man*.[43]

Heston's Neville is repeatedly identified as Christlike throughout *The Omega Man*. Dutch (Paul Koslo), the younger white man who will eventually carry Neville's cure, responds to Neville's declaration of immunity, "Christ, you could save the world." And when Matthias martyrs Neville by spear, Neville then assumes the Christ pose in death, his blood spreading across the fountain's water to signal the potency and purity of Neville's "160-proof Anglo-Saxon" blood—with sacrificial white blood offering "a powerful racial metaphor" to cure a diseased and dying world (Nama 49) (fig. 3.10). Posthumously passing on a cure derived directly from his blood, Neville's self-sacrifice ensures the rejuvenation of humanity and symbolically reinvigorates the white institutional male. A foregrounded shot of the vial, with a group of infected children-survivors massed in the background, clearly connotes his role in their survival; the orphaned children now have a symbolic father (fig. 3.11). Nama argues that Neville's sacrificial death foreshadows "the narcissistic self-pity of white male martyrdom . . . that became a signature feature" in post-Vietnam Hollywood films. Neville equally needs the children to restore whiteness and patriarchy as sacrificial and foundational. For example, the archetypically innocent little girl, by placing his military cap in front of his cruciform body, symbolically anoints the white male Christ figure as militarized and muscular. In so doing, she repairs patriarchal failings and restores institutional underpinning for society's survival. However, white male hegemony is ultimately anointed by the innocent white child and disquieted by the black teenager's knowing identification of the father figure's monstrosity, irrevocably compromising his final sacrificial restoration.

In this regard, *I Am Legend*'s similar representation is clearly not a uniquely post-9/11 response. Neither is it tied to white masculinity. Indeed, "There has often been a distinct messianic cast to [black] sacrifice" in Hollywood, with Manohla Dargis and A. O. Scott contending that Smith now holds "the mantle of the Black Messiah" in films such as *The Pursuit of Happyness*. However, while most scholars interpret Neville's blood as the cure, through which his sacrifice marks him as savior, it is not derived directly from his blood. Indeed, just as the virus is named after a female, so too is the cure drawn from the blood of the captured female vampire-zombie—whom Neville subsequently kills in the grenade blast. Neville is immune, but he is *not* unique. Unlike in *The Omega Man*, 1 percent of the general population is also immune.

The injunction to "light up the darkness," which Anna repeats at film's end when she delivers the cure to the survivors' colony, prompted critical assumptions about the revival of Christianity in the film. For Kirk Boyle, the statement

Figure 3.10. Heston-Neville assumes the Christ pose, his blood cure under his wing.

Figure 3.11. Neville's self-sacrifice and blood cure connote him as the symbolic father of humanity's rejuvenation.

becomes a supposed command (for the audience) to convert nonbelievers. Neville's use of "Let me save you" (instead of "cure") as the Alpha Male attempts to break through the Plexiglas in Neville's lab "represents a slip from medical to ecclesiastical discourse" (1). Anna's final use of the phrase may reflect her own faith but, celebrating his role in its development and protection, recalls Neville's first use of "Light up the darkness" to align the singer-activist Bob Marley's musical philosophy with virology, curing hate by injecting love and music.[44] And the Alpha Male comprehensively (and seemingly irrationally) refuses his offer. Although Neville momentarily indicates he believes the vampire-zombies can be cured—"I can save everyone"—he kills rather than converts, and the survivors ultimately leave the city to the remaining hordes of "nonbelievers."[45]

The ad hoc "holy family" gives the appearance of a postracial American postapocalyptic imaginary. Nama argues that blackness in post-9/11 science fiction cinema functions "to promote an image of a racially integrated America" through "multicultural fantasies" that function to subordinate race in the service of nation and displace difference onto the alien-monster Other (40–41). As in *The Omega Man*, Neville's sacrifice supposedly culminates in the establishment of a new world through reinvigorated nostalgic notions of America, this time evidenced in the briefly depicted village-nation colony as an ideal image of the rural American foundational township. Anna hands the vial given by Neville over to a faceless white male authority (only his hands are shown). In Anna's transfer of the cure, *I Am Legend* thus recenters whiteness, the cure not only controlled by unseen white male hands, but America's postapocalyptic future and hope located in a surviving white child. Paternal sacrifice seemingly ensures a postracial future that restores America as white and patriarchal, founded on sacrificial blackness (including the death of the black child), female subordination, and the symbolic destruction of the Darkseekers in Neville's final suicidal explosion.

"The Cure's in Her Blood": Females as Redeemers and the Survival of Difference

Females, initially demonized and maligned, are belatedly repositioned as redeemers in *I Am Legend*. Laura Copier likewise describes the tendency to link feminism with apocalypse as only ever partially successful. And Brayton claims that the film restores Neville's damaged identity "through a masculine vernacular that downplays if not excludes women from the narrative of national recovery" (73). Yet emphasizing Neville's masculine redemption overlooks how females are refigured as redeemers: they numerously rescue him; redeem him as father; carry the cure by blood, faith, and hand; and facilitate his heroism. Neville's entrapment begins the transformation of females into redeemers and refigures the significance of Neville's final sacrificial act. With Neville incapacitated in releasing himself from the trap, Sam saves her master from the vampire-zombie dog attack—having already protected Neville against security lapses triggered by debilitating memories of his family's loss. Only now, as his canine companion is fatally wounded in the course of saving him, does Neville reveal that Sam is actually Samantha, a final girl who sacrifices herself. This destroys his final living

Figure 3.12. The Alpha Male as also-butterfly.

link to his daughter, who had handed the puppy over to Neville immediately before her death, and he is compelled to kill her as she "turns."[46] Anna, subsequently, not only rescues Neville but redeems him as father and scientist. It is her speculation that the virus cannot survive the cold that leads to a cure and permits Neville's heroic sacrifice. Anna's arrival facilitates Neville's return from darkness into the light and the transition from his reliance on "seeing" to "listening." After Anna unwittingly reveals his home's location, Neville is compelled to detonate his inner perimeter defenses, reminiscent of coordinated car bombings, as the Darkseekers descend on his brownstone. Momentarily destroying his capacity to hear allows him to finally "listen" in a metaphysical sense.

Neville's daughter, Marley, is divinely figured through her posthumous redemption of the father and insistently associated with butterfly symbols—symbolizing transience before transformation and new life resurrected from old. By invoking her purity and alignment with nature, as well as postapocalyptic hopes, the film emphasizes that Neville's motivation is fatherly, marking his redemption as more paternal than professional and more familial than religious. Marley makes butterfly symbols before the apocalypse and symbolically "calls" on Neville to listen to her entreaties to save Ethan and Anna. The moment's significance, rather than signaling Neville's conversion, is more ambiguous. Tellingly, the Alpha Male terror-Other then not only creates a butterfly symbol in the cracked glass as he beats it violently—an unresolved incoherence as problematic as Neville's entrapment—but is visually associated with, and in some sense *becomes*, a butterfly (fig. 3.12). As he does this, all sound disappears from the soundtrack as Neville finally "listens" to his daughter's earlier entreaty about butterflies.[47] Neville looks back to Anna cradling Ethan, seeing the tattoo of a butterfly on Anna's neck. After he hands her the vial, he replies humbly: "I'm listening."

As the Darkseekers descend on Neville, he passes on the cure to Anna. Neville's sacrifice to save the "second family" establishes a benevolent paternalist relationship with Anna and Ethan and redeems him as father. Sacrificial death finally reunites the father with his family, an emphasis foregrounded in a final, predeath look at another photograph of his family. The repeated association of butterfly symbols with his daughter, Anna, and the Alpha Male—given his motivation to rescue his mate—reinforces their connection to diverse notions of family. Neville's sacrifice doubly assuages protective professional and paternal guilt through redemptive male sacrifice. Hollywood apocalypses invariably figure the self-sacrifice of a human agent as messianic figure, to save others, from a single family to all of humanity. As in *The Omega Man*, "a new family is born . . . from the broken body of a 'tragic man'" (King 154). This reproductive capacity, another assumption of the maternal by the final man, reiterates Neville's earlier assumption of the maternal in the home. Neville's sacrifice in *I Am Legend* both protects the cure and reconnects the family. Copier argues that such self-sacrifice in contemporary versions of apocalypse is most often identified with the continuation of the family, through marriage and childbirth, *or* "reconciliation" or "reuniting" it, often through sacrificial death (245).[48] Like the representation of Smith/Neville's body, martyrdom is a "spectacular performance, with the body as medium" (Copier 33). In willing his own death, Neville in a sense attempts both, through his reunion-death *and* in saving the "second family."

Contrastingly, the future in *I Am Legend*—more than simply multiracial—will be founded on the killed-but-not-destroyed Other, despite Neville's violence and the Darkseekers' supposedly irreconcilable difference. In Neville's sacrificial death and Anna's delivery of the cure into white hands, the film seemingly resolves social and cultural anxieties about the threat of difference, including prominent blackness. The film seemingly resolves social and cultural anxieties, "a realized harmonious social order whose antagonistic sources have been eradicated" (Boyle 3). However, although Neville symbolically destroys the Darkseekers, their actual annihilation is rather elided. As Neville himself acknowledges, "the cure's in her blood"—a line of dialogue added in the reshot theatrical version. In stark contrast to most interpretations, *I Am Legend* ultimately positions the female Darkseeker, the embodiment of otherwise horrific difference, as a redeemer of Neville—like Sam(antha), Anna, and Neville's daughter—*and* humanity. Even more tellingly, the blood cure may be derived from the female Other but *also* forms a hybrid with Neville's.[49] Such an implicit, if unwitting, avowal of difference complicates Nama's assertions about Hollywood's strict policing of racial difference in science fiction apocalypses. Indeed, the cure represents not only the survival of difference, however much disavowed, but difference as foundational (in humanity's future). Despite a seemingly idealized postracial imagination, represented by the mannequins and the "second family," *I Am Legend* instead offers a decidedly multiracial future, founded both on the surviving white child *and* on a hybridized cure derived from the blood of a sacrificial black hero and a female vampire-zombie; difference can be killed, but it cannot be eradicated.

Incoherent Endings: An *Always* Monstrous Savior

The original ending of *I Am Legend*, replaced after poor early test screenings, legitimizes the Darkseekers as a new, hybrid form of humanity.[50] This version includes an additional sequence that more fully establishes the Darkseekers' role in Neville's entrapment and his subsequent realization of the potential effects of cold on "curing" the infected. In the film's alternative ending, his daughter's call on Neville—and the audience—to "listen" more clearly represents a call to accept difference. More importantly, Neville discovers a butterfly tattoo on the female Darkseeker's neck (rather than Anna's, as in the theatrical version), and the Alpha Male more clearly creates the butterfly symbol, even greasing the symbol onto the Plexiglas for Neville. Neville, consequently, returns the female to the Alpha Male, who halts the other Darkseekers' attack. Neville finally admits the Darkseekers' alternative humanity, withdrawing the IV drip delivering the "cure" and reviving her: "I'm sorry." This moment also signals, first, the viewer's and, second, Neville's recognition *of his own monstrosity*. Again initially figured in shifting him out of focus, a shot from behind the Plexiglas, approximating Anna's (and the viewer's) perspective, positions Neville in front of the consequences of his experimentation. Sliding to the ground, the "faces of death" on Neville's wall then finally also come into focus *for him*. Passing the lioness and her cubs, the survivors thereafter leave the city to the Darkseekers and drive north in search of the (now only ever prospective) survivors' colony, leaving the city to its new, alternative human populace. The radio broadcast is now delivered by Anna: "There is hope. Keep listening. You are not alone." This alternative ending studiously avoids the violent annihilation of difference, but the reshot ending in the theatrical version implicitly acknowledges the foundational quality of the blood of the (female) Other in America's future, likewise complicating binaries of Self and Other that are violently ruptured through Neville's ultimate sacrificial monstrosity.[51]

I Am Legend seemingly satisfies Broderick's contention that hero myths in science fiction–apocalyptic cinema increasingly reinforce the symbolic order and maintain conservative social regimes through the redemption of the father and the nostalgic restoration of the nation. Yet America's imagined postapocalyptic reinvigoration as village-nation is only briefly depicted in *I Am Legend*—and is the ideologically incoherent result of a belated reshoot after negative test audience responses to a more ambivalent original ending, in which the reality of the colony remains uncertain. Not only is the cure derived from the blood of the female-Other, but humanity's continuation requires fleeing the city—overrun and presumably now occupied by the racial/ideological terror-Other—to rebuild society in the countryside.[52] The apocalypse in *I Am Legend* erases the state, but it is reborn in the fledgling survivors' colony. After Neville's sacrificial death, the surviving "holy family" delivers the cure to the foretold colony. The colony seemingly represents a return to an ideal image of the American foundational township, a nostalgic fantasy space that reinstalls white male authority. Despite the appearance of a postracial imaginary, Anna hands the vial given to her by Neville over to an unseen white male (faceless, only his hands are visible). According to Brayton, the colony "reflects a revival of Christianity and American patriotism housed in a fortified rural community" (74), merely a more remote evocation of the private security state. In Neville's death and Anna's delivery of the cure, Brayton claims that *I Am Legend* proffers diversity "working" to eradicate a more threatening Other to "revive" the nation, resonating with post-9/11 political anxieties (74–75). In Anna's transfer of the cure into white male hands and the presentation of the colony, *I Am Legend* partially recenters whiteness and again potentially implicates Smith's screen persona in the preservation of white power, as in his earlier science fiction roles. In a sense, the viral plague and the breakdown of society (negatively associated with the female scientist) lead to the resurrection of the father (through sacrifice) and restoration of society (as patriarchal) *through* female actions. Black sacrifice and female redeemers make survival and a cure possible but ultimately return it to (white) male hands.

More accurately, the colony is emblematic of *I Am Legend*'s incoherence, evident in its peculiar combination of armed militia, scientific monitoring technologies, and green energy. The retina scan Anna and Ethan submit to both signals the colony's noninfection and, compounded by an armed militia, reinstitutes the military-scientific institutional regime that failed to avert the initial collapse of civilization. A church steeple signifies sanctity and sanctuary and marks the colony as a Christian space, an earthly "new Jerusalem." It is even visually associated with Anna's body, as if the reconstituted church rises out and up from her body. Yet while the wind turbines evoke a return to a simpler way of life, they hardly represent a conservative vision, especially when taken with Anna's disavowal of the technology first aligned with Neville: the car. Even though lionizing Neville—"We are his legacy. This is his legend"—Anna is also now the voice of this future.

A shot of autumnal trees from the point of view of Anna's driver's seat offers a neat juxtaposition with the opening sequence of Neville's vehicular perspective in the postapocalyptic city. Revealingly, given that cars are persistently associated with Neville, Anna leaves her vehicle outside the colony walls. Additionally, such straightforward perspectives on the colony mandate that we overlook the foundational quality of the blood of the (female) Other, the redemptive actions of numerous females, and Neville's ultimate sacrificial monstrosity.

I Am Legend's seeming closure, rather than reassuring, leaves the twinned restorations of professional-paternal protective masculinity *and* nation unsettlingly incoherent. King asserts that because "sacrificial allegories" like *I Am Legend* must also "expose the trauma" they seek to dispel or resolve—arguably of failed normative masculinity, as much as the 9/11 attacks—they inevitably disallow closure and remain ambivalent (165–66). *I Am Legend* first seemingly advocates unencumbered, solitary consumption before demonstrating its schizophrenic effects. The film then proffers a "monstrous" black savior whose sacrifice recuperates and reunites his fragmented protective paternal-professional identities, but who is finally dependent on female redeemers. It likewise imagines a utopian-nostalgic American village-nation that reinstates failed (masculine) institutions and faceless white power but is nonetheless founded in blackness, monstrosity, and the blood of a female terror-Other. The implications of a reinvigorated American future that *precludes* the final man are significant. Neville's blood is foundational in the (re)establishment of an "America," yet he lives and dies in a monstrous urban space along with his antagonists. Laura Copier argues that martyrdom is an unstable, changeable concept, with often-conflicting historical meanings and interpretations (34). Jan Willem Van Henten, for example, finds contemporary complications of the "clear demarcation between victim and perpetrator" in his observations on "Muslim martyrs," whose very acts of martyrdom also render them "perpetrators of violence" (qtd. in Copier 39).[53] Neville's sacrificial paternal redemption requires monstrosity, leading only to more violence and dying as both "legend" and "monster." His violence may be righteous—to save a "second family" *and* rejoin his own in death—but in martyrdom, Neville also becomes America's most monstrous Other, the suicide bomber, a final incoherence that unsettles the redemptive sacrifice of the final man. *I Am Legend* variously undermines sacrificial paternal redemption, not only via female redeemers, the final breach of the home, or the survival of difference, but because Neville's redemption as father and military-scientist in *I Am Legend* is only conceivable through becoming terror-Other, an agent of terror. Neville is *always* monstrous, not only in Anna's eyes but also in ultimately *becoming* Western society's most monstrous terror-Other, the suicide bomber.

4

"A VARIATION OF VENGEANCE"
The Inadequacy of Revenge in Remasculinizing the Nation Abroad

Early in *The Kingdom* (Berg 2007), FBI agent Ron Fleury (Jamie Foxx) mounts a case to deploy an FBI forensic team to investigate a series of coordinated terrorist attacks on an American oil company's employee housing compound in Saudi Arabia. The attorney general (Danny Huston) warns Fleury—especially because secondary large-scale bombings at the housing compound also kill two FBI agents, including Fleury's friend, special agent Fran Manner (Kyle Chandler)—that his desire will likely twist the investigation into "a variation of vengeance." Fleury summarily dismisses the attorney general's words, especially since they come from the mouth of a reviled character. Yet they diagnose a seductive danger to which the FBI team—and the film—ostensibly succumbs, largely in service of remasculinizing its hero, the institution, and the nation he represents. *The Kingdom* is a seemingly reactionary and jingoistic Hollywood action-procedural, envisioning both American life after terror *and* an attempt "redo" America's response in the wake of 9/11.[1] It also clearly relates to what Linda Williams terms "male action" genres, most notably action film, war movies, and westerns. The attacked oil company housing compound represents an idea of America as an isolated, vulnerable frontier outpost in foreign territory. Even after agreeing to permit the FBI's multiethnic rapid response team to deploy to Saudi Arabia, the Saudis assume control of the investigation, further designating the American compound space as foreign. Western tropes of the insecure outpost and a fraught experience of hostile territory position the film as a frontier western, an articulation of the mythology of the often-violent struggle to secure the nation.

Masculine identity, sheathed in conflated professional-paternal protective roles, is threatened by the inhibition of professional agency and mobility in an unwelcoming foreign environment. The film counters this twinned undermining of masculine identity and American sovereignty through another jarring generic shift, from forensic procedural to "revenge fantasy" action-war movie in its final act as the film ends in a spectacular, over-the-top shoot-out in which the team kills the Orientalized terror mastermind. The return to arms and violent annihilation of the terrorist nominally satisfy the desire for retributive violence, reinstitute professional agency, and reembody militarized masculinity. Treating the film exclusively as an action-procedural, critical opinion largely claims that it satisfies supposed conservative genre expectations regarding the utility of violence.[2] Violent revenge in the film restores American sovereignty and might and revises the shame of 9/11 and the uncertainty of the war on terror. The persistent critical employment of *Rambo III* (MacDonald 1988) implies that *The Kingdom* offers a sort of cathartic revenge fantasy or "do-over" in which this time America gets to win. Critics predominantly considered *The Kingdom* to be a conventional genre movie that cloaks itself unconvincingly, even cynically or hypocritically, in "bogus seriousness," offering instead "a barely disguised wish-fulfillment fantasy" ("Hollywood Takes On the Iraq War"). Yet while the film superficially reinvigorates the muscular Vietnam War revisionism of 1980s action-war movies, *The Kingdom* is finally more ambivalent, incoherent, and discomfited.

In *The Kingdom*, Berg perhaps unwittingly troubles some of the action genre's presumed cultural functions, to satisfyingly remasculinize American masculinity and (re)Americanize foreign space.[3] The film's action-war turn ultimately offers only persistent insecurity and melancholy, rather than triumph. *The Kingdom*, intentionally or otherwise, meditates on the inadequacy of vengeance and here recalls John Ford's cavalry western *Fort Apache* (1948). This perhaps provocative association with American cinema's most fabled genre, and John Ford's famed Cavalry Trilogy in particular, is evident in each film's construction of constraining domestic and feared Other spaces—and characters' relations to them—and equally ambivalent narrative codas. In *The Kingdom*, supposedly cathartic violent retribution amplifies and extends the terror threat through intergenerational blowback, devastating efforts to reassert personal-professional *and* American national identity. The terrorist mastermind's ambivalent function as the hero's "dark mirror" highlights the corrosive personal effects of not only acting like, but also becoming the same as, the monstrous terrorist. Violent revenge deflates rather than reinvigorates, the film belatedly, if only implicitly, recognizing that remasculinization through retributive violence is finally incomplete, uncertain, and equivalent to *being as monstrous as* America's dark mirror.

Outpost America: *The Kingdom* as a Frontier Western

Despite *The Kingdom*'s animated documentary-news-style opening credits sequence, pseudodocumentary aesthetic, and overt generic structure as an action-procedural, the film structurally, formally, and thematically aligns with the frontier western film. As well as positioning the film with 1980s action movies—largely because of its violent final act—numerous critics noted the film's various western elements.[4] In his book *Cowboy Imperialism and Hollywood Film*, Mark Anderson offers the useful designation of the "frontier western": projections and explorations of the frontier myth. These films' implicit relation to colonialism, conquest, and control means they are not limited to "classical" westerns. Indeed, Anderson shows they are particularly amenable to war movies and would include films such as *The Green Berets* (Kellogg, Wayne, and LeRoy 1968), *Full Metal Jacket* (Kubrick 1987), *Starship Troopers* (Verhoeven 1997), *Alien* (Scott 1979), and *Black Hawk Down* (Scott 2001). Richard Slotkin likewise contends in *Gunfighter Nation* that the genre films that succeeded the western, like gangster, science fiction, and World War II combat films, rested on a foundation of character, setting, and plot derived from the western.[5]

While Anderson reproduces the typology approach he criticizes, his designation of the frontier western is particularly useful in examining *The Kingdom*'s contemporary articulation of the frontier. This is particularly so given his explicit relation of the frontier western to colonialism and "the vitality of the frontier myth" in post-9/11 Hollywood (10). Likewise, Geoff King observes that *The Kingdom* and *Zero Dark Thirty* highlight cinema's capacity to embody cultural understandings of the war on terror and simultaneously evoke "frontier narrative" tropes. While classical westerns were made decades after the period they depict, *The Kingdom* was produced at a time of ongoing and unresolved conflict. Still, it invokes an idea of the cinematic space of the Hollywood frontier western. Similarly set at, or just beyond, the symbolic edge of American "civilization," the film includes a beleaguered outpost, an inciting massacre, and vulnerability within hostile foreign space, and it ambivalently represents its Others (whether foe or friend). Alien, hostile space is coveted, fascinating and feared in equal measure. Analyzing *The Kingdom* formally and thematically as a frontier western also ties it more clearly to the history of Hollywood masculinities and Orientalist depictions of the Other.

Not only does *The Kingdom* share a host of western tropes with Ford's celebrated first cavalry western, *Fort Apache* (1948), especially in the presentation of space and characters' relation to it, but their significance culminates in equivalently ambivalent codas that implicitly destabilize national projects of remasculinization through retributive violence.[6] Western mythology invokes a profound, unresolved tension and contrast between domesticated and open spaces, between secure and insecure, and American and foreign. This is most beautifully represented in the opening contrast of domestic and open space in *The Searchers*, but equally in the persistent vulnerability of Fort Apache, forever needing the protection of individualistic, outsider heroes who (are willing to) transgress.[7] In *Fort Apache*, the fort-outpost, idyllic and nurturing, yet cloying and emasculating, lies isolated and surrounded by alien territory and hostile natives. In Lt. Col. Owen Thursday's (Henry Fonda) eyes, the Fort Apache outpost over which he assumes command represents the borders of civilization (or just beyond them). It is, quite literally for the stagecoach, the final stop. Yet although it is in many respects another world, the fort is clearly marked as a multicultural American space, both geopolitically and through social ritual. Its inhabitants engage in a constant struggle to civilize the space by importing and enacting social rituals and events. The dances and courtships in Fort Apache (try to) mimic society in the east of the country and seek to domesticate and transform the alien space into a community where women preside. However, the depiction of the re-creation of ideals of home and the work to sustain or (re)establish the outpost as a home is also uncertain. As the highly regarded American film critic Dave Kehr affirms, an "emotional climate of loss and uncertainty" pervades *Fort Apache*; a "sense of stagnation and emptiness has settled in . . . which the residents have attempted to fill with social ritual . . . and domestic warmth" ("How the West Was Filled with Loss"). This hostile, alien space may be fraught, oppressive, and cloying, but it is nonetheless declared to be "American," with Thursday further seeking to instill the discipline he considers required to ensure its survival. Escalating hostilities over the course of the film lead to the devastating massacre of Thursday's command, with it falling victim to his quest for military glory, his fateful disrespect of the Apache, and his unwillingness to listen to the greater field knowledge of his second, Capt. Kirby York (John Wayne).

The opening of *The Kingdom*, like *Fort Apache*, establishes the oil company compound as an isolated, vulnerable, beleaguered outpost of civilization (read: America). The film portrays the oil company housing compound via a nostalgic reimagining of an America transplanted abroad, replete with green lawns, baseballs, and "American values." Invoking the innocence typically associated with small-town America, the compound is holding a company picnic—a montage of Americana, softball, families, mothers feeding children, and barbecuing. The compound's status as an oil company employee compound—and therefore commercial and private—is deftly deflected, subsumed within an idea of America: the economic subsumed within the cultural. Lina Khatib (qtd. in

Wilkins) identifies that, in contrast to dirty, crowded Middle Eastern urban spaces or barren deserts, American spaces in cinema are represented as green and ordered, as "oases in the desert." However, fragility, anxiety, and vulnerability inevitably accompany this idea of America, one always potentially overwhelmed by all that surrounds it. This is literalized in Ford's *The Lost Patrol* (1934) as a wearied patrol of British soldiers besieged at an oasis by faceless hostiles in World War I Mesopotamia, a terrifying experience of exposure that becomes true also for the compound's residents early in *The Kingdom*.

This idea(l) of America abroad is immediately complicated, with the compound knowingly surveilled from within and without. Indeed, the first compound resident perspective is an optical point-of-view shot from a player on the softball field, looking up toward a Saudi police officer standing and watching over the community picnic from a rooftop. Acutely troubling notions of small-town security and American freedom, the compound is perhaps more accurately a protected diplomatic space and persistently reminiscent of a prison, its inhabitants surrounded, watched, and depicted behind fences. This disturbing liminality is also apparent in the opening credits sequence, which uses archival images of suburban life, families, and swimming pools inside oil company housing compounds. The juxtaposition of these nostalgic images with contrasting scenes of Saudi life implies not only the deep social roots of the American presence in Saudi Arabia but also its long-standing social tension with Arab life. As Peter Berg observes, the compound's residents live "normal" American lives—unaffected by religious and cultural laws that apply beyond/outside—but only "behind walls and security" (*The Kingdom* DVD commentary). It is not unusual to highlight the vulnerability and precariousness of the outpost in frontier westerns, and the surveillance is routinized, and residents pay no heed. Yet while the compound in *The Kingdom* simultaneously claims and cultivates "promised" land, this uncanny America—to use Williams and Linneman's term (200)—is clearly marked as precariously inside another's land and as out-of-place. This precarity and uncertainty allegorically associate it with Iraq and Afghanistan. It also stands in stark contrast to most westerns, with the irresistible, inevitable (and usually violent) American westward advance—its Manifest Destiny—asserting the land's transformability and (prospective) custodianship by (white) America, even when critiqued. However, while the oil compound in *The Kingdom* still represents American soil, a cultivated oasis-outpost in the desert, it remains a profoundly fragile, even superficial, example of American innocence and community abroad.

The opening series of coordinated terror attacks on the housing compound shatters these already fraught notions of home and America. As is typical in frontier westerns like *Major Dundee* (Peckinpah 1965), the film deploys a mas-

Figure 4.1. A literal-symbolic attack on the American suburban home.

sacre of an outpost or of representatives of America as an "inciting incident," which permits Major Dundee (Charlton Heston) to enter prohibited hostile territory (Mexico) without official backing. Howard Movshovitz observes that American cinema—and America—has often chosen to imagine the nation's conflicts as "out there," where borders confront the wilderness (68). The terror attack "out there" in *The Kingdom* is additionally connoted as an attack on a specific idea of America by emphasizing its violent disruption of the softball game and company picnic and images of American suburban life and the home. The attackers, masquerading as the same police officers who watch over the compound, shoot young girls walking dogs and, presented from the attackers' objective point of view—if the association was not yet clear enough—strafe the compound homes with bullets (fig. 4.1). The attacks culminate in a subsequent suicide bombing on the softball field, almost as if directly targeting this everyday American cultural pastime as much as the players and residents. The compound outpost-home is demonstrably fragile even before the attacks, but the terrorist attacks expose its isolation and susceptibility to attack from without. The initially nostalgic representation of all-American suburban compound life masks a more liminal, more exposed American experience abroad.

Fathers and Ambivalently Gendered Spaces

The Kingdom also connects and contrasts Saudi and American father-son relations, in recurrently gendering Saudi and American spaces. The terrorist attacks on the compound are coordinated and recorded from a rooftop, while Fleury is shown visiting his son's classroom. The terrorist leader's youngest grandson—the symbolic "Arab son," one of three grandsons present—on the rooftop is here visually twinned with Fleury's son via each boy's crayon drawing and family poster. This twinning equally conjoins antagonist and protagonist and Saudi Arabia and America. Sean Carter and Klaus Dodds argue such spatial connections show how Hollywood uses cinematic form and grammar to render "these complex/distantiated spatialities of the 'war on terror' more visible" (108). For example, the montage of the housing compound, the rooftop, and the classroom in the opening scene organizes different non-Western and Western spaces and times and "allows us to see such events [and spaces] as distantiated yet connected" (109). It also implies "the threat [as being] to both family life and the nation-state" (109), reinforcing the sense that the oil company housing compound represents an America abroad. The attacks collapse the battlefield and America and signal the perceived permeability and susceptibility of America to foreign, distantiated threats. However, although the film connects the two sons, the montage also represents Saudi space as utterly Other via crosscutting that pejoratively contrasts the two father figures.

The crosscutting between the Saudi rooftop and the American school reinforces this sense of difference as foreign violence disrupts everyday American life and security. On the rooftop, the veiled terrorist leader (unnamed until later in the film) calls his youngest grandson to his side at the outset of the attacks and puts his arm around him. The terrorist-father gives the boy his binoculars and in so doing introduces him to the "terrorist perspective." This is further shaped by his narration of what the boy witnesses. As the boy is directed to watch the softball field, the succeeding binocular shot now represents the boy's optical-but-coached point of view. After the concluding suicide bombing, the boy tries to avert his gaze from the carnage, but the terrorist-father forces him to continue watching, repeatedly using his hand to return the boy's gaze to the field. After the attacks end, *The Kingdom* again cuts directly from one son to another as news of the atrocity disrupts Fleury's classroom visit. Before he takes the phone call that delivers news of the attacks, Fleury excuses himself from the "children's space." The American father seeks to shield his son from violence, first by taking the call outside the classroom and second in subsequently mirroring the boy's innocent phraseology by describing atrocity and attackers alike as "bad." The hall here conveniently represents a transition space, marking the moment when terror figuratively enters America via the school and the American hero must leave to combat it. The terrorist-father, on the other hand, not only allows his grandsons' presence but coerces their participation through watching and filming terror. Thus although the spaces are brought closer and linked, *The Kingdom* demonizes the terrorist-father (and, implicitly, Arab/Muslim societies) for the inappropriate presence and involvement of sons in violence and atrocity.[8]

In marked contrast to American spaces such as the housing compound and classroom, where boys and girls play together and women and men congregate in public, Saudi spaces (that is, all those beyond the compound) are often male only. The rooftop, for example, is a characteristically male-only space. Saudi women are represented as veiled in, or absent from, public life throughout, beyond a voiceless, marginalized presence within the home. This is pointedly juxtaposed with the insistent suggestion that women play a prominent, vocal role in American life, from politics, security, and government agencies to the schoolroom. For example, during Fleury's visit to his son's classroom, the boy's two teachers indicate conspicuous female presence and public voices. Agent Janet Mayes's (Jennifer Garner) active participation in the Department of Justice briefing and discussion on the appropriate American response to the attacks also self-consciously accentuates *The Kingdom*'s construction of the difference between American and Saudi women. However forced—she is a forensic examiner, not a political scientist, after all—her presence implies that American society is more inclusive. The absence of American mothers in *The Kingdom* is a fascinating blind spot in this respect. Fleury's son's mother is never mentioned—even in a family poster the boy creates for his class—and when Fleury later visits Manner's son after his death, no maternal presence is invoked. Indeed, two surrounding conversations between Fleury and the boy's mother were deleted from the final cut, tellingly excising another potential female maternal presence. This ensures *The Kingdom* remains focused exclusively on father-son relations but also undermines the film's demonization of the absence, veiling, and silence of Saudi women.

The classroom scene lauds the American father, who actively participates in his child's life but shields him from terror. But it also depicts professional-paternal masculinity as symbolically confined within a remote space clearly coded as feminine and childlike when terror strikes. When the film introduces Fleury, he is uncomfortably sitting in a too-small chair, marginalized at the edge of the frame, as his son describes his family poster to the class (fig. 4.2). By depicting Fleury as immobile and identified with females, the film implies that he is distracted and unable to either prevent (or react to) the eruption of terror. Showcasing the prominence of the interrogative female teachers, Fleury must be cajoled into speaking to the children. It is even unclear in what capacity he visits the school, whether as father, FBI agent, or both. Dressed as he will be in his later FBI briefing, he subsequently describes his son's birth as if a search-and-rescue mission. His words contrast his imagined father-son relation via life (and birth) with the terrorist's father-son relations via death (and mass murder). They also conflate, even blur, his paternal and professional identities—and symbolically erase the mother, replaced by a father (with pro-

Figure 4.2. Fleury uncomfortably confined to a too-small chair and marginalized at the edge of the frame.

claimed reproductive capacity). Perhaps more significantly, his words and dress conspicuously designate this professional-paternal masculinity as protective, adapting Godfrey and Hamad's designation.

Masculinities at Home and Abroad: Immobility and Containment

Fleury is signified first as father, yet his professional identity is invoked in the story of his son's birth, before formally (e)merging when he is informed about the attacks. Sean Carter and Klaus Dodds observe that Fleury's "identity as both father and FBI agent is critical . . . to resolve the need to use extreme violence to preserve social order" and link national and familial security (106). Tied to the film's pseudodocumentary aesthetic, subtitling the main characters' first appearance with their names and professional specialty defines each main character's name and identity via his or her role. This professional identity is also associated with notions of agency and mobility (or the lack thereof)—a specific structuring device for masculinity in *The Kingdom* and many frontier westerns. The film articulates the anxiety about their absence or removal by linking professional and paternal roles within protective masculinity. After the opening attacks, the exercise of this professional (and personal) identity is numerously thwarted, at home and abroad. The initial postattack briefing ends with confirmation that the State Department has acquiesced to Saudi demands for sole jurisdiction, a willful submission to the Arab/Muslim Other that the FBI director (Richard Jenkins) resists: "We try not to say uncle." The State Department's refusal to allow an FBI team to travel to Saudi Arabia to investigate destabilizes the agents' personal and gender identity by prohibiting them from fulfilling their professional role. While western and frontier masculinities are frequently associated with movement, mobility, and open space, *The Kingdom* is primarily concerned with reversing immobility, constraint, and impotence, both within the compound and by virtue of American political and Saudi constraints on the FBI response.

This is signaled before the attacks, with Fleury depicted as huddled off-center in his too-small classroom chair.[9] Distinctly uncomfortable in a feminized space, Fleury's professional immobility is repeated in the wake of the attacks, with the director telling him that "everyone's terrified, so nobody moves. . . . You aren't going anywhere." Matthew Hannah's assertion that the myth of the frontier is tied up with ideals of masculinity *and* national identity (554) is most evident in the metaphoric figuring of Fleury initial emasculation, immediate resistance, and ultimate remasculinization with American institutional and national identity. Fleury's (professional) immobility and stasis are countered in (and by) the film, representing his resolute, persistent motion. In spite of the seeming constraints placed on the FBI response, Fleury is repeatedly depicted moving from one location to another, connoting a resistant, unbowed masculinity. Fleury's unrelenting mobility—he is shown walking to the postattack briefing, walking to the Department of Justice, and walking to Manner's house to visit his orphaned son—sets him apart from the rest of Washington.

As is characteristic in westerns and action films, Fleury's masculinity is defined as much in opposition to politicians and bureaucrats as the enemy. Fleury must act outside official channels to counter bureaucratic constraints and unwillingness to respond, including by initiating informal negotiations and issuing veiled threats to obtain entry into Saudi Arabia. As in *Fort Apache*, *The Kingdom* immediately implies a gulf between bureaucratic (or diplomatic) and "frontier" (or field) knowledge.[10] This notion of "can do" *as* "know-how" acquired through on-the-ground experience is a root mythology of American culture. A feeling of mobility is even articulated through elliptical editing that highlights the efficacy of Fleury's unconventional back-channel approach as the film, in Lisa Purse's words, "substitute[es] the reality of grappling with complex political situations for a fantasy about instant access and instant action" (156). In Fleury's impromptu "negotiation" with the Saudi ambassador to the United States—in a diplomatic car he jumps into unannounced as it leaves a hotel—he demands immediate access for his rapid response team. A straight cut then propels the narrative from this preliminary discussion to his team's imminent departure from Andrews Air Force Base. This strongly connoted sense of movement is reinforced when Fleury is again shown walking, striding from hangar to plane.

The interplay of mobility and stasis throughout visualizes the current state of Fleury and his rapid response team—comprising forensic examiner Mayes, intelligence analyst Adam Leavitt, and bomb technician Grant Sykes—and their initial impotence and immobility are reinstituted when they arrive in Saudi Arabia. After the team lands, the Saudi police take the Americans' passports, markers of national identity and protection. Fleury and Sykes (Chris Cooper)—the team's most conventionally masculine characters—must also surrender their weapons.[11] The team is rapidly disidentified, disarmed, and disempowered, with American masculinity abroad distinguished by (continued) submission, inaction, and impotence. Male identity is not only intimately linked to a professional role but destabilized upon its disruption. The team's investigation—and thus its members' professional identities—is likewise circumscribed, inhibited, and limited. The Saudi prince additionally constrains the team by defining (away) its agency, consigning it to a bureaucratic rather than policing role: "We brought an American team ... not to make arrests, but to give advice and reports." Colonel Al Ghazi (Ashraf Barhom), the team's chaperone, adds that the prince also said that "there are more rules," controls, and prohibitions. The team cannot touch evidence, question anyone without Al Ghazi's presence, touch a dead Muslim, or leave his sight at any time.

The movement of Fleury's team from the airport highlights the fragility of American presence in the space of the Other, especially when entering or traveling through open, unprotected space. This is highly characteristic of frontier westerns. In *Fort Apache*, for example, although generally dismissive of the Indian threat, Colonel Thursday immediately panics when he learns his daughter (Shirley Temple) is out riding with a cavalry suitor, Second Lieutenant O'Rourke (John Agar): "This country's not safe!"[12] Ford's camera similarly communicates this sense of anxiety, rarely venturing outside or away from (tenuously) protected spaces, like the cabin of the stagecoach, the cavalry escort, or the fort. Travel through open space is frightening and uncertain, and the cramped stagecoaches mimic the claustrophobic confines of the outposts and homesteads. *The Kingdom* mimics this frightening stagecoach experience, the team notably fearful, unsafe, and exposed when traveling outside areas marked as American. For example, in the opening escort convoy ride along the freeway from the airport, the team's SUVs must travel apace through open space to avoid detection and in numbers for protection. Throughout the trip, the camera, approximating a passenger's point of view, wanders nervously and warily across suspicious vehicles.

An emasculating sense of imposed impotence—whether by disdained bureaucracy or the feared Other—is also typical of frontier westerns.[13] The sense that Fleury's team remains under the control of others is confirmed when they are escorted to their accommodations. Recalling Cold War films in which a visiting American law enforcement representative is always assigned a minder, the Saudis' control of American movement further threatens Fleury's professional identity. The Saudis not only lock the team down in the compound gymnasium at night but even define day and night, emphasized in Al Ghazi's reply to Fleury's dogged questions about the exact time of sunrise (when they will be allowed to visit the bomb site): "When I open this door." Al Ghazi then closes the door on Fleury, who is walking behind him, halting the insistently peripatetic mobility that had otherwise countered his professional immobility. Another example of how the American experience inside the compound is likened to prison, the camera is similarly "locked down" inside the compound gym. Marking the gym as a liminal American space ensures audience sympathy and identification with the team, the viewer likewise positioned as immobile (and under foreign control). The gym is a site of imposed confinement, containment, and inaction, the team only allowed to leave it accompanied.

Mayes is asked by an American official, US embassy deputy chief of mission Damon Schmidt (Jeremy Piven), to "cover up" before the prince arrives at the bomb site. *The Kingdom* buttresses Fleury's masculinity in opposition to Schmidt.[14] Fleury's ongoing resistance, however ineffectual at this stage, and preference for action over speech (or speech that leads directly to action) are heroically contrasted with Schmidt's willingness not only to bow to Saudi demands but to avow supposed Muslim attitudes. Schmidt is demonized for being corrupted by (association with) the Other, for his willful submission to foreign cultural and political demands and his embodiment of supposedly "foreign" behavior in his attitudes toward women. Schmidt's desire to spin the FBI presence and the later success of the joint raid on a suspected terrorist command center is contrasted with the team's frustrated desire for material results through action. Immediately after Mayes is asked to "dial down the boobies," a shot of Saudi police and guards in prayer at the bomb site cuts to Mayes, now in a singlet top, playing basketball with Fleury in the gym. Although a site of immobility, the gym is nonetheless defined as an American space through Mayes's body. Unlike spaces marked as foreign, which the massed prayer implies the compound has become in the wake of the attacks, the gym represents a space for female freedom and inclusion. Fleury's near silence throughout his first encounter with Schmidt privileges measured speech over incessant talk—"You talk a lot. A little too much"—and connotes Schmidt's contrasting volubility as effeminate. Typical of action and western heroes, ideal masculinity is marked as inexpressive in *The Kingdom*. Such inexpressiveness may be deemed heroic in male action genres, but it is also historically signified as debilitating, particularly in the field of personal relationships, including in *Fort Apache* for Thursday and *The Searchers* for Ethan Edwards (John Wayne). Nonetheless, in implying that Schmidt's preference for spin effectively aligns him as (with) the Other, Schmidt's lecherous demand not only sexualizes Mayes's body but conveniently displaces supposed Saudi attitudes to women onto an "ugly American" *in order to* emphasize them.

Rehistoricizing and Resituating 9/11: Crime and Emasculation

Post-9/11 Hollywood films are routinely accused of depoliticizing and dehistoricizing events by ignoring the political for the personal. This tendency is amplified in action-war movies that concentrate on the individual experiences of soldiers over the wider political causes and ramifications of conflict. Berg even declares his goal was "to present an act of terror and . . . divorce that from politics and religion" (*The Kingdom* DVD commentary). Yet in contrast to dominant discursive political and media responses in the aftermath of 9/11, *The Kingdom* uses the action-procedural genre to rehistoricize 9/11 and reframe terrorism as a crime. *The Kingdom*'s opening credit sequence (re)historicizes the attacks of 9/11, using archival images and footage that imply its seeds were established by the United States' growing long-term dependence on Saudi oil. In this sense, the sequence mirrors a central concern of *Fahrenheit 9/11* (Moore 2004), spotlighting America's geopolitical and geoeconomic relationship with the Saudis as opposed to its regional rivals. At the same time, it implicitly establishes America's perceived historical (right of) presence in the Middle East. Yet the opening credit sequence perhaps most interestingly figures the relationship as gendered. After the terms of the historically asymmetrical relationship shift—with US dependence on oil during the 1973 trade embargo "redefin[ing] the balance of power" in Arab favor—a montage of Saudi leaders with subsequent presidents follows. Each president, from Nixon through to George W. Bush, is depicted as subordinate, uncomfortable, and emasculated, implying the negative effects of this redefinition for American national identity and (presidential/American) masculinity, cultural sensitivity positioned as weakness. More significantly, it mirrors typical rhetorical constructions of the 9/11 attacks as caused by the predating emasculation of American national identity.[15]

Introducing Osama bin Laden, declared architect of the 9/11 attacks, in explicit connection with the buildup to the first Gulf War and subsequent US military presence in the region further resituates 9/11 in contrast to conservative American discourse. In later observing that fifteen of the nineteen hijackers were Saudi, the sequence reinforces the Saudi connection to the attacks and reframes al-Qaeda as rooted in Saudi history, rather than as stateless (or born of Afghanistan or Iraq). The sequence swiftly demonstrates how 9/11 is connected to US reliance on Saudi oil, as twin bar graphs showing Saudi production and

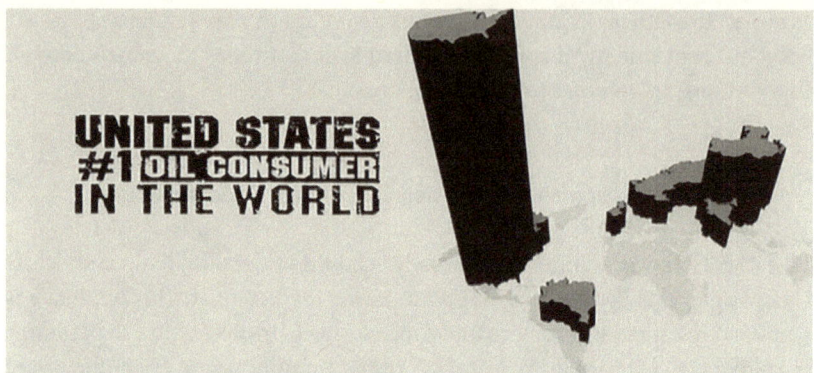

Figure 4.3. An infographic visually connects 9/11 to US reliance on Saudi oil, depicting US consumption as a high bar graph.

Figure 4.4. This morphs into "twin towers," with the US "consumption tower" mutating into the first World Trade Center tower hit on 9/11.

US consumption morph into "twin towers," and the US "consumption tower" shockingly mutates into the first World Trade Center tower hit on 9/11 (figs. 4.3–4.4).[16] Towers, like the Twin Towers, may be indicative of power, excess, and influence, building and communicating wealth, yet also conversely connote a bared vulnerability that invites attack. Concluding the opening credits sequence with 9/11, *The Kingdom* reframes the attacks as criminal rather than an act of war.[17] The response to the succeeding terror attacks on the housing compound is therefore most appropriately forensic and procedural rather than military. Fleury's team repeatedly characterizes the terrorists as criminals, a persistent designation that becomes particularly important in the film's representation of American masculinities and remasculinization in the final act.

The contemporary news aesthetic employed in the opening credits sequence seeks to establish the subsequent narrative's historical veracity. It also ties wider real-world political events to the film's fictional world to afford it greater weight and imply al-Qaeda's orchestration of the fictional attacks that subsequently open the narrative. Integrating stock news footage into (especially the opening of) Hollywood genre films during wartime is common, including in World War II combat (propaganda) films like *Objective, Burma!* (Walsh 1945). The multiethnic squads of World War II combat movies alluded to by the FBI team's multiethnicity, in combination with the film's stylistic-generic blend of pseudodocumentary and action, extend this association.

Unveiling and Conquering the Space of the Oriental(ized) Other

Scholarship on *The Kingdom* routinely characterizes its (and the team's) representation of Saudis and Saudi society as Orientalist.[18] The film supposedly uncritically invokes Hollywood's persistent stereotyping of Arab/Muslims, especially the contemporary terrorist, through long-established Orientalist conventions and shorthand visual codes. Williams and Linneman contend that despite detailing the complexity and long-standing US relations and vested interests in the Middle East, post-9/11 films like *The Kingdom* and *Syriana* (Gaghan 2005) nonetheless portray Arabs as untrustworthy, crude, and uncivilized and identify them as Islamic extremists (199).[19] Equally, the corrupting influence of (oil) wealth and Western influence subtly shifts responsibility for Islamist attacks onto corrupt Saudi leaders, rather than the US presence, downplaying US complicity and provocation. By coding particular acts as Islamic and fundamentalist, Nayak argues that films equate religion and ideology. Michelle Aguayo, writing about *The Kingdom*, concurs, arguing they produce "the collective myth of the Arab—who is *always* Muslim" (44, emphasis in original). *The Kingdom* conflates Arabs, Muslims, and terror and represents Arab/Muslims as culturally and technologically inferior, barbaric, and violent, as well as irrational and antimodern. It also seemingly installs the Orientalist fantasy of so-called good and bad Orientals. Aural and visual Orientalist codes equally establish Oriental space as threatening, dangerous, and alien in *The Kingdom*. Identifying how the Middle East is safely contained via a limited and repetitive repertoire of sound, Corey Creekmur observes how "aural Orientalism" is constituted to connote dread and threat, with Muslim prayer equated with political violence (87). Even before the team departs for Saudi Arabia, the country is recurrently described as alien. Before they board the plane for Riyadh, Sykes tells Leavitt (Jason Bateman), whose inexperience and lack of knowledge not only locate him as an audience cipher but also narratively permit his emasculation, that Saudi Arabia is "a bit like Mars."

158 The Inadequacy of Revenge in Remasculinizing the Nation Abroad

Figures 4.5–4.6. A current affairs television technique—a series of step-ins before a sudden shift to a black-and-white image of the Saudi spokesman—invokes the manipulative duplicity of the Arab/Muslim.

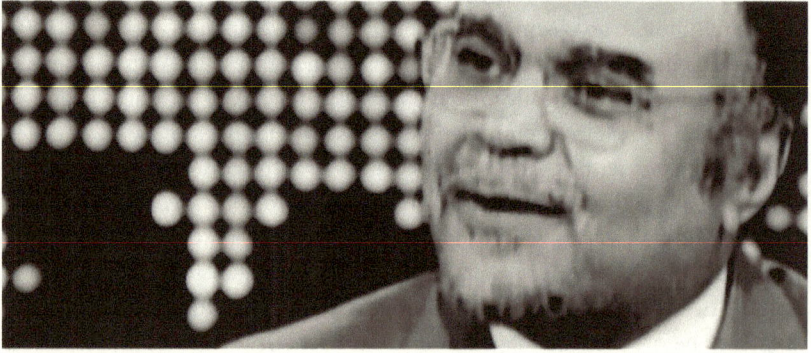

Figure 4.7. The sudden shift to a black-and-white image of the Saudi spokesman confirms the manipulative duplicity of the Arab/Muslim.

Despite (re)historicizing the attacks of 9/11, the opening credits sequence inaugurates an Orientalist construction of Saudi society. The sequence foreshadows—or delineates—the narrative's more explicit Orientalism, in which the representation of Saudi masculinity broadly conforms to Orientalist notions most famously outlined by the Palestinian scholar Edward Said. The sequence implies the despotism, hypocrisy, and corruption of Saudi royalty and stokes fears—and (mis)perceptions—about strict religious fundamentalism, including the oppression of (always veiled) women and the willingness to "hold the Western world hostage" to oil. For example, even though a subsequent title declares that "the Saudi monarchy quickly condemned the [9/11] attacks," the use of current affairs television techniques—a series of "step-ins" and a sudden shift to a black-and-white image of the Saudi spokesman—invokes not only the manipulative duplicity of such PR more generally but also that of the duplicitous Arab/Muslim (figs. 4.5–4.7).[20]

The opening credits sequence also presents Saudi society as socioculturally backward—even schizophrenic—with a rapid series of negative images of Saudi society, following the "news" of 9/11, which depict "a nation where tradition and modernity are in violent collision." It similarly invokes contemporary American fears of the Arab/Muslim Other and Islamic terror. Indeed, archival images of the Saudi kingdom's origins in noble battles for independence are supplanted by subsequent images that imply its eventual establishment by an army of violent "anti-Western" Muslim warriors, analogously massed for war and in prayer, conflating religion and violence.

In Riyadh, Fleury's sense of his masculinity is further undermined via enforced submission, disarmament, and immobility at the hands of foreign Others. Threatened male and professional identity must consequently be (re)defined and restored in opposition to this Other. The deployment of binary generic character types seeks to overcome the supposed "shapelessness" that David Holloway contends effects other Hollywood representations of the war on terror. The film's title implicitly contrasts the Saudi monarchy to American democratic structures—at least before the Trump era. The FBI team's diversity—comprising an African American, a southerner, and, arguably provocatively, a female and a Jew—additionally represents a laudatory marker of cultural difference in contrast to the seemingly undifferentiated and archetypally malevolent Other. *The Kingdom* Orientalizes so-called good and bad Arabs to remasculinize Fleury, the FBI, and the nation. The FBI team's experience echoes American experience after 9/11, attacks that Meghana Nayak argues compelled the conscious, concerted coding of "constitutive differences between Self/Other" to "*resurrect* a strong, impenetrable" America (42–43, emphasis in original). By infantilizing, demonizing, and dehumanizing the Oriental

Other, Nayak claims that the West could strongly justify military action (48). As well as shaped by political context, Hollywood Orientalism, including the representation of Native Americans in many westerns, is molded by generic expectations and typical film structure, including the perceived necessity for a clear antagonist. This potentially has material effects on audience beliefs and (support for) foreign policy, especially absent counterexperiences from everyday life. In *The Kingdom*, too, inverted positions of dominance and subordination are countered by conspicuously defining American identity in contrast to the Arab/Muslim Other, a notion foreshadowed in Fleury's initial confrontation with the Othered Schmidt.

The sustained Othering of the Arab/Muslim contains—including within a reassuring, familiar genre and narrative structure—his threat to (American) masculine identity. As the fictional terrorist leader in *The Kingdom*, Abu Hamza's archetypal monstrosity is figured not only in his actions but in his literal disfigurement—he has lost two fingers—a horrific consequence of his bomb-making deeds. Through Hamza and his terrorist group, *The Kingdom* establishes the barbarism and treacherous deception of the Arab/Muslim. The opening attacks in *The Kingdom* swiftly conflate terrorist violence, Islam, and Arab cultural dress. Both Hamza and the suicide bomber he deploys invoke Allah in relation to the act of violent terror, and all of the attack's remote coordinators wear recognizable Arab dress. Hamza's barbarism is confirmed when his first attacks target women and children. In particular, the attackers gun down a father as he desperately runs toward a small boy wearing a gray cap on a tricycle, as bullets strafe toward the unsuspecting child. The boy's death is implied through a close-up of a small gray cap, which, viewed from Agent Manner's disconsolate perspective in the aftermath, becomes a cipher for the compound's innocence: "How old were you when your hat was this small?"[21] A baby's cry—a mother is earlier shown feeding—can also be distinctly heard after the first suicide bombing, elevated in the film's sound design and overlaid over images of the dead and injured. Such barbarism outwardly confirms the villain's wickedness and will justify Fleury and his team's ultimately violent response.

Further linking the frontier western with colonialism and Orientalism, this characterization connects *The Kingdom* to earlier "colonial outpost" films, such as *Gunga Din* (Stevens 1939) and *The Lost Patrol*. Matthew Hannah observes that descriptions of the Oriental Other often repurpose a vocabulary reminiscent of popular cultural stereotypes about combat with Native Americans, of a cowardly enemy opposed to civilization itself (555). Ziauddin Sardar and Merryl Davies also briefly link "colonialist films" such as *Beau Geste* (Wellman 1939) to westerns, which feature a "lone and beleaguered outpost of a fragile and imperiled civilization that must fight for its very existence against an implacable barbaric enemy" (247). As interesting as these connections may be, it is vital to recognize and interrogate the ambivalence of films like *Fort Apache*, including in its acknowledgment of white America's complicity in the escalation of violence, or the general unsavoriness of *Beau Geste*'s so-called defenders of civilization.

A consequence of its apparent genre conventionality, the majority of scholarship on *The Kingdom* declares the ostensibly xenophobic, racist, or Orientalist construction of Saudi characters in the film. Berg's *Lone Survivor*, based on the autobiographical recount of a Navy SEAL whose team battles for survival after their mission to kill a Taliban leader is derailed, certainly seems to satisfy critics of his depictions as Orientalist and binarist. However, *The Kingdom* was released at a very different juncture in American life and is clearly more ambivalent about America's responses to 9/11. While *The Kingdom*'s representation of Arab/Muslims superficially reproduces Orientalist constructions, it also complicates them. Critics and scholars predominantly mock the team's chauvinism and willful ignorance.[22] Yet this chauvinism and bombast are contrasted critically with Colonel Al Ghazi's stoicism and dignity in the film. Not only, then, does the Other destabilize and trouble normative American masculinities, but the film seems to be in on the joke to an extent: Leavitt even reads *The Complete Idiot's Guide to the Koran* in the gym *after* the team's arrival in Saudi Arabia.

Further complicating Orientalist characterizations of the film, Fleury's (and America's) own "dark fantasies" muddy distinctions with the supposedly evil Other. In westerns like *The Searchers*, the uncivilized Other, Comanche chief Scar (Henry Brandon), also represents the hero's dark mirror. The Other embodies what the hero desires and what he despises about himself. *The Kingdom* defines Fleury (and America) in opposition to Saudi use of torture. Yet in a wider sense, Nayak argues that the violent Other represents America's "dark fantasy" and even signposts the post-9/11 reality of displaced, subcontracted torture. For example, the first FBI briefing after the attacks foregrounds the agents' frustrations, angered by the enforced impotence of bureaucratic acquiescence to Saudi demands. This is immediately succeeded—and ambivalently remedied—by a sequence depicting the Saudi interrogation-torture of Al Ghazi's deputy, Sergeant Haytham (Ali Suliman), who actually saves multiple lives in the first attack (including the boy in the cap). The placement of the torture, conducted at the behest of a National Guard general, serves two functions. It first defines Saudi methods as backward and brutal but likewise reflects American desire for revenge, a dark wish fulfillment that ordains but displaces the desired savagery onto the Oriental Other.

Hamza is associated with invisibility and concealment and is (morally) coded as despicable, treacherous, and "unmanly."[23] Such a representation has

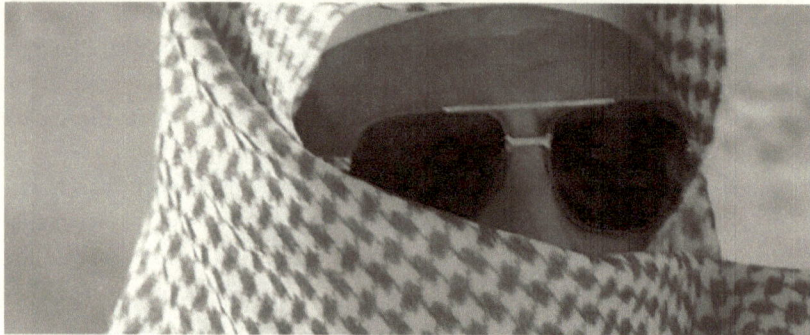
Figure 4.8. The Orientalized terrorist mastermind, veiled even from the film-camera.

been remarkably stable across male action subgenres, including westerns, World War II combat pictures, colonial outpost films, and Vietnam War movies. Indeed, a reformed Saudi terrorist bomb maker's description of Hamza as "like a ghost" echoes opening titles and character dialogue in *The Lost Patrol* seven decades earlier. The facelessness associated with modern terrorism reworks long-standing Orientalist descriptions for a contemporary audience. The first time Hamza appears, he is on the rooftop, concealed from his unwitting victims. His face is hidden even from the camera (fig. 4.8). Hamza's persistent concealment of his face in his video messages is pragmatic, evading possible identification. However, given how he also does this on the rooftop, Hamza's consistent veiling signals his mendacity and, evocative of Orientalist images of women, his effeminacy. The film's inciting attacks are also committed by attackers posing as police officers, a monstrous masquerade completed when one suddenly becomes a suicide bomb(er), violently revealing what the uniform temporarily concealed. Also duplicitously veiled as an apartment building, like Hamza and his operatives, the terrorist group's hideout only masquerades as civilian. Transformed into a terror space, its holes and tunnels recall typical representations of Arab cities "as dark, exotic, labyrinthine and structureless places" (Graham, 256, qtd. in Dodds).[24] As in many frontier westerns, the Other treacherously tries to blend in among women and children. During the final shoot-out, when Fleury's team enters the terrorist group's building, Hamza uses the women and children in his family to shield himself from identification, masquerading as infirm and helpless to obscure himself from the FBI's perspective (which approximates the camera's).

As observed earlier, all space outside the compound is alien and hostile in *The Kingdom*, leaving Fleury's team persistently exposed and uneasy. As well as immobile, Fleury is unable to read this foreign space. This reiterates the fragility of the outpost and lionizes the threat beyond but also admits a discomfiting lack of local knowledge. When Fleury looks out from the safety of the compound "green zone," his request to visit a building in the near distance is rejected by Al Ghazi because "it's outside the walls." The compound, again both fortress and prison, is now marked as foreign space by dint of Saudi control over it. The hostility of foreign space even within—it has been infiltrated by Hamza's members and is under continued surveillance—is communicated by the camera's persistent approximation of a sense of suspicion and wariness, a fearfulness Fleury and his team are desperate to reverse.

The Kingdom partially shores up Fleury's and the team's undermined masculinities by containing the threat, menace, and unknowability of Arab/Muslim space—an Orientalist desire for mastery. During the opening terror attacks, the attack coordinators on the rooftop orient the film-camera. Their binocular and video camera points of view, the "terrorist perspective," repeatedly identify forthcoming phases in the attacks, to which the film-camera must then, in a sense, catch up. *The Kingdom* builds the impression that the terrorist perspective precedes and structures the film-camera, as if the film must orient itself to an unfolding spectacle orchestrated and known only to the terrorist-Other. This gives the sense that the film, like the attacks, is being directed by the terrorist perspective, whether directing the audience to the two masquerading police officers who begin the attack or the soon-to-be suicide bomber walking onto the softball field. This repeated reorientation does more than build an impression of a lack of control, but rather builds on it. Berg's early preference for a handheld, pseudodocumentary aesthetic, connoting a stylized lack of control, contributes to this feeling. Shooting on location, he studiously avoids (the appearance of) blocking scenes in his predilection for partially obscured or slightly removed action to mimic the aesthetic of a "fly-on-the-wall" documentary. Yet this also signals how the film manages the attacks and swiftly reinstates symbolic control, particularly given that this "terror perspective" is never revisited. *The Kingdom* equally contains the perceived threat of foreign space by using Arizona to re-create (and thus de-Other) Riyadh. The frontier western identifier here also accurately describes *Gunga Din* (as a sort of "boy's own" western) and *The Lost Patrol*, films that, though putatively set in the "Orient," were likewise filmed in Arizona. In so doing, *The Kingdom* enacts the geographic containment of the Other, with American space masquerading as Other, able to represent anywhere and appear as if Other.

A key characteristic of western mythology celebrates individualistic heroes and transgressive masculinities. The hero's relation to space and the Other are equivalent, each (to be) feared and conquered in equal measure. In *The Kingdom*, a sense of control over the compound as an American space, along with the team's professional agency, is destabilized both by the attacks and by subsequent assertions of Saudi jurisdiction. To reverse this loss, Fleury's team must reterritorialize, remasculinize, and (re-)Americanize foreign space. As with all popular genres, westerns represent a nexus of cultural fears, desires, and politics. Richard Slotkin argues that conquering the frontier, twinned with the destruction of the Other, was politically and culturally integral to America's national identity. Yet, as John E. O'Connor observes, the western ideology of space "both disavows [American] colonial intention and affirms colonial hegemony" (32). In *The Kingdom*, the film-camera's rapid reorientation (away from the terrorist perspective) late in the opening attacks foreshadows the like struggle of Fleury's team to reassume control, the film's efforts to master Arab/Muslim perspective and space repeated by the FBI team. The use of FBI investigators rather than the CIA or military not only depoliticizes and demilitarizes the national-institutional response but redesignates the compound-bomb site as both domestic *and* international. The sense that the oil company housing compound signifies an America abroad is thus restored in the course of the FBI investigation. The FBI presence, routinely connoted as a domestic organization, seeks to governmentalize and Americanize the space, especially in the wake of Saudi assertions of jurisdiction.[25] The team will also (re)claim the bomb site—and thereby the compound—as an American space through the imposition (and implicitly assumed cultural and technological supremacy) of American investigative methods and practices. The significance of it becoming such a site in *The Kingdom* facilitates the restitution of destabilized identities sheathed in (the performance of) professional roles.

In Fleury's case, he reprises his talents for negotiation and persuasion by identifying a loophole in the Saudi rules: he can still interview compound inhabitants as witnesses. Reiterating its material function in sustaining his identity, Fleury is again shown walking, this time toward a compound home. Tellingly, he no longer follows Colonel Al Ghazi but leads him to the door, further erasing enforced immobility. This symbolic reterritorialization via professional agency is affirmed when Fleury subsequently refuses to be positioned as a subject of the prince in a palace meeting. Ignoring cultural sensitivities and Al Ghazi's advice, Fleury surprisingly secures Saudi agreement to continue the investigation through so-called American methods: "America's not perfect . . . but we are good at this," he tells the prince. Klaus Dodds recognizes that the Middle East is often "a site for US personnel to demonstrate their superior skills and technical expertise" in film (1633). In *The Kingdom*, each team member's consequent return to performing his or her specialized role reestablishes professional identities destabilized by the attorney general's initial acquiescence to Saudi jurisdiction and upon their arrival in Saudi Arabia. Mayes, for example, returns to her role as a forensic examiner, and Sykes to his as bomb technician. Mayes and Sykes then concurrently reassemble the attack's components, Mayes via extracting a marble from shrapnel embedded in non-Muslim victims, and Sykes, after finding a gurney in the bomb crater, by discovering the second round of bombs that killed Manner were delivered via an ambulance. Transforming the investigation and bomb site through performance rather than mere presence, the resumption of their professional roles restores previously contested spaces as unambiguously American. The gymnasium even becomes a mini-investigation headquarters, reversing its previously ambivalent signification as a liminal American space and a site of immobility, constraint, and inaction.

Americanizing the Interracial Buddy and Inculcating Sons into Violence

Fleury's team nonetheless needs a so-called good Other to help it navigate opaque Saudi cultural and institutional customs. The good Other, or "good Indian," is an ambivalent figure in Hollywood history. Persistently used in westerns and war movies, the good Indian is a typical characteristic of frontier westerns, from *Major Dundee* to *Black Hawk Down* and *The Missing* (Howard 2004). Underscoring how the convention has transferred to the representation of Arab/Muslims, Karin Wilkins and John Downing contend the pre-9/11 *The Siege* (Zwick 1998), in which a wave of terrorist attacks in New York result in the imposition of martial law, largely explores the western dilemma of whether good Indians can be trusted (426). Often scouts, informants, or "natives," their local knowledge and greater capacity to blend into their environment are coveted as much as they are *also* portrayed as backward, uncivilized, and inferior. Never fully trusted, their intelligence and allegiance are considered equivalently invaluable and unreliable.

Peter Berg intended Fleury and Al Ghazi's relationship to also mimic the structure of an interracial buddy film relationship (*The Kingdom* DVD commentary). Fleury and Al Ghazi's initial antagonism is established when Fleury lands in Saudi Arabia. The two men are presented in a mirrored-but-oppositional stance that also foreshadows their equivalence. The film further establishes the men's adversarial relationship through a series of shot–reverse shots throughout the team's convoy escort from the airport. Al Ghazi eventually dominates these shots, affirming his precedence in this new foreign space. Al Ghazi notes that the FBI team does not understand the dangers beyond the compound, and he is unwavering and unflinching in standing up to Fleury: "There is me telling you what you may or may not do, and there is you doing it." Yet far from oppositional, Al Ghazi mirrors Fleury's besieged, beleaguered (professional) masculine identity. He too must navigate dysfunctional institutional structures, and interagency conflict between his police and the National Guard. The team members initially deride and dismiss the colonel as a "babysitter," a gendered term that seeks to emasculate their chaperone. However, pointing to the film's overall ambivalence, Al Ghazi both exposes and resists the team's persistent, patronizing chauvinism. His stoicism and dignity, reinforced in critical praise of Barhom's performance, stand in stark contrast to the team's (naive and misguided) jingoism and bombast. In contrast to Jack Shaheen's claim that the inclusion of "good" Saudis is "mere tokenism" ("Stereotypes Reign in *The Kingdom*"), the film implicitly critiques—as much as it revels in and reproduces—the team's cultural ignorance and bigotry toward Arab/Muslims. Initial mockery even becomes empathy after Al Ghazi details the competing agencies he must negotiate and admits his impotence under the control of the National Guard general. Fleury finally recognizes that the two are equally disempowered and so must cooperate. Reframing Al Ghazi from antagonist to "buddy" is then advanced through the identification of shared values and attributes clearly denoted as American.

Al Ghazi's early dominance underlines the team's loss of professional agency. While it must eventually be blunted so as to reestablish threatened American/masculine identity, the representation of this good Indian reproduces and complicates straightforward Orientalist readings. This notion is affirmed in a short, lyrical scene midfilm depicting the home life of the film's good Indians, Al Ghazi and Sergeant Haytham, which extends the film's central concern with the relations of fathers to sons. The montage first shows Al Ghazi at home playing with his children and then, panning down and left from Al Ghazi to his son, depicts both in prayer. Most poignantly, however, the scene shows another father-son relationship as Haytham returns home to his invalid father. Subverting audience expectations, it is the distraught sergeant, recently interrogated and beaten, who, comforted by his visibly frail father, weeps and becomes child again. Michael Cieply observes that this so-called softer scene "went in and out of the movie several times" but was finally retained to avoid accusations the film was anti-Muslim ("*The Kingdom* Gambles"). Cynical or otherwise, the scene "offers a portrayal of Saudi domestic life" and Islam as "embedded in everyday life," with prayer familial rather than male only (Dodds 1628). A straight cut to Fleury on the phone from Riyadh with his son reinforces the shared import of family and further associates Fleury and Al Ghazi, this time as fathers.

The Kingdom visually and thematically links American and Saudi sons throughout, variously connecting and contrasting Fleury, Al Ghazi, and Hamza (through his two youngest grandsons) as father figures. After Al Ghazi's death at film's end, Fleury pays his respects to Al Ghazi's father. The camera moves to

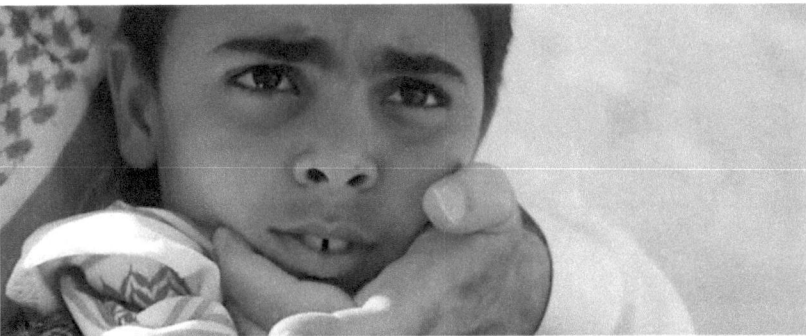

Figure 4.9. The Arab/Muslim terrorist-father forces his grandson to watch the attacks, seeking to inculcate him into the terrorist perspective.

the old man's hands, locating him as a "good Other" by showing that he—unlike the reformed bomb maker and Hamza—retains all his fingers. Even though Al Ghazi also has two daughters, Fleury only encounters his son in the visit. His words to the silent boy, "Your father was a good friend of mine," mirror sentiments he earlier expressed to Manner's surviving son. Fleury here assumes figurative responsibility for the Saudi son, as he has for the American.

Yet the clear links between Fleury and Al Ghazi also foreshadow the twinned induction of American and Saudi boys into cultures of violence by father figures and the (potential) intergenerational consequences of fathers' actions. Throughout *The Kingdom*, looking at terror invariably occurs at a mediated distance, through either binoculars or the camera. This simultaneously brings the watcher closer while marking a separation from what is watched. Yet "mediated looking" also induces a capacity, even willingness, for Saudi sons to watch scenes of violence. It also contributes to a growing sense of hatred toward American presence. *The Kingdom* erroneously posits a gateway structure to the indoctrination of Arab/Muslim boys into terrorism; that is, looking through binoculars—the massacre narrated by the terrorist mastermind—leads first to filming and finally to actively participating in terrorism. The path on which Hamza has set his youngest grandson is corroborated during the opening attacks as the camera pans from the terrorist mastermind's concerted efforts to compel the child to watch the attack to his older teenage grandson, who calmly videos the carnage even after the suicide bombing (fig. 4.9).

This gateway structure is reinforced when the teenager, now thoroughly inculcated into the terror perspective, is shown actively involved in preparations to later attack Fleury's team. *The Kingdom* repeatedly implies that Arab/Muslim culture quickly transforms the child's desire to look away into the teenager's pleasure in not only watching but participating in violence. The

Figure 4.10. Hamza delivers a video address praising the attacks and the sacrifice of his "sons."

Figure 4.11. Rather than the camera, the focus of Hamza's address is his teenage grandson.

film reinforces that mediated looking leads inexorably to participation by cosituating bomb making and Hamza's propaganda video recordings. Hamza's video address celebrating the first attacks' success further reinforces the film's interest in the impact of father figures on sons. As Hamza speaks, praising all his "sons," including those sacrificed, the film offers Hamza's objective point of view. Yet it is his teenage grandson, rather than the video camera, who is Hamza's central focus, as if he is communicating with the boy before his wider audience (figs. 4.10–4.11).

As much as *The Kingdom* implies that Arab-Muslim father figures coach sons into bomb making, weaponry, and terror, American sons are likewise implicitly introduced into a culture of violence and militarism. Superficially reproducing but partially destabilizing too-simplistic Orientalist interpretations of the film, this inevitably complicates assumptions about Fleury's paternal redemption. After Manner's death, Fleury visits his surviving son. Underlining the significance of symbolic father-son relations in the film, this scene, like Fleury's later visit to Al Ghazi's son, was included in the final cut only at the last minute. The boy plays with a model of a military chopper—presumably built with his deceased father—throughout his conversation with Fleury, and military toys and photos of the boy and his father dominate the bedroom. Such gender socialization through toys and games normalizes militarism and masculine violence for American boys. Fleury's earlier arrival at the boy's house is briefly offered from the boy's perspective, watching Fleury's arrival through curtained windows from the confines—and assumed protections—of the home. Further linking terror abroad to the American home, the scene spotlights anxieties about the impossibility of shielding the home from terror manifested by 9/11. It predominantly, however, suggests a certain ambivalence, with the American son's innocence equally threatened by his inculcation into a culture of militarism and violence, one firmly embedded in paternal relations.

In interracial buddy film relationships, the expression of shared values or experiences affirms the pair's growing allegiance and developing (earned and mutual) respect. Williams and Linneman correctly identify that "the noble traits displayed by Al Ghazi are not connected to Arab culture, but are norms shared by Americans and Saudis" (202). More than this, Al Ghazi and Fleury's relationship is importantly cemented *through* American (global) popular culture, as Al Ghazi describes for Fleury how he wanted to become a cop as a child because of the "green beast" (the Hulk) on television.[26] Bonding via American popular culture serves not only to erase otherwise troubling cultural and ethnic difference but begins to reestablish threatened American masculinities through notions of equivalence. Al Ghazi is not so much humanized through universal values as he is assimilated via American popular culture. Al Ghazi's embrace of American culture (and the values it articulates) here recalls the overtly colonialist *Gunga Din*, whose titular character, a water bearer and consistent object of ridicule for three British sergeants in the former British India, openly aspires to the virtues and values of the colonial master.

This eradication of difference is secured when Al Ghazi admits his heretofore-concealed desire—beyond merely safeguarding Fleury's team—for vengeance: "When we catch the man who murdered these people, I don't care to ask even one question. I want to kill him." Al Ghazi's words again recall the Hulk, whose transformation into the "green beast" is fueled by rage and who has limited control over his subsequent actions. Al Ghazi's admission voices what Fleury cannot. Not only does Al Ghazi share Fleury's popular culture values, but his desire for violent revenge again articulates Fleury's suppressed "dark fantasy." As much as a moment of bonding, this perhaps signals America's violent duality and foreshadows the corrosive effects of uncontrolled rage and violent vengeance. Their buddy relationship is (generically) ordained through a physical altercation with a National Guard officer, when Fleury comes to Al Ghazi's aid after he is beaten. This bonding through violence culminates in the very merging of the men's perspectives and actions. Late in the film's climactic apartment building shoot-out, the two men turn together, ending in a close-up of their weapons pointing in the same direction, their bodies and weapons perfectly aligned and shooting in unison.[27]

The fidelity of the good Indian can only truly be confirmed through sacrificial death, as is the case in *Major Dundee*, *Gunga Din*, and *The Missing*. His goodness requires sacrifice, and invariably death, as a performative display of allegiance. Only Al Ghazi dies in *The Kingdom*; the good Indian must be sacrificed, especially because his early dominance threatens Fleury's masculine identity. Al Ghazi's death also marks the death of the Americanized Other, a death precipitated by American intervention. One unsettling implication is the impossibility of being (and surviving as) the much-heralded conservative political construct of the "moderate Muslim." That is, to be both Arab-Muslim and American is not only to be caught in between but fatal. In the final shoot-out in the apartment building, Fleury and Al Ghazi join Mayes in a room in which Hamza hides *in plain view* among women and children. Al Ghazi's face darkens when he realizes the terrorist may be present. A series of shot–reverse shots shows Al Ghazi and Hamza "reading" each other, before Al Ghazi cannily compels Hamza to divulge his monstrosity by revealing his missing fingers, his disfigurement finally betraying his identity. The supposed necessity to sacrifice the good Indian here implies that the good Indian cannot be divorced from the evil Other, an intrinsic duality often explicitly visualized through physical struggle and twinned death in the cause of eliminating the evil.[28]

Taking Up Arms: Female Masculinity, Remasculinization, and Gender Reversal

The renewed impression of American control and agency via the resumption of the rapid response team's individual professional roles is exemplified when Mayes performs an autopsy on victims of the bombings. Michelle Aguayo claims this scene reinforces Orientalist discourses of the Other as scientifically backward and culturally primitive, especially through their sexist treatment of Mayes. This underplays Mayes's empathic relationship with Sergeant Haytham, one that arguably mirrors that of Fleury and Al Ghazi. Her professional expertise enables her to reconstruct and visualize his commendable earlier efforts to kill some of the first attackers. In a flashback-like scene, Mayes nimbly reassembles details of Sergeant Haytham's disruptive intervention from spent bullet casings, blood patches, and collision points. Then, when a guard is angered when

Mayes touches a dead Muslim during the autopsy, the sergeant becomes her surrogate, an adjunct who follows her instructions. The autopsy scene does, however, depict the transformation of Arab/Muslim cultural attitudes and acceptance of American values and methods. Through the (re)establishment of female professional agency, Saudi males *perform* American methods *under* American female instruction.

The Kingdom incorporates women, along with multiethnicity, into public/professional roles to mark American exceptionalism. Mayes is also coded as (female and American) masculine through her equally enthusiastic taking up of arms with the team at film's end. Mayes is the rare female character whose assumption of masculine traits, roles, or positions does not appear to be overtly punished or demonized. As possessing agency, being tough, resourceful, and competent with weapons, she persuasively embodies Yvonne Tasker's definition of military masculinity ("Soldiers' Stories"). However, Mayes's female masculinity, reiterating Jack Halberstam's scathing criticism, is ambivalently framed "in order that male masculinity may appear to be the real thing" (1). *The Kingdom* repeatedly and pejoratively delineates Mayes's difference from that of her male colleagues. Aguayo identifies that Mayes's clothing (military pants and tight T-shirt) seeks to both "masculinize her body while still show[ing] her female curves, with specific emphasis on her breasts" (52). More subtly, in her first appearance, during the first briefing, Mayes is the only FBI agent to cry when Fleury reports that Manner has been killed. Fleury chokes back his tears—tears subsequently displaced onto Mayes—and he somewhat theatrically draws attention to hers by halting his briefing to whisper in her ear. It is only after this, when she speaks in her professional capacity in the briefing, that Mayes is identified by name and area of expertise. While her identity is similarly tied to her professional role, it is wholly prefigured by a feminine-coded response.

Unsurprisingly, Mayes's supposed difference is amplified in Saudi Arabia and again displaced onto the Oriental Other. Making an *explicit* issue of her body and presence is marked as culturally misplaced, even perverse, in the film. Mayes first laughs off well-meaning but clumsy Saudi attempts to create a "feminine" space in the gym for her when Al Ghazi apologizes for not being able to place a pink screen around her cot for privacy. And her body is the only one sexualized, by Schmidt as proxy for the Saudi prince. Finally, preparations for another, later car bomb attack prominently display a surveillance photo of Mayes as a designated target—but not of Sykes or Leavitt.[29] The perversity of the exaggerated focus of the terrorist perspective on Mayes is reinforced at the close of the apartment shoot-out when Hamza's teenage grandson chooses to direct his gun sideways at Mayes rather than forward at Fleury, who actually holds the teenager in his gun's sights. While the film derides such cultural attitudes, it consistently designates her body as less resilient and more liable to suffer, however accurate and appropriate her bodily response may be. Mayes, for example, is the only team member who falls to the ground when a jeep-mounted machine gun is fired into the air after the physical altercation between Fleury and a National Guard officer. *The Kingdom* again conveniently displaces male pain and suffering onto the female body.

Yet Mayes's dual embodiment of female *and* military masculinity develops over the course of the film. Through Mayes, masculinity "becomes legible as masculinity" and as performative (Halberstam 2). This is first foreshadowed when she regenders the gym's space, relocating "pink" onto Leavitt, as she points to an imaginary line on the floor: "Don't cross this: pink line." As the least conventionally masculine team member, Leavitt is seemingly aware of this implication, and his response is telling: "You're real butch after a long flight."[30] Leavitt's words weakly attempt to transform Mayes's "barely butch" gender into deviance (Halberstam 217), a connotation Mayes will soon upend in rescuing the soon-to-be male abductee. In *Courage under Fire* (Zwick 1996), Capt. Karen Walden (Meg Ryan), a chopper commander posthumously investigated over her worthiness for the Medal of Honor, is also pejoratively described as "butch." Tasker argues that Walden is ultimately both masculine coded and normalized, the film establishing the "coexistence of her military *masculinity*" and "her status as a military *woman*" ("Soldiers' Stories" 212). While Tasker ("Soldiers' Stories" 217) claims that "becoming 'butch' is insistently not about becoming male," Walden's female masculinity nonetheless relies on metaphorically militarizing motherhood, with Walden comparing being shot to childbirth, and her father describing Walden's motherhood as *also* a duty.[31] Tasker also observes that cinematic military masculinity is also associated with star persona, clothing, and appearance, and Ryan's performance was accordingly critically panned as unpersuasive and unconvincing ("Soldiers' Stories"). Garner-Mayes, on the other hand, is persuasively normalized through discourses of military masculinity. Unlike Walden, Mayes's female masculinity does not require militarizing motherhood and is reinforced by Garner's action pedigree as the star of *Alias* (Abrams 2001–6), in which she portrayed a CIA double agent adept in martial arts, and the eponymous superhero in *Elektra* (Bowman 2005).

Mayes's representation of female military masculinity is literalized when the team's convoy is attacked as it departs for the airport, following a series of nominally successful joint raids that disrupt the second attack. In the ambush, Leavitt is abducted, his kidnappers again masquerading as officers in the FBI team's escort. Without sanction, the remaining team members promptly arm themselves. As much as the restoration of professional agency, Fleury's and

Sykes' rearming after being disarmed on arrival is integral in reasserting their masculinities. Mayes's taking up arms likewise firmly aligns her with military masculinity. This alignment is initially uncertain. In Hamza's apartment building hideout, as Al Ghazi and Fleury rapidly clear out rooms, Mayes, initially overwhelmed, cowers in the hall as explosions and bullets tear through the walls around her. A hall again represents a significant transition space, this time signaling the realization of Mayes's militarization. Stumbling upon a room of terrified women and children, she resolves to act (as gun-wielding action hero). Moving on, she finds and shoots a number of Leavitt's captors and would-be executioners. In a final, frenzied kill scene, she wrestles, shoots, and—cue Freudian symbolism—stabs the largest captor, who still masquerades as a police officer, in the groin. Wielded by a militarized action film final girl, Mayes's knife is penetrative and "unmanning" as she rescues Leavitt—an unarmed and bound man. Mayes's armed rescue of Leavitt complicates claims by Susan Faludi about how a post-9/11 revival of "captivity narratives" prefigured American women as passive, fragile victims of uncivilized "Indians" and (re)inflated the role of their male rescuers. Rather, Mayes's rescue of Leavitt surprisingly disrupts this representational code and, in Halberstam's words, "produce[s] radically refigured notions of proper gender" (41). Leavitt's rescue certainly remasculinizes American masculinity, but remasculinization is embodied by Mayes. At the same time, Purse observes that this "emphatic reinstatement of Mayes's narrative and physical agency subtly undermines the Muslim prohibitions" on her presence and participation (161). The scene also confirms long-standing suspicions about American male insufficiency—coding Jewishness as urban—with Leavitt's persistent emasculation redoubled by his abduction and need to be rescued.

Replaying debates about Hollywood's role in the depiction of recent national traumas, *The Kingdom*'s allusions to the imagery and iconography of real-world terror in the planned execution scene attracted substantial criticism.[32] L. Susan Williams and Travis Linneman assert the use of imagery reminiscent of beheadings in *The Kingdom* and *Syriana* "is a powerful device to help the audience connect a fictional portrayal of Arabs to real-world violence" (199).[33] In this regard, clear allusions to real-world events, such as the beheading of the journalist Daniel Pearl—in concert with the film's news-style credits sequence and handheld documentary aesthetic—garner greater-than-typical weight for an action genre movie. However, critics considered such allusions within conventional—even "low"—genre form problematic, to say the least.[34] Considered too reminiscent of the horrific fates of Pearl and other beheading victims, the film's blurring of reality and fiction does inspire an uncertain viewing experience. Taken into a room with a video camera, Leavitt's panicked apprehension of the mise-en-scène of the modern execution video communicates an understanding that recording not only makes an event "real" but is to ultimately mark death. A fast-paced montage that follows one abductor's order to "start the camera," which variously includes the reading of a missive of accusation and judgment, the camera's spotlight, and the knife, confirms its familiarity in global discourse.[35] When the spotlight subsequently falls on Leavitt's face, he stares fearfully into the camera. A slight zoom in from Leavitt's optical point of view terrifyingly connotes how this "apparatus of death" pulls him in. Roused from his trance by outside gunfire that marks the arrival of the FBI cavalry, Leavitt's resistance is reactivated, and his subsequent toppling of the camera tripod forestalls his death and gives time for Mayes to rescue him.

Leavitt's disruption of the videoed execution highlights how events must be recorded to index their existence and communicate terror to others. Hamza's group films the first attacks and later posts them on the internet to both communicate their success to sympathizers and terrorize beyond their immediate targets. Absent recording, Leavitt cannot be executed; his survival lies in averting spectacle, in not being made the object of terror. In repeatedly linking terror and the recording of images, including in Hamza's video address at the site of preparations for additional attacks, *The Kingdom* implicitly defines the act of recording as also an act of terror. Establishing Hamza as more than a distantiated figurehead, this association also signals the function of communication technologies in creating and communicating terror. Ostensibly the film least connected to 9/11 and New York in this book, *The Kingdom* seems the only one able to overtly represent the spectacle of terror for its audience—both terror and cinema similarly interested in spectacles of violence. Corey Creekmur claims that an online video of the first attacks confirms them as "an event staged for a camera and given a 'new' soundtrack [of prayer and chanting] at least as troubling as its more realistic, 'original' sounds" (91). The attacks become horrifyingly real when watched on screens—in the first FBI briefing and later when the team watches the online video—but their horror is also symbolically contained and managed within a small screen.[36] Until the shoot-out, Fleury's team have only watched killing at a mediated distance, on screens and through binoculars. The team's flippant jocularity as they lounge among the corpses of militants killed in the raid, whom Fleury calls "kids," highlights this, as much their willingness to dehumanize the Arab/Muslim Other. The macabre scene also demarcates the world of difference between watching violence at a mediated distance and doing violence, a difference that becomes all too real in the aftermath of the team's final turn to vengeance and apparent celebration of military masculinity.

Genre Schizophrenia: The Impossibility of Concealing Vengeance

Before Leavitt's abduction, Fleury's team orchestrates raids in which they can observe but cannot participate. After their superficially successful conclusion, the team's—and the film's—forensic-procedural response comes to a sudden and unsatisfactory halt. Their criminal investigation simply stops: Hamza remains unpunished, and the militants they kill are "insignificant." The team, subsequently informed by Schmidt that they are leaving Saudi Arabia immediately, is also again immobile and constrained. As if in response, *The Kingdom* joltingly shifts from a crime procedural into an over-the-top action-war revenge fantasy. Leavitt's abduction initiates *The Kingdom*'s final-act generic transformation into an action-war film, with the measured quest for criminal justice disconcertingly giving way to vengeful violence. The remaining team members—and the film—seemingly submit to a long-repressed desire to take up arms in vengeance. Adapting Richard Slotkin ("Our Myths of Choice"), the shift affirms that when American manhood "feels" profoundly threatened, the desire for "savage war" overwhelms the nation's commitment to "good war." Similarly, Klaus Dodds suggests American soldiers in action films in part "consolidate their militarized identities and institutions" and secure America through violence (1628). Critics decried this sudden turn, identifying it as the film's "schizophrenia," as if character and film alike become driven by vengefulness rather than justice (Lane, "Outlaws").[37] Restoring professional agency, reterritorializing space, and solving the crime are ultimately insufficient. Remasculinization requires violent revenge.

Until this point, Fleury's long-standing but subliminal desire for vengeance is masked and displaced. Only Fleury's revelation in the film's coda, after killing Hamza, that he "told [Mayes] we were gonna kill them all" in the first FBI briefing belatedly discloses the driving centrality of vengeance, just as the attorney general suggests early in the film. The team numerously masks Fleury's (and their own) thirst for vengeance. Before arriving in Saudi Arabia, Mayes evades telling Leavitt what Fleury whispered in the briefing, and Fleury and Sykes also sidestep enunciating Fleury's motives. Fleury's vague confession that he has a "beast in [his chest]" perhaps unintentionally reveals his true motivation but also symbolically associates him with the uncontrollable rage of the "green beast" whom Al Ghazi later celebrates. Fleury's desire for vengeance is thus displaced onto the good Indian, solemnly concurring with Al Ghazi's vow "I just want to kill him," highlighting his/America's persistent desire to conceal its "dark fantasy" within the body of the Other. Multiple deleted scenes further uncover how Fleury's motivating desire for vengeance is obscured (*The Kingdom* DVD bonus materials). In one, the FBI director elicits an admission from Fleury that he "just wants to hit somebody." And in two surrounding conversations with Manner's widowed wife—excisions that further erase female-maternal presence from the film—Fleury promises her that he will "make 'em pay."

Vengeance, and the schizophrenic mutation into an action-war film, offers the team the secretly yearned-for opportunity to remasculinize via a showdown. *The Kingdom*'s spectacular—and plainly absurd—shoot-out finale simulates the siege experience of the outpost in frontier westerns like *Fort Apache*, *Gunga Din*, and *Black Hawk Down*. After pursuing Leavitt's abductors into Suweidi—a neighborhood, characterized as entirely hostile, that recalls Mogadishu in *Black Hawk Down*—the team is surrounded by overwhelming numbers attacking from a high vantage point.[38] The rearmed team and its good Indians—Al Ghazi and Haytham—ride into an ambush within the unreadable space of the Other, the hostile district and the apartment cum terrorist hideout. Stephen Graham notes that Arab spaces need to be "unveiled" to facilitate the production of "order"—and thus become mere "terrorist nests" and "killing fields" (256). Fleury's team's incursion into the apartment building embodies Hannah's identification of post-9/11 American foreign policy's invocation of frontier masculinity, articulating not only the need to uncover "hidden" targets but the assumed right to violate boundaries—legal, official, and spatial—in doing so. More than this, their incursion invokes the need to "unveil" the terrorist-Other and designate their actions *as also* self-defense via simulating a siege experience.

Fleury's principal motivation is all the more troubling for its long-held concealment and displacement, marking him an uncertain moral figure and coloring the team's entire investigation. According to O'Connor, the western ideology of space also justifies military presence based on self-defense (32), a justification often provided by the represented kidnap or massacre of women and children, such as in *She Wore a Yellow Ribbon* (Ford 1949) and *Major Dundee*. *Fort Apache* similarly stages graduated instances of so-called Indian savagery, including splaying cavalry dead across wagon wheels and colluding with other tribes, to justify a violent response. In *The Kingdom*, it is not the targeting of women and children but the abduction of a male agent that ultimately unbridles Fleury's repressed desires and transforms him (and the team) into the "green beast." This act offers them supposed cause for (re)militarization and retributive vengeance, typically celebrated in male action genres, but also critiqued in westerns like *The Searchers* (Ford 1956). The film tracks Ethan's (John Wayne) journey to rescue his eldest niece, kidnapped by Scar, an Indian chief on the warpath. However, Ethan's obsessive drive to recover the girl and avenge the killing of his brother's family (and the sister-in-law he silently loved) slowly but surely erodes his humanity. Likewise, *The Kingdom*'s genre schizophrenia, far from offering resolution, ends on an unclear future, suggesting that retaliatory violence not only fails to remasculinize but may make matters worse.

The Inadequacy of Vengeance and the Reality of Blowback

Far from necessary and restorative, violence is ultimately cyclical, intergenerational, and blows back. A CIA term coined in relation to the 1953 Iran coup to denote the unintended and undesired adverse repercussions of political or military action, blowback is a recurrent trope in post-9/11 American cinema. Relatively unacknowledged critically, it is noteworthy in films including *Rendition* (Hood 2007), *The American* (Corbijn 2010), and *The Missing*. Examining the codas of four films—*The Kingdom*, *Munich* (Spielberg 2005), *Zero Dark Thirty* (Bigelow 2012), and *Fort Apache*—underscores the acknowledged inadequacy of vengeance for masculinized heroes and its negative consequences.

Fort Apache's famously ambiguous coda in a sense presages the concept of blowback and its impact on the violent remasculinization of national identity. Colonel Thursday, who does not respect Native American cultures, breaks Captain York's promise of peace in his vainglorious quest for personal military glory. Thursday, who cannot distinguish the Apache from the landscape—and so concludes the former are not there—leads a calamitous charge into a fatal ambush, largely provisioned by guns sold to the Apache by an unscrupulous Indian agent. This results not only in the massacre of his entire command but in a renewed Indian campaign by the previously peripheral young warrior Geronimo. Likewise exploring the frontier struggle between "savagery" and "civilization," Ford "provokes a thoughtful uneasiness about the very myths" that westerns present (Heffernan 147). *Fort Apache*, much like *The Searchers*, "acknowledges a need for heroes while undermining the notion of heroism" (Kehr, "How the West Was Filled with Loss"). Thursday's twin legacy may be fame and discipline, but his chauvinism and ignorance provoke an escalated cycle of intergenerational war. Thursday becomes a mythic figure (despite the dishonorable reality of his death), and York remains representative of good. The coda, however ambivalent, even ends hopefully. As much as lamenting the passing of an era, and a particular sense of history, it announces a secure(d) future in Thursday's daughter's union with Lieutenant O'Rourke, who is excused from Thursday's command just before the massacre. Clearly recalling the earlier departure of Thursday's command on its ill-fated final journey, a shot shows the fort's women again watching from a fort balcony as another military campaign begins, this time under York's command, to combat the more threatening Geronimo. The presence of a new wife and young son implies a firmed sense of home, one built on and defended through paternal sacrifice, as the failed officer becomes the redeemed father. Despite the folly of the cavalry's massacre, Thursday safeguards the family, nation, and civilization by shielding Lieutenant O'Rourke *and* provoking an escalated conflict. Ford's famed coda indicates that York's military campaign successfully concludes with the cavalry symbolically raising the American flag over once contested land. Although this communicates ownership of and over the land as American, Ford finally equivocates on the validity and means through which (fragile) white dominion is achieved.

> Complicating such meditations on the efficacy of retributive violence through another rare instance of incorporating female masculinity, the climax of Kathryn Bigelow's *Zero Dark Thirty* outwardly represents the cathartic culmination of a period of American national anxiety after 9/11 and the ensuing war on terror. Bigelow's Oscar-nominated film also deploys 9/11 as an initiating device, but without the historical context *The Kingdom* offers in its opening (and then largely ignores, admittedly). Not only is 9/11 again visually unrepresented, merely a chaotic cacophony of overlapping, disembodied, anonymous voices over a black screen, but nothing except blackness precedes the attacks in the film's diegesis. Ironically, *Zero Dark Thirty* is less historically complex, in effectively extracting the attacks out of history, than the seemingly base *The Kingdom*. The attacks open the film and motivate its protagonist, Maya (Jessica Chastain), a CIA operative new to fieldwork, in her quest to locate Osama bin Laden. Maya's resilience and perseverance counter the national uncertainty triggered by 9/11 and exacerbated by ongoing failures in Afghanistan and Iraq. Undaunted by her initially shocking exposure to torture tactics, Maya will become the most conventionally masculine figure in the film. Bigelow's portrayal of the successful search for, and violent destruction of, the feared terrorist-Other in *Zero Dark Thirty* seems to cinematically mark the reassertion of American national identity. The killing of bin Laden in May 2011 represents the ultimate erasure of the terrorist-Other, the retributive redemption of America for 9/11 and reversal of the emasculating humiliation it marked. Yet the film's deflating ending suggests the persistence of national uncertainty, ambivalence, and turmoil. Maya boards a transport flight back to America after successfully concluding her

Figure 4.12. Emptied rather than triumphant, Maya begins to cry, no longer having an anchor of purpose.

quest to avenge the attacks of 9/11 and the subsequent deaths of colleagues. Maya is changed by her experience, both her encounter with America's terrorist-Other and what she has become in the course of destroying it. The final shot in the film shows Maya, alone with her irresolvable grief, begin to cry, no longer having an answer for the pilot's question: "Where do ya wanna go?" (fig. 4.12). Rather than triumphant, she is emptied and, finally—without the terrorist-Other—without anchor or purpose. This unrelieved melancholy is also partly a symptom of situating the crisis of the terror threat, and thereby its remedy through violent remasculinization, in a single figure and event. Even with bin Laden's elimination, American masculinity and national identity are uncertainly recuperated in *Zero Dark Thirty*. Remasculinization through retributive violence depends on the tenacity and suffering of a young American woman, but the American Self is changed irrevocably by the encounter with the terror-Other: annihilation neither satisfies nor recuperates.

Spielberg's *Munich* perhaps offers the most sustained interrogation of the scarring consequences of vengeance and blowback, for hero and nation alike. Ostensibly about the experiences of the Mossad assassination team established to avenge the Black September attacks in 1972, and based on a creative nonfiction book by George Jonas titled *Vengeance*, *Munich* is as much an American film *about* America. After completing his mission, Avner Kaufman (Eric Bana), the team's leader, is unresponsive to congratulations and scarred psychologically. In the film's final scene, Avner, disillusioned

Figure 4.13. Avner, exiled in New York, is spurned by handler and country.

Figure 4.14. The unsettling presence of the Twin Towers in the background foreshadows the blowback America would experience on 9/11.

and now exiled in New York, has a final meeting with his Israeli government handler. He explicitly questions the value of Israel's violent retribution: "If they committed a crime, why not arrest them?" Avner's query is reinforced by the consequent escalation of terror as his team is killed one by one in retaliation: a prospective fate that will forever loom over him. Such blowback is portended by Avner's bomb maker—a former toy maker thereafter blown up by a bomb secreted in one of his own toys—who observes, "All this blood ... comes back to us." Even more explicitly, after Avner walks away alone, spurned by his handler—and, symbolically, the nation—the film-camera pointedly looks across toward 1970s Manhattan. The Twin Towers stand silently in the background in a shot that, held over end titles and credits, links the bomb maker's words to the blowback America would experience on 9/11 and after the war on terror (figs. 4.13–4.14). Vengeance changes Avner and nation alike: "There's no peace at the end of this, you know this is true." Emptied, Avner's exile lies as much in no longer having an unsullied home (or place of return) as in his fears of reprisals. Far from conclusive and restorative, Avner—and the film's final shot—acknowledges how retributive violence initiates only an unending cycle of violence and terrifying irresolution.

Becoming the Avenging (Action) Hero: Hollowness, Inadequacy, and Blowback

Although a less developed articulation of the consequences of vengeance, the future in *The Kingdom* is equally fraught, acknowledging vengeance to be not only hollow but counterproductive. David Thomson asserts that cinema can "distil and tame the rage for mere vengeance" (30). As in *The Searchers*, the immense buildup toward and need for violent revenge "collapses in the face of abiding kinship." However, in *The Kingdom*, revenge collapses not in the face of kinship but rather *in on itself*. Although Arab/Muslim space is transformed and (re-)Americanized through the symbolic return of American methods and values, its status as American is temporary and tenuous. Not only does violent action—the traditional masculine, national, and generic response to emasculation and threat—fail to provide solace to Fleury's team, but it seemingly leads only to further violence. Indeed, Berg intended to highlight the "cyclical nature of the violence," violence that "certainly isn't solving the problem" (*The Kingdom* DVD commentary). Yet rather than inspiring catharsis, *The Kingdom*'s turn to action-war and revenge fantasy only deflates, vengeance neither redemptive nor reassuring. When Fleury's hands are finally bloodied, he is left shocked and cradling the dead. A long-held shot of Al Ghazi's unblinking eyes devastates Fleury's repeated but uncertain invocations of "we got him." The film registers this by reworking a stylistic device used earlier to communicate restored mobility and investigative momentum, as the team strides with purpose after the prince agrees to let the FBI investigate. The slow-motion aesthetic employed throughout Fleury's visit to Al Ghazi's grieving family bleeds unsettlingly into the team's departure from Saudi Arabia, now associated with immobility, grief, and disintegration. Rather than triumphant, the extreme close-ups fragment their faces, their thirst for revenge emptied but inadequate.

In contrast to typical understandings about the cultural function that violence plays in American popular culture, violent action in *The Kingdom* resolves neither threatened professional, national, nor gender identities. This is emphasized in the film's coda, when the team, visibly bruised and scarred, reassembles in the FBI offices.[39] Their director tells them they "did outstanding work over there" and should "hold their heads high." Yet the team is immobile and silent, and each character stares blankly into offscreen space. Stephanie Zacharek observes that the ending resists jingoism; the team learns it cannot fix the Middle East ("*The Kingdom*"). Earlier signifiers of idealized masculinity in the film are also inverted. Inexpressiveness now connotes uncertainty, and mobility lacks purpose or destination. Fleury, after disclosing his early promise of vengeance whispered to Mayes, merely turns and walks back in the direction from which he entered; his undaunted mobility no longer has direction. While earlier he had appeared to comfort Mayes when he halts his postbombing briefing, we now learn that Fleury instead initiates the process of incorporating Mayes into military masculinity. Her embodiment of military masculinity now assumes greater ambivalence in the wake of the mission. The abrupt shift from crime procedural to action-war in *The Kingdom* nominally satisfies the team's motivating lust for vengeance but offers no such consolidation. Despite being just what the team—and audiences, it seems—believes it needs, violent revenge is unsatisfying, corrosive, and incomplete, a reality they can recognize but cannot speak.

More than this, their act of vengeance invites blowback, a prospect projected uncertainly beyond *The Kingdom*'s narrative close. Much like the Winchester rifles unscrupulously provided to the warring Apache in *Fort Apache*, the toys/bombs that kill the "toy maker" in *Munich*, and the rise of ISIS that succeeds the death of bin Laden and marginalization of al-Qaeda, the military detonator used in the opening attacks in *The Kingdom* is identified as American made. Violence in the film numerously causes actual *and* symbolic scarring and disfigurement of the perpetrator: the deleterious consequences of violence and hatred made manifest on the body. When Fleury and Al Ghazi visit a Riyadh games arcade to question the reformed former bomb maker—another father figure ambivalently associated with "sons" through a culture of violence in another male-only Saudi space, as teenagers gleefully shoot and kill American soldiers in video games—the informant explains the cause of his (and Hamza's) lost two fingers: "Every bomb maker at some point gets bitten by his own work."[40] Most troublingly, the film's coda further projects the prospect of intergenerational blowback as a direct consequence of killing Hamza, tacitly acknowledging that neither the team nor America can predict the consequences of its actions. The FBI director's declaration that Fleury's team "did outstanding work over there" is laid over an image of Hamza's surviving youngest grandson. Berg then intercuts Leavitt's and the grandson's mother's questions about what Fleury and Hamza respectively whispered, visually connecting the distantiated spaces and the opening FBI briefing with the film's violent culmination. The boy relates his grandfather's dying words, unsettlingly repeating Fleury's: "We are going to kill them all." Fleury's team may be chastened by the demoralizing realities of vengeance fulfilled, but the sentiment is alive in the Arab grandson. The film's final shot is an extreme close-up of the grandson. The shot mirrors the extreme close-up of his panicked eyes after the opening terror attacks, desperately trying to avert his gaze. Yet after Fleury kills Hamza, the boy progressively dons the clothing his grandfather wears when he coordinates these first attacks. First wearing the red *ghutra* head scarf and finally adopting the white *thobe* robes in the film's coda, the boy's inculcation into the terrorist perspective is seemingly complete. A purposeful, controlled stare accompanies his first spoken words in the film—the words of the terrorist-father—not only faithfully transmitting but also perhaps promising to realize the threat whispered by the dying Hamza. A slight zoom concludes the extreme close-up, as if the film-camera vainly attempts to "read" the Arab son's eyes—the only uncredited character—to know his mind and see his (and America's) future. More than an Orientalist representation of the supposedly inscrutable Other, *The Kingdom* reflects and extends the team's uncertainty, with hatred transmitted across generations, rather than extinguished, by retributive violence.

Killing the elusive terrorist disconcertingly fails to satisfy; violent redemption is hollow, uncertain, and incomplete. Vengeance cannot extinguish the threat of terror and may even exacerbate it through intergenerational blowback, and the American outpost and nation alike remain vulnerable. In the team's own estimation, revenge proves inadequate despite—and perhaps because of—its very fulfillment. It neither secures America nor persuasively remasculinizes the FBI team or the hero. Remasculinization through the restoration of professional agency, reterritorialization of space, and taking up of arms is ultimately not recuperative. In the emptied appetite for violent retribution, we find neither victory nor redemption, only exhaustion, doubt, and deflation. Paternal-professional retributive violence not only fails to satisfyingly resolve destabilized masculinities but also infects succeeding generations. Vengeance even renders militarized masculinities monstrous, in mirroring and being the same as the supposedly evil terrorist-Other. Ultimately, *The Kingdom* ends not as a call to arms or celebration of violence but as a disquieting—and surprising—marker of American masculine uncertainty, ambivalence, and monstrosity.

CONCLUSION
"How Do You Love Your Family and Leave Them to Go to War?"

In a phone conversation at the end of *World Trade Center*, former marine Dave Karnes (Michael Shannon), defiantly standing atop the rubble of the Twin Towers on September 12, 2001, informs his boss: "They're gonna need some good men out there to avenge this." Karnes's presence in uniform at Ground Zero remilitarizes masculinity and reasserts American certitude at what was a site of emasculation. The revenge fantasy *The Kingdom* seems to make good on Karnes's promise-threat when the FBI director tells Ronald Fleury's (Jamie Foxx) reassembled team, having killed the Saudi terrorist who masterminded the slaughter of American families and colleagues, they "did outstanding work over there." Yet the team finds their quest for revenge is not only emptied but hollow: the violent destruction of the monstrous terrorist-Other can neither slake their thirst nor secure the nation.

My singular focus throughout the book on screen masculinities in encounters with terror in American film reveals the recurrent incoherence of the presumed remasculinization of normative American masculinities and national identity in post-9/11 Hollywood cinema in the face of uncertain redemptions, uncontainable terror, and even male monstrosity. The films I have examined seek to manage the chaotic threat of terror by variously containing—visually, narratively, and generically—the horrific spectacle of 9/11 and the ongoing irresolution of the war on terror. Yet purported remasculinization unravels repeatedly across films peppered with recuperations that are ultimately undermined, partial, and ambiguous. David Holloway outlines a post-9/11 cinematic trend toward "allegory lite": a "commercial aesthetic so packed with different hooks pitched at different audience groups that a degree of aesthetic and narrative fragmentation has become intrinsic to the way Hollywood tells stories" (83). In this vein, representations of 9/11 and the war on terror are rendered incoherent and political critique dulled in the attempt to cover—or appease—all ideological positions.[1] A broader cinematic trend, rather than a specific characteristic of post-9/11 American cinema, Holloway's claim also disregards how contemporary

Hollywood film remains, even in an era of "intensified continuity," to use David Bordwell's term, a highly coherent cultural system. The genre schizophrenia, jolting midfilm subgeneric shifts, discomfiting narrative fissures, and ambivalent endings seen in these films denote politically and culturally significant ruptures. This incoherence troubles male redemption and inhibits the capacity to exorcise the threat of terror, marking moments in which the dominant fiction of male and national remasculinization does not hold.

Such narrative and formal cinematic incoherence has been identified in previous eras. Rather than the return of "muscular" American masculinities and violent remasculinization reminiscent of 1980s action cinema, the representation of encounters with terror in post-9/11 American cinema accords with the pervasive cultural anxieties witnessed in post–World War II and Vietnam cinema. These films recall the relative incoherence associated with 1970s American film, in which Julian Smith contends that the "disorienting" and "indeterminate nature of that war we couldn't seem to win or abandon, was reflected in our filmmakers' inability to find an appropriate format for presenting [it] to a mass audience" (22). Robin Wood likewise argues that dramatized issues and conflicts in the 1970s "no longer even appear to be resolvable within the system, [and] within the dominant ideology" (62). These post-9/11 films in many ways also extend Kaja Silverman's observations about post–World War II war and film noir masculinities. Yet rather than signaling profound disquiet about American masculinities at Hollywood's *margins*, the book reveals that post-9/11 American films foreground instabilities at the *center* of mainstream representations. That long-standing gender and national anxieties are only ever temporarily relieved is reiterated in popular American cinema's need to repeatedly vanquish them and its insistent desire to reassert hegemonic masculinity, but these films cannot persuasively foreclose anxieties about their fundamentally unstable, uncertain, and troubled men.

The book's core arguments distinctly pivot toward the broader meanings of the displaced filmic representations in American cinema post-9/11 of the terror threat that materialized so violently on September 11, 2001. In examining the complex discursive relation of American film and Hollywood genre to 9/11 and the war on terror, I have also shown how mainstream cinema perhaps served as cultural herald or portent. The shocking victories of the terror group ISIS across Iraq and Syria in 2013 and 2014, and the unexpected ascension of Donald Trump to the American presidency in 2016, were each, in their own way, abrupt, violent, and geopolitically ground shaking. The welcome diminishment of the former has been similarly spectacular, and it remains to be seen if the same will be said of the latter, forever mired in investigation and scandal. Yet each was born of a long and complicated historical tail.

Conclusion

The linking of American national identity and (white) hegemonic masculinity has again come into sharp relief in the hypermasculine politics—both hyperbolic and parodic—of the Trump era. Likewise venerating the return of so-called traditional gender roles, Trump's venal "strong man" persona, like the hypermasculine action hero, spotlights and even magnifies vulnerability and weakness in seeking to abolish each. Rather than an antidote to these anxieties, Trump amplifies them, one tweet at a time, highlighting deep white male and national anxieties the more he tries to expunge them. Perceptions of external threat have, rather than weakened, hardened and grown, out of proportion to any actual threat. Inflaming and then exploiting widespread fears of foreign Others, as well as social anxieties about a lowered (white) Self, propelled Trump into the White House. These concerns have since mutated from rhetoric advocating (white) "America first," equivocating white supremacy, and lashing out at weaker Others into systemic, if scattershot, policies of cruelty and exclusion.

This book articulates how films across a range of genres underscore the grave consequences of an unwillingness or inability to engage the terror-identified Other. As Kirk Combe and Brenda Boyle assert, monsters function culturally as portents or warnings (24). Across the films, representations of Orientalized and monstrous terror figures thwart the supposed project of remasculinization *because of*, rather than in spite of, efforts to annul frightening difference. Redemptions of hegemonic American masculinity consistently founder against the unrelieved invisibility, elusiveness, and uncontainability of post-9/11 monsters—both literal and metaphoric. The insistent cinematic framing of these Others in relation to prior conflicts, villains, and monsters reflects a broader, long-standing American political rhetorical stance. Never meaningfully addressing the systemic drivers of terror—or American complicity in its rise—inhibits both representational and real-world attempts to combat it. The real-world consequences of this were shockingly writ large in the metastasization of al-Qaeda into ISIS, even more malevolent and heinous than its predecessor. The terror-identified Other *remains* frightening and threatening, with American anxieties about the Self and fears of the Other undiminished, fatally undermining the remasculinization of male protagonists and nation alike.

American masculinity and manhood are also not only unredeemed in these films but finally *made monstrous* in the willingness to become or be *the same as* the reviled terror-Other. This monstrosity manifests in numerous ways, with male protagonists either incapable of eradicating the terror threat, marking them as failed men in some sense; becoming like the monstrous Other; or exposed as having been *always already* monstrous. Combe and Boyle's axiom that "monstrous is as monstrous does" (20) is highly resonant here. This mirrors not only American governmental failures to defeat terror—whether that is even possible, it remains an insistent political goal—but also evokes almost two decades of political rhetoric and military practices post-9/11. Since former vice president Dick Cheney's infamous advocacy of America's need to "work ... the dark side," like responses have and continue to shape American rhetoric and policy. The preparedness not only to adopt the tactics but to assume the mind-set of terrorists—to become, in effect, like the supposedly monstrous Other—has resurfaced during the Trump era. Trump's presidential campaign rhetoric about torture and waterboarding in a sense doubled down on this, and in office he has since elevated Gina Haspel, previously a chief of a CIA black site in which prisoners were tortured, to direct the CIA. The films examined in this book represent the first full cinematic expression of pervasive cultural unease and establish a pattern that reverberates into American cinema today. These popular cultural responses shaped subsequent cinematic representations of masculinity and threat. Despite appearances, anxieties about the inability to either eradicate the threat of terror or persuasively remasculinize American manhood or national identity in post-9/11 American film remain.

The Continued Incoherence of Cinematic Remasculinization

In recent years, American films about the wars in Iraq and Afghanistan have largely met with critical disinterest and box office failure. For every *American Sniper* (Eastwood 2014), there were ten more like *Billy Lynn's Long Halftime Walk* (Lee 2016). Yet the Jerry Bruckheimer–produced *12 Strong* (Fuglsig 2018), which tells the story of the first Special Forces team deployed into Afghanistan in the immediate wake of 9/11, seems tailor made to neatly reassert American national identity and manhood. Under the leadership of Capt. Mitch Nelson (Chris Hemsworth), a commander without prior combat experience, the team works with an Uzbek-Afghan warlord to defeat the Taliban and al-Qaeda and recapture a key northern city. Exemplifying Mark Anderson's designation of the frontier western, and based on a nonfiction novel by Doug Stanton, *12 Strong* sanctions the frontier myth of conquest and control through a return to the immediate aftermath of 9/11. In many respects, the film explicitly works through the trauma of 9/11—Mitch even buries a piece of the World Trade Center in Afghanistan at the end of the mission—by returning to the originary terror attacks and "redoing" America's initial military response.[2]

The film superficially resolves many of the anxieties discussed throughout the book. *12 Strong* ostensibly promotes traditional gender codes and roles for men and women. Men are fathers and soldiers, and women are mothers and housewives. Women are either confined to conventionally gendered spaces and traditional

Figure 5.1. Footage of the attacks breaks into the home and the everyday while the hero is confined to a feminized space and distracted.

roles or marginalized or absented entirely. Heteronormativity is "natural," and gender roles are presented as sex aligned or biologically determined. The film thus defines common values or ideas of the feminine conservatively—and when pejoratively associated with any of the Special Forces team, as an insufficiency to be vehemently denied or displaced. The film also represents 9/11 as an attack on the American home as much as the homeland. Yet home and homeland are again presented as incomplete, unprepared, and vulnerable. The film opens with Mitch and his young family moving into a new home, he having sought a desk job to spend more time with his daughter and wife. Again, as in *World Trade Center* and *Cloverfield*, terror breaches the home—filled with still-unpacked boxes—via television.[3] Doing his daughter's hair, Mitch has his back to early coverage of the attacks, and his daughter must draw his attention to the news (fig. 5.1). No longer a vigilant warrior, Mitch is distracted, confined in a domestic setting, and symbolically feminized when terror strikes, like Ronald Fleury in *The Kingdom*.

The attacks initiate the first of a series of broken promises by members of Mitch's former Special Forces team. These strangely compel an emphasis on *needing* to desert the home so as to *promise* to return to it: "I'm coming home," Mitch promises his wife (Elsa Pataky). These signal an anxiety in the compulsion to ensure that responsibility for their decision is jointly assumed by wives. When each man apologizes for undertaking his proposed mission, his wife absolves him, subsuming herself within her husband's professional identity: "I'm a soldier's wife," and "I knew what I signed up for." Mitch protests to Sam Diller (Michael Peña)—"What I did, I did for my family"—when he is accused of jeopardizing his team's participation in the impending conflict by leaving the field. Conventionally establishing war as a rite of passage, Mitch must go to war to become—and return home—a man.[4]

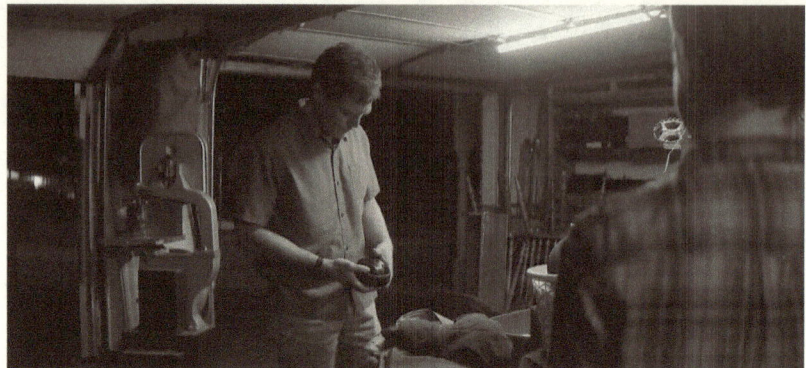

Figure 5.2. Hal is never shown inside the home and meekly informs his son he is leaving for Afghanistan.

The film twins the professional and the paternal within uniformed protective masculinity. On the night before their final battle, Mitch looks at a photo of his daughter, and his team members do the same before embarking on the mission. The film implies the team's actions prevent more attacks and secure the home(land): "But if we quit now, then what happened back home is gonna happen again and again." And in a conversation during their later mission to recapture a northern Afghani city from al-Qaeda and the Taliban, Mitch and Diller describe their fathers as violent and abusive. However, the Special Forces soldiers are ambivalently presented as fathers. And fears that the two are irreconcilable persist, with Hal Spencer (Michael Shannon), Mitch's deputy, tellingly asking only when he is *already* in country: "It's a hell of a thing we do. How do you love your family and leave them to go to war?" Shannon's character is again first shown watching the attacks on television before resolving to rescind his planned retirement to, effectively, go "out there to avenge this"—doubly recalling *World Trade Center* in being introduced while watching television coverage of 9/11 before another symbolic return to uniform. Spencer, whose broken promise is the most poorly received by his family, is never shown inside the family home, his domestic scenes confined to the garage. His wife—"I'll love you when you get back"—refuses to do his "dirty work" and inform his son: "You know I love you, right?" he offers with a weak, forced smile as his visibly angered son wordlessly walks away (fig. 5.2).

A central concern in *12 Strong* rests in becoming a man *through* violence; a warrior without combat experience is a warrior in name only. In showing Mitch's arrival on his military base immediately after the scene in the home, the film swiftly relocates him from a feminized domestic setting and into a masculinist institutional one. When Mitch's first request to rejoin his team as leader is refused, he returns to his new office, kicking over his desk in impotent frustration. His inexperience is questioned repeatedly, here, when he petitions to lead the mission, and on his first meeting with the Uzbek-Afghan warlord General Dostum (Navid Negahban). Dostum, similarly motivated as a husband-father in seeking revenge for al-Qaeda's killing of his family, even defers to the older and more experienced Spencer, who served in Somalia and during Desert Storm. The warlord implies that Mitch must earn his "killer eyes" if he is to lead: "What did you kill?" Only after Mitch leads his men in to cover the general's retreat—killing multiple al-Qaeda fighters in the process—does Dostum welcome Mitch into their brethren: "Now you have killer eyes." An imprimatur of becoming also-barbaric, to be a man-warrior requires killing.[5]

The broadly Orientalist depiction in *12 Strong* of the Other, enemy and citizen alike, attempts to annul their difference in making them "knowable" but finally admits insistent anxieties about an enemy *also* fundamentally indeterminate. The local Afghan population, predominantly represented through the perspectives and words of the soldiers, are unscrupulous yet backward, snatching most of the team's supply drop to sell it back. Even those few presented positively, namely, a boy soldier and Dostum, largely accord with long-standing Orientalist Hollywood constructions of the "good Arab/Muslim." The film further seeks to make the enemy knowable—and killable—in conflating Osama bin Laden and the Taliban as if a unitary body, the "brains" and the "muscle." It also establishes their monstrosity and barbarism via their treatment of women, as members of Mitch's team watch a video of the public stoning of a woman accused of adultery. In one scene, in an act of caricatured villainy, the region's commander, Mullah Razzan, executes a mother for secretly educating her daughters—followed by de rigueur cries of "Allāhu akbar" and wild bursts of gunfire into the air. The terror-Other is yet again consistently presented as mendaciously hidden and veiled. Opening titles describe bin Laden as "hidden in the mountains of Afghanistan," and most treacherously, a suicide bomber emerges from among a surrendering group of fighters, seriously wounding Spencer.[6] Invoking not only fears of all Others—both enemy and ally—but anxieties about the capacity of the (white male) Self, Mitch admits he and his soldiers "can't tell enemy from allies." Even their CIA contact admits he cannot read Dostum, who even conceals his ability to speak English before revealing, "It's good to know the language of your enemies." In this sense, the film admits its unrelieved anxiety about an enemy *also* fundamentally unknowable to the Americans.

To assuage these abiding concerns—both domestic and foreign—the film stages the return of numerous reassuring male action subgenres and codes, from the cavalry western to the World War II combat film. Mitch leads a cavalry charge and charges a missile launcher on horseback—the team progresses from novice riders to being akin to cowboys in the space of a few weeks—with Dostum's fighters immediately electing to follow him before the general's reinforcing charge enables the two men to lead in unison. The film also bears distinct cultural echoes of John Wayne's apologist Vietnam film *The Green Berets* (Kellogg, Wayne, and LeRoy 1968), a World War II fantasy of the Vietnam War, in nostalgically recalling its singing of "The Ballad of the Green Berets" for the first time on-screen. These comforting genre associations unsuccessfully mask profound genre, gender, and national anxieties. Wholly unconventionally for a combat film, along with the audience's learning next to nothing about nine of the twelve men, no team member dies. Although the film's action is based on real events, this profound trepidation to represent American military deaths is implicitly acknowledged as the film score's most rousing moment occurs when the team stretchers the seriously injured Spencer to an awaiting medical evacuation chopper. David Edelstein's review of the film confirms the depth of this anxiety, noting the potent omission from the film's celebratory closing titles that a number of the team later died in Iraq. *12 Strong* is a combat film in which no team member *is allowed* to die.

Related to this, the film's fixation on the notion of victory signals its desperate desire to counter the irresolution of the war on terror. As the team begins its mission, Colonel Mulholland (William Fichtner) commands them: "Go win this thing." Mitch also repeatedly declares, first to Spencer and later to Dostum, "The only way home is winning," and "I'm gonna win you this thing." Recalling John Rambo's plaintive plea at the beginning of *Rambo: First Blood Part II* (Cosmatos 1985)—"Do we get to win this time?"—Mitch's declarations reflect a deeper, anxious cultural need *to return to* the war's beginnings for a second chance at victory. Mitch's team, by its own admission, only wins a battle, and this is a war they can neither win nor abandon. As Dostum tells Mitch immediately after their apparent success: "Today, you are our friend, tomorrow, you are our enemy. It won't be any different for you. You will be cowards if you leave. And you will be our enemies if you stay." Recognizing what the American cannot countenance, Dostum warns Mitch: "You will not win here because you are not honest with yourself." His—and the film's—fantasy of individual remasculinization and national reinvigoration can only be partially fulfilled.

The anxious need to celebrate a victory in a war that was never won is compounded by numerous incoherences that repeatedly inhibit remasculinization. *12 Strong* strangely resuscitates al-Qaeda, needing to imagine its supposed defeat rather than acknowledge its eventual eclipse by the even more radical and violent ISIS. And, somewhat mirroring the initial rhetorical construction of 9/11, America's experience in Afghanistan is both unprecedented and has been forever repeated. The extreme altitude on the flight into northern Afghanistan establishes

Conclusion 193

Figure 5.3–5.4. Adopting Mitch's optical point of view, the film-camera stages Mitch's return from inside the home.

Figure 5.5. As the film-camera assumes his wife's perspective from outside, Mitch continues moving toward the window, his duffel bag slung over one shoulder.

the extraordinary nature of their mission, yet notions of eternal recurrence are repeatedly cited—and then elided. One team member, after reading inscriptions at the staging post—nicknamed the Alamo—recognizes America's place in this "graveyard of empires," and Mitch observes they are in a "minefield of history of one hundred wars." The Special Forces team—and the film—also presents itself as outnumbered and outgunned, repeatedly disregarding that the capacity to call on the overwhelming firepower of bombers—reiterated in multiple, fetishistic aerial shots invoking the bombs' perspective—means that "we own the sky." This is such a blind spot that Mitch can in one sentence lament that his team is facing fifteen thousand men and "fighting with horsemen against tanks"—conveniently ignoring Dostum's fighters—before boldly declaring: "General, I'm your link to the greatest weaponry in the history of civilization."

The strange prerequisite to abandon home so as to return home—at film's end, Mitch declares to Diller, "I'm pointing us home"—is finally starkest in how the film chooses to envisage Mitch's homecoming. Adopting Mitch's optical point of view, the camera dollies forward, before a shot from outside—his wife's perspective—shows him moving toward their picture window (figs. 5.3–5.5). Conventionally, his duffel bag is slung over his shoulder; the returning hero smiles, having kept his promise of return. Yet with his wife and child welcoming him home from outside, the film ends incoherently on the image of the combat hero returning from war *from within the home*, as if he never left. Even Bruckheimer's cheerleading film is unable to coherently or convincingly represent supposedly resurgent male triumphalism or satisfyingly recuperate American national identity. Ultimately, in American cinema, anxieties about these "troubled men" and the nation they represent remain unrelieved in encounters with terror, both "over there" *and* back here.

NOTES

Introduction: Remasculinizing American Cinema Post-9/11

1. While 9/11 was not initially configured as a predominantly American event and experience, its subsequent (re)configuration by the Bush administration and news media commentators as such came to dominate public discourse.

2. The term "war on terror" has changed numerously over time, before being officially dropped by the Obama administration in 2009, but the term remains resonant in international geopolitics.

3. See, e.g., Baudrillard; Žižek; Dixon, *Film and Television after 9/11*; King, "'Just like a Movie'?"; Page.

4. Hollywood implicitly acknowledged these criticisms, readily self-censoring by pulling productions related to terrorism, digitally altering promotional materials, and deleting film images depicting the Twin Towers. Hollywood support for the administration's response was enlisted in meetings with the White House and also publicly offered by the president of the Motion Picture Association of America (Valenti).

5. Specifically, Eric Avila finds that postwar 1950s science fiction "captured white preoccupations with the increasing visibility" (88) of racialized Others, extending wartime anxieties about "alien invasion" to domestic fears associated with increased black urbanization and white flight.

6. Critics have consistently castigated spectacle's vacuity "as cosmetic, mechanical thrill-seeking" that "eliminat[es] character development" and overwhelms narrative (Keane 5).

7. Page significantly observes that such cultural representations were preceded by the graphic, near-apocalyptic, and oft-disseminated imaginings of scenarios of terror by policy makers and politicians.

8. Drew argues that the mediated construction of President Bush as determinedly eager to reassert control "reveal[s] the cultural and media enthusiasm" for this remasculinization of American identity (74).

9. Marita Sturken argues in *Tourists of History* that the attacks engendered a new kind of nationalist political discourse of "historical exceptionalism" centered on the belief "that history itself was transformed on 9/11" (167). The notion of a "post-9/11 America" is mirrored in the before-and-after dualism attached to Bush's presidency and character (Hannah).

10. Constance Duncombe argues that parallels to Pearl Harbor figured 9/11 within the same representational frame, as a surprise attack resulting in the loss of American innocence. Nilges also argues that the attacks and their impact were also linked to a psychological perception created by socioeconomic transformations related to globalization, which long predate 9/11: "the fear of lack of control and stability" in a world perceived as chaotic,

confusing, and threatening, but "ideologically connected to and dramatically amplified by the 'war on terror'" (Nilges 27, 32).

11. See, among innumerable others, Savran; Robinson; Durham; C. S. King.

12. Raewyn Connell identifies a multifaceted cultural movement to reinstall men from their perceived redundancy to their perceived place of privilege from 1980 to 2000 ("Studying Men and Masculinity").

13. See, e.g., Silverman; Tasker, *Spectacular Bodies*; Savran; Robinson.

14. See, e.g., Drew; Faludi; Melnick; Godfrey and Hamad.

15. Parallel to this, Gallagher argues that women in 1980s action are "absent or incapacitated," ensuring that heroism "becomes the *de facto* province of men" (14).

16. For a transcript of Bush's address, see http://www.nytimes.com/2003/09/23/international/22TEXT-BUSH.html. While Carter and Dodds correctly observe 9/11 was discursively portrayed by Western media as "an attack against the nation" (107), it was also more broadly characterized as attacks against "the West" or "civilization," although the United States was invariably the implicit, unspoken stand-in for each designation. American responses to the 9/11 attacks were multiple and multifaceted, including nonviolent responses such as large public concerts, but in this book I focus on the aspect that ostensibly came to dominate global perceptions of America's response.

17. The imperiled home is a typical trope of horror, disaster films, and westerns, although 9/11 also exemplifies horror's fascination with the sudden, violent intrusion of evil into the everyday (including the home).

18. See Dodds; Svendsen.

19. Sardar and Davies also note that, despite the so-called unprecedented nature of 9/11, by "referring to and feeding off all the conventions and associations of ideas that have gone before," the contemporary Arab/Muslim terrorist "emerges less from the world of political reality than . . . the western imagination" (248; see also Shaheen; Wilkins; Williams and Linneman).

20. See, e.g., Aguayo; Nayak; Duncombe. And Ken Nolley observes that cinematic representations of Indians, much like Orientalism, come from a long intellectual and cultural tradition built up over centuries, particularly through popular westerns.

21. Stephen Joyce also notes that terrorists were configured in relation to 1990s Hollywood film, including *Independence Day* (Emmerich 1996) and *The Siege* (Zwick 1998).

22. Although this definition falls slightly outside conventional academic definitions of terrorism, given the lack of discernible political goals, it coheres with popular and contemporary political usage.

23. Steffen Hantke ("Return of the Giant Creature") and Stephen Prince share the view that the post-9/11 years are broadly analogous to Cold War life under persistent nuclear threat, reflected in a (re)turn to 1950s Cold War–era science fiction–horror films or genres, most notably through remakes of invasion films such as *The Invasion* (Hirschbiegel 2007) and the revitalization of the giant creature or monster trope.

24. Rather than a specifically post-9/11 condition, Nama acknowledges that experiences and conditions of race, and blackness in particular, are historically ignored in science fiction—and arguably in mainstream narrative cinema more generally.

25. It is also true that a consideration of masculinities in film has arguably long been central, if implicit, for example, in analyses of westerns and auteurist discussions of directors like John Ford.

26. Scholars expressing this view in relation to (sub)genres examined in this book include, but are by no means limited to, Broderick on science fiction–apocalypse; Kakoudaki on disaster and science fiction–disaster; Carroll, Clover, and Hantke ("Historicizing the Bush Years") on horror; Slotkin (*Gunfighter Nation*) on westerns; and Wood (*Hollywood from Vietnam to Reagan*) on 1970s buddy films.

27. A number of genre studies, in science fiction and horror in particular, examine contemporary American film in relation to national identity post-9/11, but multigenre anthologies on post-9/11 American popular culture do not assume a specific gender focus.

28. The multigenre scope of the study and focus on American narrative cinema largely preclude a focus on televisual texts. Post-9/11 television series like *Battlestar Galactica* (2004–9) and *The Looming Tower* (2018), especially serials and "complex narratives," are better able to represent and develop ambivalent ideological positions and characterizations (Charles).

29. As during the Vietnam War, American cinema largely (yet conspicuously) avoided directly exploring the impact of 9/11 on the American psyche in the first half of the 2000s.

30. Although American film has long been produced as much for a global market and audiences, this study predominantly considers the domestic resonance and implications of the films.

31. This approach mirrors the Bush administration's discursive strategy to prosecute and justify the war on terror through binary divisions (see Carter and Dodds).

32. For example, Robert Leigninger observes a filmic interest in problems related to the embodiment of masculinity in post–World War II westerns.

33. *World Trade Center* (released August 9, 2006): $US 65 million budget, $US 163 million total box office—$US 70 million domestic and $US 93 million foreign; *United 93* (released April 28, 2006): $US 15 million budget, $US 76 million total box office—$US 31 million domestic and $US 45 million foreign; *25th Hour* (released December 19, 2002): $US 5 million budget, $US 24 million total box office—$US 13 million domestic and $US 11 million foreign.

34. *Cloverfield* (released January 18, 2008): $US 25 million budget, $US 170 million total box office—$US 80 million domestic and $US 90 million foreign; *The Strangers* (released May 30, 2008): $US 9 million budget, $US 82 million total box office—$US 52.5 million domestic and $US 29.5 million foreign; *War of the Worlds* (released June 29, 2005): $US 132 million budget, $US 591.5 million total box office—$US 234 million domestic and $US 357.5 million foreign.

35. *I Am Legend* (released December 14, 2007): $US 150 million budget, $US 585 million total box office—$US 256 million domestic and $US 329 million foreign; *The Book of Eli* (released January 15, 2010): $US 80 million budget, $US 157 million total box office—$US 95 million domestic and $US 62 million foreign.

36. *The Kingdom* (released September 28, 2007): $US 70 million budget, $US 86.5 million total box office—$US 47.5 million domestic and $US 39 million foreign; *Munich* (released December 23, 2005): $US 70 million budget, $US 130 million total box office—$US 47 million domestic and $US 83 million foreign; *Zero Dark Thirty* (released December 19, 2012): $US 40 million budget, $US 96 million box office—$US 37 million domestic and $US 133 million foreign.

37. *12 Strong* (released January 19, 2018): $US 35 million budget, $US 69.5 million box office—$US 45.5 million domestic and $US 24 million foreign.

1. "Shielding Us from What We Are Not Yet Ready to See": The Uniformed Hero as Victim and in Masquerade

1. The officers were two of only twenty survivors pulled from the rubble of Tower Two.

2. See the introduction and chapter 2 for additional discussion.

3. Only Clint Eastwood's *Sully* (2016), which dramatizes pilot Chesley Sullenberger's miraculous emergency landing of a US Airways flight on the Hudson River in 2009, has visualized—traumatically restaged as Sully's (often waking) nightmares—the skyscraper-level perspective of a passenger plane flying below the Manhattan's skyline and of a plane slamming into Twin Tower-like buildings.

4. Officers are even asked to keep particular watch on their patrols for a young runaway girl ("This is important!"), an especially strange request given the size and population of New York City. Such unambiguously positive connotations of police uniforms are not evident in representations in 1970s police procedurals, for example, but are repeatedly established in the opening of *World Trade Center*.

5. The officers continue to encounter and debate contrary information, rumor, and third-hand fragments of information and speculation garnered from other first responders, family members, and radio and TV, uncertain even whether the initial impact marks an attack or if there has been a second impact. In this sense, the film parallels *Tora! Tora! Tora!* (Fleischer 1970) in its representation of how communication breakdowns inhibit America's ability to respond to, let alone prevent, the Pearl Harbor attacks in 1941. However, in *Tora! Tora! Tora!* a slow bureaucracy and the accumulated effects of individual failings are the problem, as opposed to communications chaos and the excessiveness of events.

6. This has been extensively explored only in Denis Leary's *Rescue Me* (2004–11), which focuses on the professional and personal lives of a group of New York City firefighters traumatized by their experiences on 9/11.

7. This perhaps highlights the film's timid construction of "authenticity," standing in marked contrast to Stone's repeated use of the Zapruder 8mm film—and his fetishization of the image and the death moment of JFK's assassination—in *JFK* (1991).

8. Of the three surviving officers, only Pezzulo is able to move, but he is killed shortly thereafter while trying to free Jimeno in the succeeding collapse of Tower One.

9. McLoughlin, as leader, assumes Jimeno's guilt for the deaths of the officers he took into the buildings, a guilt that deepens into shame because of their failure to rescue anyone—"I took 'em in, for what? What good did we do?" However, Jimeno reminds McLoughlin that their deceased colleagues had collectively volunteered to enter the buildings, compelled because of "who they were"—equating who they are with what they do. Jimeno's declaration reiterates the tension between wearer and uniform, invoking conflicting notions of choice (they volunteered because they wanted to go in) and compulsion-obligation (they were compelled by the duties associated with their uniformed roles).

10. See the introduction for a discussion of Robinson's work.

11. See Haschemi Yekani for a discussion cautioning against universalizing crisis as a concept inherent to masculinity, using *World Trade Center* as a direct case.

12. See the introduction for additional discussion of the cultural response to Hollywood's first forays into representing 9/11.

13. The film's deemed authenticity lies in Greengrass's extensive research and interviews with participants and families, his documentary-realist aesthetic, and his use of minor actors and real participants in prominent roles. As in his earlier *Bloody Sunday* (2002), Greengrass uses nondiegetic sound sparely, prefers naturalistic lighting, and

primarily restricts the narrative to perceptual subjectivity, that is, the point of view a character would presumably hold. Edelstein's otherwise positive appraisal reflected this critical unease: "If it was indeed a saga of heroism, its heroes weren't conventionally introduced, and all, unconventionally, perished." At the same time, the *Slate* and *New York Times* reviews of *United 93* and *World Trade Center* note that each merely "did precisely . . . what other cultural representations of 9/11 have done before and since: replicate, not delve" (Faludi 3).

14. All other televisual representations of Flight 93, while avoiding the plane's crash, do nonetheless represent or acknowledge it by including images of its aftermath, which *United 93*'s cut to black does not.

15. See B. Johnson, "Oliver Stone: Redemption in the Ruins"; Lewis, "Hollywood Does 9/11"; Klawans; Stevens, "Stone Cold."

16. Such concerns were only fueled by controversial comments Stone made shortly after 9/11. As part of a film panel in New York, Stone attested to the political ambiguity or complexity of the events and envisioned a 9/11 film that would offer historical context and include the terrorists' point of view (Kendrick).

17. As A. O. Scott opines, Cage "turns all his intensity inward" ("Pinned under the Weight"); see also Denby; Edelstein, "Up from the Ashes"; Hoberman, "Fight Them over There"; Rich, "Out of the Rubble"). Stone similarly commends Cage's atypically subtle, "restrained performance" as evidence he "could . . . play 'against type'" ("*World Trade Center* Production Notes").

18. See Denby; Edelstein, "Up from the Ashes"; Hoberman, "Fight Them over There"; Scott, "Pinned under the Weight"; Zacharek, "*World Trade Center*."

19. As Brian Johnson rightly observes, *World Trade Center* "never lets you forget" you are watching a movie; Stone personalizes the tragedy "and surrenders to the most elemental form of Hollywood mythmaking" (49, 51).

20. Some commentators similarly lamented the film's "smallness," related to its refrain from spectacle (Jaafar).

21. The value of such narrativization is poignantly observed by the real John McLoughlin: "Revisiting these events became a form of therapy for the real men . . . became cathartic for all of them" ("*World Trade Center* Production Notes").

22. This reimagining of the disaster hero as someone who survives rather than prevails coheres with Freda's contention that survival became a form of heroism in post-9/11 popular culture (qtd. in Takacs 499).

23. This is an aspect ratio Stone had used only irregularly since *Wall Street* (1987) almost twenty years earlier, typically preferring wider screen ratios.

24. See the introduction for further detailed discussion.

25. The film literally contained the disaster through its construction of a 1/16th scale set of the zone at Ground Zero ("*World Trade Center* Production Notes").

26. The ambivalence of Stone's portrayal of television's role on the day is highlighted in his clear disdain for the mass media, which he says "entrances and pollutes and trivializes . . . with fragments of information that [present] an incomplete, confusing and finally abstract picture of the world" (qtd. in Gentry 57).

27. The stark absence of uniformed females from Ground Zero in the film makes it reasonable to assume the children's rescuers are male.

28. The real McLoughlin and Jimeno appear in the film as extras.

29. Stone does not completely or accurately convey the space of the hole, so the audience does not get a clear sense of how impacted in the rubble the trapped men are. Other than

in the establishing shot of the Ground Zero "hole," space is thereafter collapsed for the audience, and Stone breaks down the space separating the trapped men.

30. This refigures an earlier scene in which McLoughlin tells Jimeno to ensure he does not go to sleep, for he will never wake, and "If you die, I die." This interrelatedness is especially reiterated in the characterization of the men's ultimate rescue, the collective bonds that motivate men to rescue their own (country)men evoked in the uniform.

31. I discuss the use of tropes from the interracial buddy film in chapter 4.

32. When he reaches hospital, Jimeno has rocks suctioned from his mouth and insides.

33. Just as the only female PAPD officer remains at reception throughout, so only one among the pantheon of rescuers when the men are disinterred is identifiably female, glimpsed only briefly from behind and in the background.

34. Although three-quarters of 9/11's casualties were male, the only victim-body—implied rather than represented—is also female, with Karnes inadvertently stepping on a single high-heeled shoe when he arrives at Ground Zero.

35. Jesus's radiance in Jimeno's vision was created using the 3M Scotchlite reflective tape used on emergency service uniforms, so that "it completely exploded in light" ("*World Trade Center* Production Notes"). This enables Stone to recount Jimeno's documented experiences in the hole without submitting to his Christological worldview and equally sacralizes the rescuers, and the uniform specifically.

36. Aaron DeRosa and Stacey Peebles even contend that Karnes's character makes explicit the broader rhetorical comparison between accounts of the heroism of first responders at Ground Zero and the sacrifice of soldiers during war.

37. I discuss the pre-9/11 cinematic emphasis on "disaster response" in chapter 2.

38. See the introduction for further detailed discussion.

39. This markedly contrasts with the uniform's status in Stone's earlier films *Platoon* and *Born on the Fourth of July*. As Lichty and Carroll note, while similarly about confusion, disorientation, and survival, *Platoon* focuses on the enemies within as much as those without, exemplified in Taylor's (Charlie Sheen) concluding narration: "We fought ourselves. And the enemy was in us" (398–99). Ambivalent masculinities are not unusual in Stone's oeuvre, with the conflicting masculinities in *Platoon*, for example, representing not only basic distinctions between good and evil but also contrasting notions of "America."

40. For example, B. Ruby Rich labels Karnes "a biblical warrior out of the New Testament by way of Vietnam" (see also Klawans; Liss; Zacharek, "*World Trade Center*"); Brian Johnson describes Karnes as a "vigilante GI Joe action figure—a born-again Christian soldier" (51; see also Denby); and Edelstein even considers the film better for Stone's ambivalent representation of Karnes "as both a valiant savior and a monomaniac Holy Warrior" ("Up from the Ashes").

41. Shannon's later film and television work adds further weight to the considered ambivalence of both Karnes's character and Shannon's performance, particularly in repeated portrayals of religious zealotry and mental illness in *Revolutionary Road* (Mendes 2008), *Boardwalk Empire* (2010–14), and *Take Shelter* (Nichols 2011).

42. Stone seemingly admits as much, privileging Strauss's "legitimate" professional authority over Sereika's masquerade. Significantly, while Strauss enters the hole before Sereika in the film, Rebecca Liss details that Sereika was actually the first person to reach Jimeno—a fact that would have further unsettled the restitution of uniformed masculinity after the former marine has located the trapped men.

43. Similarly, Robinson considers *Deliverance* (Boorman 1972) ultimately unsuccessful in closing down anxieties associated with its troubled men's masculinities, even after their apparent recuperation and reassertion.

44. This effective absence of represented victim bodies in *World Trade Center* is not unique to a post-9/11 context, and the film's unwillingness to depict American dead killed in a foreign attack has a long pedigree. For example, the only confirmed, clearly represented casualties of the attack on Pearl Harbor in *In Harm's Way* (Preminger 1965) are incidental and indirect: an adulterous couple driven off the road by a military truck.

45. This moment mirrors a similarly constituted absence of firefighters in a pub scene in Lee's *25th Hour*.

46. In an interview, Stone affirms this duality, agreeing that the film is at once a small story and "conveys the arc of America on that day" (Jaafar).

2. "I Don't Know Why This Is Happening": Shamed Everymen and America's Own Unknowable Monsters

1. It only becomes clear at film's end that Central Park's "formerly known" status is a direct consequence of concerted military action.

2. I discuss this point in detail in the introduction.

3. While their fate is unclear and the film's conclusion ambiguous, the couple's demise is formally implied in the trope of the handheld camera's transfer to another owner-operator (in this case the Department of Defense) after the previous operator's death and the manner in which the video abruptly stops, akin to when its previous operator, Hud, is killed.

4. The film's only loosely associated sequel, *10 Cloverfield Lane* (Trachtenberg 2016), arguably represents a commercial rather than narrative association, and the third film in the series, *The Cloverfield Paradox* (Onah 2018), was poorly received, deemed to represent cynical commercial exploitation. At best, the films are now more interested in referencing their own franchise universe than contemporary events.

5. I discuss this point in detail in the introduction and chapter 1.

6. For example, monsters traverse oceans to descend on it in *The Beast from 20,000 Fathoms* (Lourié 1953) and *Godzilla* (Emmerich 1998), and floods wreak havoc in *When Worlds Collide* (Maté 1951) and *Deluge* (Feist 1933).

7. More broadly discussed in the introduction and chapter 1. For similar sentiments on *Cloverfield*, see Phillips, "*Cloverfield*"; Berardinelli; Dargis, "We're All Gonna Die!"; Ebert, "*Cloverfield*"; Lane, "Monstrous Times"; Stevens, "When Monsters Attack Pretty People."

8. Even before an attack on New York is confirmed, *Cloverfield* explicitly locates itself in a post-9/11 world, with multiple characters asking if it is "another terrorist attack."

9. See Tony Shaw's highly regarded *Cinematic Terror: A Global History of Terrorism on Film* for an intriguing examination of each of these aspects.

10. David Bordwell contends that *Cloverfield* conforms to the principles of classical structure and narration despite its technical fit to the premise of amateur video recording, with jumps or gaps "*justified as* constrained by the physical circumstances of filming" by handheld video ("A Behemoth from the Dead Zone," emphasis in original).

11. Walliss and Aston implicitly note this ambivalence, calling the film "both a mechanism to comment on post-9/11 fears and a way of crudely appropriating 9/11 imagery" (56). Steen Christiansen considers *Cloverfield* "a willed attempt at articulating cultural anxieties and frustrations." See also N. Lee "*Cloverfield* Is One Giant, Incredibly Entertaining 'Screw You!'"; Savlov; Totaro).

12. For example, James MacDonald similarly discusses how the film dialogues with its giant monstrous predecessors while reflecting contemporary anxieties after 9/11. See also

Berardinelli; Ebert, "*Cloverfield*"; Schwarzbaum, "*Cloverfield*"; Totaro; Pile; and Coyle—although critics and scholars oscillated between defining the film predominantly as horror or science fiction. This is not unusual, with *The Thing* (Carpenter 1982) and *Alien* (Scott 1979) similarly exploring claustrophobic, restricted, frighteningly intimate and close encounters with monsters. Such encounters with monstrous Others explore anxieties associated with the transgression of borders and the dissolution of individual subjectivity (or the nation-state).

13. The threat is also characteristically global, with the monster in *Godzilla*, for example, traversing great distances on its way to Manhattan. Moreover, much of the damage is often the result of overzealous military action, most notably in blowing up the Chrysler Building.

14. *Cloverfield*'s closing credit theme, "Roar" (Michael Giacchino), explicitly invokes the theme from *Gojira*. Reeves also inserted stills from *King Kong* (Cooper and Schoedsack 1933), *Them!* (Douglas 1954), and *The Beast from 20,000 Fathoms* into the film—first identified by avid film fans and circulated online. King Kong signifies the clash of primitive and modern but also more ambivalently represents the enslaved Other's revolt against the West, while the other two monsters specifically evoke anxieties about the consequences of atomic testing.

15. Gojira wreaks havoc that recalls the firebombing of Tokyo and the aftermath of the atomic bombing of Hiroshima and Nagasaki. Breathing radioactive fire across the city, the monster's call and heavy footsteps are also aurally reminiscent of a bombing raid. Roused by atomic experimentation and further provoked by the Japanese military, Gojira critiques Japanese society as much as the nation that dropped the atomic bomb. The young scientist's guilt about his scientific "overreaching" finally compels his redemptive act of self-sacrifice and also signals the reinvigoration of the professional elite and partial exorcising of the scars of defeat in World War II.

16. I discuss this point in detail in chapter 1.

17. Bordwell's analysis of the film reflects this in describing the film's "shooting-gallery plot" ("A Behemoth from the Dead Zone"), while Lisa Schwarzbaum observes its "masterstroke of lovingly staged banality" ("*Cloverfield*"). Dargis, "We're All Gonna Die!"; Lane, "Monstrous Times"; McCarthy, "*Cloverfield*"; and Franklin also implicitly recognize the film's slasher-like characteristics. The film also bears the hallmarks of survival horror, which Donato Totaro observes as a growing trend in horror in the first decade of the twenty-first century, portraying vulnerable and often unarmed victims focused more on evasion than confrontation.

18. The pseudodocumentary aesthetic, of course, is not a new phenomenon, with *The Blair Witch Project* (Myrick and Sánchez 1999) offering a key earlier American example. More than merely tied to the events of 9/11, the pseudodocumentary's resurgence is also linked to technological developments in ultraportable cameras (Bordwell, "A Behemoth from the Dead Zone").

19. Although they are typically described as "found footage" films, Bordwell prefers the term "discovered footage," primarily because "found footage" has a long history in film criticism to denote experimental assemblages by artists like Bruce Conner ("A Behemoth from the Dead Zone").

20. For example, *Godzilla* is populated primarily by professionals who, however maligned, possess the skills required to collectively counter the monstrous threat.

21. Even in *When Worlds Collide*—like *2012* a reworking of the Noah's ark story—the supposed everyman is a pilot who eventually performs a vital specialist role, landing the

ship-ark on which survivors flee Earth on a passing planet to ensure the continuation of human society.

22. The subgenre is highly gendered, as Dean Conrad finds in *Space Sirens, Scientists and Princesses: The Portrayal of Women in Science Fiction Cinema*, with the exception of Dr. Helen Benson (Jennifer Connelly) in the remake of *The Day the Earth Stood Still*. Even this privileges a personal response above a disaster response, with Benson primarily using the apocalypse to symbolically become "mother."

23. See Sean Redmond for an early discussion on how extensively the film recasts 9/11 imagery ("When Planes Fell Out of the Sky" 29).

24. Jason is swept along the bridge by fleeing fellow citizens and climbs a column to ascertain the group's whereabouts, as Hud—and the camera—stops with Rob, distracted from the escape attempt by a phone call from Beth.

25. I discuss this point in detail in chapter 1.

26. This is as an oft-used iconic image in American cinema, including the promotional poster for the more "serious" *United 93*. The filmmakers' confirmation that the promotional poster for *Escape from New York* (Carpenter 1981) is an explicit influence on *Cloverfield* strengthens the sense that the film implicitly indicts the attack's victims.

27. After only a few minutes of an emerging love story—for character and audience alike—the video shifts to a new time signature as Jason and Lily discuss preparations for Rob's going-away party, one narrative erasing the other. In the monster's subsequent disruption of the party narrative, "images of the catastrophe" also effectively obliterate "images of the couple's shared bliss" (Hantke, "Return of the Giant Creature" 247). In this respect, not only does the party narrative record over the fledgling love story, but the party narrative is likewise disrupted by the entrance of the monster.

28. A watermark over the opening announcing "DO NOT DUPLICATE" is more than a military-governmental injunction in this sense (fig. 2.1). Playfully associating the film with those sent to voters for Oscar consideration, it also mimics antipiracy consumer warnings, an implicit Hollywood injunction.

29. The opening scene is shot by Michael Stahl-David (Rob) on a prosumer camcorder (which was later transferred to film), and T. J. Miller (Hud) likewise shot a good deal of the footage associated with his character, particularly that of the party.

30. Television screens also communicate an overwhelming and horrific spectacle, with Hud numerously filming television screens, such as in the electronics store, so that they fill the entire frame. In this respect, television screens further underscore *Cloverfield*'s generic shift from an omniscient perspective to the individual, street-level experience of terror and the personal—frightened, helpless, limited—experience of spectacle.

31. Rebecca Coyle, who observes the way sound is crafted in *Cloverfield* to augment the impression of the documentary aesthetic, similarly notes that sound in the film "trigger[s] anxiety, tension and dread" in its identification with characters' limited, subjective experience (234).

32. The camera to an extent shields Hud from the horrific events unfolding around him, akin to the "aesthetic distance" common for science fiction–disaster audiences.

33. Celebrating his impending move to Japan to take up an executive position, Rob's suit is appropriately evocative of the Japanese salaryman.

34. I discuss this point in detail in the introduction.

35. The film's sequel, *The Strangers: Prey at Night* (Robert 2018), was both poorly received and unsuccessful, making less than half of the box office of the first film. This

failure is particularly significant in light of the many successes in the horror genre over the last few years.

36. As Hantke observes in relation to recent science fiction–invasion narratives, the invasion—or breach in the case of *Cloverfield*—"is not the cause of instability but . . . takes place under pre-existing conditions of instability" ("Bush's America" 147).

37. Hud's later direct address, "If this is the last thing you see, it means I died," similarly both predicts his own demise and signals how the (originally) private has become public testimony.

38. According to online viral promotional materials for the film, this object could be a satellite operated by a Japanese underwater drilling company, which either awakens or gives birth to the monster—and further ties the monster to *Gojira*'s Japanese origins.

39. The military is associated with light when the group reaches the final military airlift point but, as with Marlena's imminent death, again foreshadows violent demise. The marine establishment of a command center in the department store collapses the military, terrorism, and the commercial, subversively signaling the uneasy conjoining of America's capitalist interests and consumer lifestyle with its military endeavors.

40. Much of the annihilation in *Cloverfield*, including undoubtedly massive civilian casualties, is attributable to the military's final (and seemingly unsuccessful) attempt to obliterate the monster—and Manhattan in the process. In *Them!*, on the other hand, the FBI and police refuse to confront the giant radioactive ants until they can determine whether two children possibly in the tunnels are safe. They are dedicated to avoiding even inadvertent harm to civilians, even after government officials urge haste in destroying the monsters. The police officer will even sacrifice his life to ensure the children's final rescue and repatriation.

41. This feature of RKO Radio Pictures horror films in the 1940s contrasts to an earlier tradition in Universal horror films in the 1930s predicated on the monster's full visibility.

42. Although Carroll notes there must be some films in which both confrontation and discovery of the monster are absent, the lack of clear examples is telling, given the detailed and classificatory nature of his philosophical project.

43. Characters in giant monster movies also often film or photograph the monstrous threat. In *Godzilla*, for example, the network cameraman (Hank Azaria) professionally "captures" the monster with his camera, while the scientist-daughter in *Them!* repeatedly photographs the film's giant ants.

44. In *The Strangers: Prey at Night*, the invaders' faces are finally revealed, but their motivation remains frighteningly unclear, and they are very much presented as America's creation (linked with Kim Wilde's 1981 song "Kids in America").

3. "I Can Still Fix This": Restoring Protective Masculinity and/but Becoming a Monstrous Savior

1. This expression playfully repurposes Clover's (1992) influential designation of the "final girl" in slasher horror.

2. As in *Cloverfield*, the film also bears the hallmarks of survival horror; see chap. 2, note 17, for additional detail.

3. Relatedly, when Neville later enters a hive of the creatures, he is startled by his reflection—as if he no longer recognizes himself or who he has become.

4. The fridge still holds sticky notes detailing appointments and reminders, with a calendar (forever on December 2009) and a quarantine notice underneath the magazine

cover. These objects imply time stopped for Neville when his wife and daughter were killed, acknowledging only a frozen *always-present*.

5. The novella details the psychological struggles of its everyman survivor, Robert Neville, in the aftermath of a viral vampire plague outbreak. Neville daily kills and experiments on vampires in an attempt to find a scientific cure and is nightly besieged by vampires (led by a former acquaintance). The novel's description of state-operated burnings and mass graves and the protagonist's Aryan visage clearly invoke the specters of World War II and the Holocaust. It is also claimed to represent "a stark concretization of white racial [and cultural] anxieties in 1950s America," particularly in relation to changes in urban populations (Patterson 24).

6. Although many reviews of the film, despite noting that *The Omega Man*'s scriptwriters receive a story credit, concentrate on Matheson's original, Matheson declares the film bears little relationship to his novella (Bradley).

7. An earlier Italian/American coproduction, *The Last Man on Earth* (Ragona and Salkow 1964), starring Vincent Price, with a script written pseudonymously by Matheson (credited as "Logan Swanson") but later altered, is the first film version to make Neville a scientist and Christ figure. The film self-consciously evokes World War II horrors and Cold War atomic fears, and its slow-moving vampires are a precursor to Romero's zombies. The foregrounding of civil rights in Vietnam-era America is also evident in Romero's *The Night of the Living Dead* (1968), avowedly inspired by Matheson's novella but only loosely evoking the Cold War as the outbreak's cause. The film transforms Matheson's vampires into zombies to engage national American conflicts, particularly over race and civil rights, through its everyman black protagonist.

8. I discuss this point in detail in the introduction.

9. For similar claims regarding an increase in apocalyptic themes and imagery in post-9/11 Hollywood, see Totaro; Pollard; Wallis and Aston; Ford and Mitchell. Sean Brayton further claims that *I Am Legend* is representative of a recent spate of Hollywood films that visualize "multicultural" disaster or apocalyptic worlds (66).

10. Each film represents apocalyptic disaster only in partial, decontextualized fragments—either protagonist flashbacks or found media snippets—and the films focus on life postapocalypse. Per Weaver's finding on secular apocalypses, each overemphasizes disaster and judgment, largely—though arguably tellingly—omitting any real vision of the establishment of a new world.

11. Warner Bros. first restarted development in 1995, and numerous stars, including an Arnold Schwarzenegger–Ridley Scott partnership, were attached. *I Am Legend* was the sixth highest-grossing film and DVD in 2007 and 2008 respectively.

12. Matheson's novella is set in Los Angeles, as is *The Omega Man*, and *The Last Man on Earth*—although putatively set in New York—is perhaps more reminiscent of Los Angeles, filmed around the outskirts of Rome.

13. For example, it is described as presenting both "a sense of wonder mingled with dread" (Zacharek, "*I Am Legend*") and "a haunting, desolate, plausible beauty" (Ansen, "The 'Legend' of Will Smith"); see also Ebert, "*I Am Legend*"; McCarthy, "*I Am Legend*"; Puig, "Will Smith Is Powerful"; Scott, "Man about Town"). While critics praised the film's initial meditation on loneliness and despair, they disparaged its final act's generic shift to B-movie horror and abrupt religious turn. For example, Zacharek describes the final act as a "false and flashy faux-religious climax" ("*I Am Legend*"), and Dana Stevens suggests that the representation of postapocalypse New York provokes thoughts about imperial decline and 9/11, before the arrival of the terror-Other supposedly signals the audience is "safely back in Hollywood" ("*I Am Legend*").

14. This trope recalls many similarly emasculated males in Hollywood history, such as Ransom Stoddard (James Stewart) in *The Man Who Shot Liberty Valance* (Ford 1962) and Clifford Groves (Fred MacMurray) in *There's Always Tomorrow* (Sirk 1956).

15. *TWTFTD* and *The Omega Man* also showcase (self-conscious) star performances in Harry Belafonte's singing and political persona and Charlton Heston's star body and performance aesthetic.

16. For a recent example, see Lobalzo Wright, *Crossover Stardom: Popular Male Music Stars in American Cinema*.

17. Smith's success in music, television, and early Hollywood roles cemented his star image as "sexually non-aggressive" and heterosexual but not hypersexual (Magill 128).

18. Likewise, when Smith helms a project originally created for a white actor, such as Arnold Schwarzenegger in *I Am Legend*, racial messages are invariably altered as the black body carries racial messages not contained in the original material (Tolliver).

19. Tolliver also attests that Smith's iconicity is also given meaning domestically by a "growing visibility and awareness of a black middle class," the cultural "reconstruction of the black male image" in the 1990s, and the establishment of a new black cultural presence by the post-civil-rights generation. Equally, the centrality of Smith's social and cultural mobility to his star image is evident from his beginnings in music and television, particularly *The Fresh Prince of Bel-Air* (1990–96).

20. Numerous pieces conflate Smith's star persona with Neville, especially in relation to racial discourses. Ansen, for example, explicitly associates the masculine star body, the "buff and chiseled Will Smith"—who seemingly subsumes the character he portrays—with the car and the gun ("The 'Legend' of Will Smith").

21. For example, Neville is identified both as representative of the nation's trauma (C. S. King) and as a black military hero who serves to revive the state (Brayton).

22. Mulligan, for example, claims that these moments act "as critical reflections of US military and governmental errors" on 9/11 and in Iraq and after Hurricane Katrina (32). Claire Sisco King suggests the depiction of governmental failure "unsettles claims of American blamelessness on 9/11" (146; see also Mitchell; Brayton; Westwell).

23. The centrality of consumption as an appropriate, even ideal, response to 9/11 was also clear: "Bush proceeded to make a plea to US citizens to show their patriotism and commitment through consumerism" (Nayak 55).

24. The preservation of capitalist ideology by the final man is similarly evoked in the film's sports car opening and Neville's later casual discarding of the car, after which he callously reenacts "buying" another car from the skeleton of a car salesman. And although his love interest first presents herself as a store mannequin, Neville's ambivalent consumer experiences partially critique contemporary consumer life. He displays ongoing hostility toward (the emptiness of) capitalism when "shopping" for clothes and cars, and the dead bodies and skeletons that litter the city remain posthumously tethered to their professional roles, as car salesman or guard, signifying the dehumanizing impacts of capitalism.

25. Issues of performance and performed identity have been integral to Smith's persona since his breakout film role as a homeless gay hustler, Paul, who talks his way into the lives of privileged white New Yorkers, the Kittredges, in *Six Degrees of Separation* (Schepisi 1993). Again highlighting intersections of race and class in the articulation and construction of (Smith's on-screen) identity, Paul's class masquerade—he first falsely claims to be the son of Sidney Poitier before later separately claiming an unlikely interracial heritage as the son of Flan Kittredge—signifies not a merger of race and class but the subsuming of race by class. However, as in *I Am Legend*, performance exposes, and perhaps even encourages, identity

instabilities. Tolliver observes that Paul must discard his own identity to adopt a more amenable postracial self, which also implies that to be black and "successful" requires deracing.

26. Heston's Neville is engaged in monologic "conversation" throughout (with the dead, his own image, and Caesar's bust), to simulate and reconstruct civil society through (self-)conscious performance of identity.

27. Class and race mark Burton's encounter with the mannequins: when he first carries the female mannequin out to his car, the film satirizes racial fears of the threat posed to white women by black male lust, and as he labors to repair the city's infrastructure, the white mannequins lounge in evening dress. At a birthday dinner party Burton organizes for Sarah—white and female—he plays multiple African American service roles, as waiter, cook, and entertainer, implicitly connecting his performance to the history of black representation in film. In *Six Degrees of Separation*, Paul also fulfills numerous of these prescribed roles over the course of his evening with the Kittredges—cook, cleaner, entertainer—and even becomes a stereotypical victim of violence. In a sense, by performing a hybrid blend of postracial privilege and black service roles, Paul seeks to conceal his "real" identity (as homeless gay hustler).

28. Confirming the mannequins' alignment with race, a third survivor—white and male—who disturbs Burton's tenuous steps toward forming the final (or first) interracial couple with Sarah is speedily likened to Snodgrass: "Don't laugh at me, okay." This is reinforced when the white man declares his interest in Sarah: "You know, you remind me of a guy called Snodgrass. I never knew what was in his mind either."

29. That Neville can only sheepishly steal looks in her direction may also in part be due to Smith's mainstream appeal. In *The Omega Man*, Neville's sexual desire (and frustration) is similarly transferred onto mannequins, and he is reaching toward a mannequin's breast just before his future love interest Lisa presents herself as a mannequin.

30. In each film version, Neville puts himself in danger with almost deliberate lapses in regimen—invoking the persistent struggle to persevere and the "losing" of control and discipline.

31. This characterization of the "zombifying" effects of consumption also suggests comparison with Romero's *Dawn of the Dead* (1978/2004) and even *Land of the Dead* (2005).

32. In this sense, "whiteness becomes a threatening presence through alien alterity, which is reified by the racial identity of the film's reluctant black hero" (Brayton 70–71).

33. For example, and despite also categorizing them as colorless, Subramanian claims that Smith's "star image affirms the multicultural values of the US in implicit contrast with the supposedly fanatical and intolerant Arab terrorist" (45; see also Heyes).

34. The terror-Others are labeled variously as zombielike vampires ("non-linguistic animalistic vampire," yet more zombie than human [Lavoie 279]); zombies with vampiric qualities ("predatory zombies . . . with fangs for teeth" [Ebert, "*I Am Legend*"]); or both ("white-skinned vampire zombies" [Ansen, "The 'Legend' of Will Smith"]). Even Richard Matheson observes that they are no longer vampires in the film but rather have vampiric qualities (Bradley 265). Regardless, or perhaps because of this, the terror-Others—part of the contemporary resurgence in zombie narratives—in part articulate anxieties about the terror that proliferates within and fears of being besieged.

35. Critical disdain for the CGI monsters was widespread (see Ebert, "*I Am Legend*"; Morgenstern; Puig, "Will Smith Is Powerful"; Rosenblatt; Scott, "Man about Town"; Bradley).

36. After Neville's declaration, a flashback implies people were *already-monstrous*. Although most people have not yet "turned," Neville tells his daughter: "Daddy will make the monsters go away." This is a common feature in films like *War of the Worlds*, *The Book of*

Eli, and *The Road*, where the invasion or apocalypse reveals people to be the monsters they *always already* were.

37. The images—of creatures who were previously fellow citizens—echo Meghana Nayak's observation that the "assertion of the US Self is as much about disciplining the Others at home as it is about objectifying Others 'elsewhere'" (51).

38. I have not called the terror-Others "Darkseekers" before this point to mirror their like status in the film.

39. Perhaps this more properly renders Neville as Joseph rather than Christ, that is, defending the cure rather than being the cure.

40. A photo of his daughter with the recently deceased Sam also confirms his daughter's death, which is never depicted on-screen.

41. Likewise, Sean Brayton contends that the film "privileges both militarism and masculinity," despite the "appearance of diversity and multicultural tolerance" in its black hero and multicultural postapocalyptic family (75); and Michael Heyes claims that the film dichotomously recodes the Darkseekers as radical Islamic terrorists to portray Neville's struggle as a means to "fix" Ground Zero.

42. The various aspects of Neville's hybrid identity arguably remain confused and split, as he gives contradictory signals to the Darkseekers throughout the final encounter—claiming "I can save you" (as scientist) as he shows an open palm, yet alternately pointing his pistol and picking up the grenade (as soldier).

43. Christ figure iconography stems from *The Last Man on Earth*: when Neville is speared—also akin to his repeated staking of vampires—he cries, "My blood has saved you," before dying on a church altar, albeit declaratively as a man: "I'm a man! The last man!"

44. A warning to "stay in the light" appears on an earlier quarantine notice, and *Legend* is also the title of the Marley compilation album from which Neville sings songs throughout.

45. Anna's eulogy regarding "the restoration of humanity" could imply the cure is used on the Darkseekers, but Neville's characterization of them as "unstoppable" suggests otherwise.

46. A shot from Neville's perspective thereafter highlights the empty screen space in the passenger seat that Sam typically inhabits. Neville abruptly stops the SUV, but the dolly shot continues, the retreating camera spotlighting his solitude and immobility.

47. Butterflies are also seen on Marley's pillow, in the cornfield at Central Park, and in a glass case in the home.

48. For example, in *End of Days* (Hyams 1999), Jericho Cane's (Arnold Schwarzenegger) sacrifice likewise reunites him with his deceased wife and daughter.

49. Christopher Moreman mistakenly claims the cure is derived from Neville's "own special blood," in thereby contending that Neville's martyrdom marks the hero as "divine savior" and the film concludes in a "blatant Christ-figuration" (see also Pak; Subramanian; Brayton).

50. See Hantke, "Historicizing the Bush Years," for an alternative to the scholarly tendency to interpret the original ending as substantially different from the theatrical release (see, e.g., Boyle; Brayton; Walliss and Aston; Westwell; C. S. King; Joyce). Hantke observes that recognition in the alternative ending remains discomfortingly tied to anthropomorphic values and thereby supports integration over difference.

51. Guy Westwell, for example, claims that it "goes some way to undoing their irreconcilable difference" and toward Neville's acceptance of a measure of culpability (833).

52. While civilization's continuation in *The Omega Man* similarly requires fleeing the city, this is more an image of 1970s urban decay.

53. Neville's deployment of mines as part of his defenses is also highly reminiscent of coordinated (suicide) car bombings.

4. "A Variation of Vengeance": The Inadequacy of Revenge in Remasculinizing the Nation Abroad

1. On the other hand, Clint Eastwood's *The 15:17 to Paris* (2018), about the actions of three young American men in successfully halting a terrorist attack on a French train in 2015, in a sense seeks to "redo" America's response to the attacks of 9/11.

2. Shaheen, e.g., labels the film as a "jingoistic *Rambo*-in-Arabia" ("Stereotypes Reign in *The Kingdom*"; see also Bradshaw, "*The Kingdom*"); Richard Corliss claims that *The Kingdom* is finally "a retro-fantasy . . . culminating in politico-military triumph" ("Americans Win the War on Terror!"); and A. O. Scott further posits that *The Kingdom* "can be seen as a wishful revisionist scenario," offering "a cathartic counternarrative" of completion and "mission accomplished" ("F.B.I. Agents Solve the Terrorist Problem").

3. Unseen and underappreciated experiences of masculinity at the edges of American "civilization" are a preoccupation of Berg's work and are similarly evident in *Lone Survivor* (2013) and *Deepwater Horizon* (2016).

4. See Scott, "F.B.I. Agents Solve the Terrorist Problem"; Smith, "*The Kingdom*"; Rainer, "*The Kingdom* Plays like *CSI: Riyadh*"; M. Johnson, "*The Kingdom*."

5. Linda Williams's linking of westerns, action-thrillers, and war movies as "male action" genres further supports their blended consideration in *The Kingdom*.

6. I focus here predominantly on *Fort Apache* of the so-called Cavalry Trilogy, which includes *She Wore a Yellow Ribbon* (Ford 1949) and *Rio Grande* (Ford 1950), because the different screenwriters for each film in the trilogy resulted in very different politics, particularly given Ford's famed lack of interest in overt political questions.

7. While men in the home are often represented somewhat pejoratively in contrast to the individualistic hero in westerns, confined to domestic spaces marked as the domain of women, *Shane* (Stevens 1953) and *The Searchers* also deal with the reorientation of ideas of masculinity and the incorporation of males (the hero, who cannot be incorporated into civilization, notably aside) within the refigured home.

8. I here employ Meghana Nayak's term "Arab/Muslim," which she uses "to politicize and denote the[ir] conflation . . . into a singular entity" (58).

9. The western hero most famously emerges from the wilderness, like Ethan in *The Searchers* or the Ringo Kid (John Wayne) in *Stagecoach* (Ford 1939). Fleury's introduction, on the other hand, aligns him more with these films' effete stagecoach passengers or emasculated homesteading husband-fathers.

10. This well-worn trope is employed in *Syriana* (Gaghan 2005), *Lions for Lambs* (Redford 2007), and *Rendition* (Hood 2007). *The Kingdom* lionizes field experience over government officialdom and a so-called Washington mind-set, most evident in the FBI director's encounter with the attorney general, quietly tolerating the latter's threats before sharing wisdom gleaned from his service in Vietnam. The gulf is often visualized through dress/uniform or slavish adherence to rules and regulations, although frontier westerns such as *Fort Apache* and *Fort Apache: The Bronx* (Petrie 1981) ultimately—and critically—also recognize the ambivalent necessity of both.

11. Despite implying that the Saudi request is unreasonable and unexpected, Berg admits that FBI agents always have to surrender their weapons when they enter a foreign country, and entry to Saudi Arabia is prohibited for anyone with an Israeli stamp in his or her passport (*The Kingdom* DVD commentary), further signaling the team's willful cultural insensitivity in choosing a member whose travel history clearly contravenes this requirement.

12. Robert Leigninger observes that few western heroes are simultaneously husband-fathers *and* professionals, but *Fort Apache* foregrounds the hybrid (and often conflicting) identities of the soldier-fathers Lieutenant Colonel Thursday and Sergeant O'Rourke.

13. For example, the opening of *Black Hawk Down* highlights the restrictive rules of engagement confronting US Army Rangers. Subsequent scenes clearly seek to counter this perceived impotence, showing Rangers detaining a suspect and firing wildly at the training range.

14. Audience understanding of Schmidt's character is also likely informed by Piven's seminal role as an amoral talent agent in *Entourage* (2004–11).

15. See the introduction for detailed discussion of this rhetorical construction.

16. As discussed in chapter 1, the attacks on the Twin Towers are again not represented, with the screen cutting to black before the graphically simulated collision.

17. The tonal dissonance between the opening credits sequence, centered on 9/11, and the ensuing genre narrative can largely be explained by the fact that *The Kingdom* was in development well before 9/11 (and its initiating attacks modeled on the bombing of the Khobar Towers in 1996).

18. See, e.g., Shaheen, "Stereotypes Reign in *The Kingdom*"; Aguayo; Williams and Linneman.

19. This tendency extends beyond the portrayal of Arabs, with *Black Hawk Down*, completed before the 9/11 attacks but released subsequently, similarly conflating Islam and violence in Somalia: a man immediately picks up his automatic weapon after concluding morning prayer on the beach. Playing on ideas of the Vietnam conflict, US Rangers in the film describe the area as "the Wild West" and consider all locals as hostile: "We're fighting the entire city." Akin to *The Kingdom*'s "stagecoach" SUVs, the rangers are especially vulnerable when driving through gauntlet-like urban space.

20. This predilection toward manipulation is reinforced in the prince's repeated association with spin and photo opportunities, as much as by royal excess.

21. Only frame-by-frame analysis confirms the boy survives, saved by Sergeant Haytham's intervention.

22. See, e.g., Shaheen, "Stereotypes Reign in *The Kingdom*"; Aguayo; Creekmur; Williams and Linneman.

23. I discuss the "invisibility" that especially defines modern terrorism as monstrous in chapter 2.

24. The building evokes the networked structure of modern terrorism and implies its cultural embeddedness in everyday Arab life, reinforced by the use of everyday objects (such as fridges) to conceal or hide terrorist activity. By planning and conducting terror from everyday spaces, terrorist-Others reposition those spaces as sites of violence.

25. The FBI's little-known role after foreign attacks on US citizens is outlined in *The Kingdom* DVD bonus materials, which note that FBI investigators were also on the ground in Saudi Arabia after attacks in 1996 and 2003.

26. Along with *The Incredible Hulk* (1978–82), Al Ghazi also mentions *The Six Million Dollar Man* (1978–82).

27. This violent unity is reiterated even in death, with Fleury wearing a bandage on the right of his neck, matching the fatal wound suffered by Al Ghazi.

28. *The Missing* also visualizes the connection between "good" and "bad" Other as an internal struggle to invoke the confused identity of the good Indian. In the film's finale, Samuel Jones / Chaa-duu-ba-its-iidan (Tommy Lee Jones) and a malevolent witch-medicine man—who leads a wave of violence and wears the photographs of female victims around his neck—die entwined in violent struggle, the good Indian only fully redeemed in death.

29. Only Fleury, as team leader, is otherwise similarly "targeted."

30. Leavitt learns before the team's departure that Manner was sent to Riyadh for breaking the jaw of a man who insulted Mayes when they celebrated graduation together, perhaps in relation to gender (in being butch).

31. In her father's memory, Walden as captain and mother is both doting and militaristic, a militarized mother who does push-ups in fatigues at play with her daughter.

32. I discuss this widespread critical reticence in the introduction and in relation to *Cloverfield*, another genre film, in chapter 2.

33. Likewise, Stuart Price observes that when a fictional film refers to 9/11 or the wider war on terror, there is "a logical transference from the fictional environment to a wider social universe of political meaning" (64).

34. For example, Stephanie Zacharek deemed it "opportunistic and creepy" ("*The Kingdom*"), and Pete Vonder Haar ("*The Kingdom*") was unsure whether he was supposed to be entertained or nauseated.

35. The fatal potential of recorded images is signaled when Schmidt informs Fleury after the team's first meeting with the Saudi prince: "I'll tell you why this is a win. You documented it and you're still alive."

36. I discuss this tendency to contain catastrophe and horror inside small screens in chapter 1.

37. See also Vonder Haar, "*The Kingdom*"; Lumenick, "The King-Dumb"; Puig, "Action Aces Cohesion in *The Kingdom*"; Hoberman, "Fight Them over There"; and Bradshaw, "*The Kingdom*."

38. It is not unusual for an inordinate ratio of Indians to be killed in frontier westerns, even from seeming positions of weakness, but Fleury's team display weapon skills that their professional roles cannot explain. In this sense, *The Kingdom* resembles contemporary action cinema and the "boy's own" colonial world of films like *Gunga Din*, in which the wildly inferior Others are easily routed when their treacherous concealment is exposed. A similar siege experience is represented in other contemporary frontier westerns such as *The Alamo* (Hancock 2004) and *300* (Snyder 2006), but the absence of either overwhelming enemy numbers or clear front lines in the war on terror may explain the paucity of post-9/11 "outpost" films.

39. The film's coda prompted wildly diverse critical responses. On one side, David Ansen decried audience applause during the shoot-out, claiming that the film "whip[s] the audience into a bloodthirsty frenzy" before a "discordant and disingenuous" coda unconvincingly attempts to suggest the error of such bloodlust ("Torrents of Arabia"). On the other, precisely because of audience cheers when Mayes stabs Leavitt's would-be executioner, Maryann Johnson interprets the subsequent coda as deliberately shaming ("*The Kingdom*"). Berg admits that in a test screening in Sacramento, the audience cheered when Mayes kills the would-be executioners, but he chooses to interpret this—given a similar response in London, with 25 percent of the audience self-identified as "Arabs"—as registering a universal desire to see extremism punished (*The Kingdom* DVD bonus materials).

40. After the raid, the team finds a collection of photographs that connect the militants to planned real-world blowback: "The Coalition: all these countries have troops in Iraq." In the original draft of the final scene, the team bid fond farewells to Al Ghazi before Haytham, who has been tortured and whose brother was killed in Iraq, detonates a suicide bomb vest, killing Fleury and his team.

Conclusion: "How Do You Love Your Family and Leave Them to Go to War?"

1. For example, Michael Cieply observes that the politics of films such as *300* (Snyder 2006) earned praise and criticism in equal measure.
2. This compulsion to return to the originary attacks in *12 Strong* extends even to the World Trade Center and Ground Zero, with the film ending on a final shot of the Horse Solider Statue erected in 2012. The limited series *The Looming Tower* goes back even further, replaying the years before 9/11.
3. The wives are later shown watching television, again coming together within the home, watching an address by Donald Rumsfeld in search of traces of their fighting husbands.
4. Diller also promises his wife he will return home—as she stoically hides her fears by cleaning the oven. Michael Peña's character in *World Trade Center* again rails against seeming marginalization and immobilization when it seems his team will not participate because Mitch has taken a desk job: "And thanks to you, we're gonna be watching this whole thing go down on fucking CNN."
5. The film's closing credits song, "It goes on" (Zac Brown), is primarily about the bonds between (presumably) men: "We'll be together at the rising of the dawn, even when we're gone."
6. The opening title sequence also seemingly signals its Trump-era politics in showing Russian president Vladimir Putin positively, kindly volunteering a warning to America before 9/11.

FILMOGRAPHY

Adamson, Andrew, and Vicky Jenson. *Shrek*. DVD, DreamWorks Home Entertainment, 2001.
Alias. Television series, American Broadcasting Company (ABC), 2001–6.
Antal, Nimród. *Vacancy*. DVD, Sony Pictures Home Entertainment, 2007.
Battlestar Galactica. DVD, Universal Pictures (Australasia), 2004–9.
Bay, Michael. *Armageddon*. 1998; DVD, Walt Disney Home Video, 2001.
Berg, Peter. *Deepwater Horizon*. Motion picture, Roadshow Films, 2016.
Berg, Peter. *The Kingdom*. Motion picture, Universal Pictures, 2007.
Berg, Peter. *Lone Survivor*. Motion picture, Walt Disney Studios Motion Pictures, 2013.
Bertino, Bryan. *The Strangers*. DVD, Universal Studios Home Entertainment, 2008.
Bigelow, Kathryn. *Zero Dark Thirty*. Motion picture, Columbia Pictures, 2012.
Boardwalk Empire. Television series, Home Box Office (HBO), 2010–14.
Boorman, John. *Deliverance*. 1972; DVD, Warner Home Video, 2000.
Bousman, Darren Lynn. *Saw II*. DVD, Lionsgate, 2005.
Bowman, Rob. *Elektra*. DVD, Twentieth Century Fox Home Entertainment, 2005.
Carpenter, John. *Escape from New York*. 1981; DVD, Universal Pictures (Australasia), 2004.
Carpenter, John. *The Thing*. 1982; DVD, Universal Studios, 2003.
Chandor, J. C. *Margin Call*. Motion picture, Becker Entertainment (Australia), 2011.
Cooper, Merian C., and Ernest B. Schoedsack. *King Kong*. 1933; DVD, Warner Home Video, 2005.
Corbijn, Anton. *The American*. Motion picture, Focus Features, 2010.
Cosmatos, George. *Rambo: First Blood Part II*. 1985; DVD, Artisan Entertainment, 2002.
Craven, Wes. *The Hills Have Eyes*. 1977; DVD, Umbrella Entertainment, 2005.
Cronenberg, David. *Cosmopolis*. DVD, Icon Film Distribution, 2012.
Cuarón, Alfonso. *Children of Men*. DVD, Universal Studios, 2006.
Darabont, Frank. *The Mist*. DVD, Dimension Films, 2007.
Dassin, Jules. *The Naked City*. 1948; DVD, Universal International, 2002.
Daves, Delmer. *Dark Passage*. 1947; DVD, Warner Home Video, 2003.
Derrickson, Scott. *The Day the Earth Stood Still*. 2008; DVD, Twentieth Century Fox Home Entertainment, 2009.
Dominik, Andrew. *Killing Them Softly*. Motion picture, Hoyts Distribution (Australia), 2012.
Douglas, Gordon. *Them!* 1954; DVD, Warner Home Video, 2002.
Dowdle, John Erick. *Quarantine*. 2008; DVD, Sony Pictures Home Entertainment, 2009.
Eastwood, Clint. *American Sniper*. Motion picture, Roadshow Films, 2014.
Eastwood, Clint. *The 15:17 to Paris*. Motion picture, Warner Bros. Pictures, 2018.
Eastwood, Clint. *Sully*. Motion picture, Warner Bros. Pictures, 2016.
Emmerich, Roland. *The Day after Tomorrow*. Motion picture, Twentieth Century Fox Film Corporation, 2004.

Emmerich, Roland. *Godzilla*. DVD, Columbia TriStar Home Video, 1998.
Emmerich, Roland. *Independence Day*. 1996; DVD, Twentieth Century Fox Home Entertainment, 2007.
Emmerich, Roland. *2012*. Motion picture, Sony Pictures Releasing, 2009.
Entourage. Television series, Warner Bros. Entertainment Australia, 2004–11.
Feist, Felix E. *Deluge*. Motion picture, RKO Radio Pictures, 1933.
Fleischer, Richard, et al. *Tora! Tora! Tora!* 1970; DVD, Twentieth Century Fox Home Entertainment, 2009.
Ford, John. *Fort Apache*. 1948; DVD, Warner Home Video, 2006.
Ford, John. *The Lost Patrol*. 1934; DVD, Warner Home Video, 2006.
Ford, John. *The Man Who Shot Liberty Valance*. 1962; DVD, Paramount Home Entertainment (Australasia), 2002.
Ford, John. *The Searchers*. 1956; DVD, Warner Home Video, 2006.
Ford, John. *7 Women*. Motion picture, Metro-Goldwyn-Mayer (MGM), 1966.
Ford, John. *She Wore a Yellow Ribbon*. 1949; DVD, Warner Home Video, 2006.
Ford, John. *Stagecoach*. 1939; DVD, Warner Home Video, 1997.
The Fresh Prince of Bel-Air. Television series, Warner Bros. Television, 1990–96.
Friedkin, William. *Rules of Engagement*. 2000; DVD, Paramount Home Entertainment, 2007.
Fuglsig, Nicolai. *12 Strong*. Motion picture, Roadshow Films, 2018.
Gaghan, Stephen. *Syriana*. Motion picture, Warner Bros. Pictures, 2005.
Garnett, Tay. *Bataan*. 1943; DVD, Warner Home Video, 2006.
Granik, Debra. *Winter's Bone*. Motion picture, Curious Films (Australia), 2010.
Greenfield, Lauren. *The Queen of Versailles*. Motion picture, Magnolia Pictures, 2012.
Greengrass, Paul. *Bloody Sunday*. DVD, Paramount Home Entertainment, 2002.
Greengrass, Paul. *United 93*. DVD, Universal Pictures (Australasia), 2006.
Hancock, John Lee. *The Alamo*. Motion picture, Touchstone Pictures, 2004.
Hillcoat, John. *The Road*. Motion picture, Dimension Films, 2009.
Hirschbiegel, Oliver, and James McTeigue. *The Invasion*. 2007; DVD, Warner Home Video, 2008.
Honda, Ishirō. *Gojira*. 1954; DVD, Eastern Eye, 2004.
Hood, Gavin. *Rendition*. Motion picture, Anonymous Content, 2007.
Hooper, Tobe. *The Texas Chain Saw Massacre*. 1974; DVD, Umbrella Entertainment, 2007.
Howard, Ron. *The Missing*. 2003; DVD, Columbia TriStar Home Entertainment, 2004.
Hughes, Albert, and Allen Hughes. *The Book of Eli*. Motion picture, Warner Bros. Pictures, 2010.
Hyams, Peter. *End of Days*. 1999; DVD, Universal Studios, 2000.
Iliadis, Dennis. *The Last House on the Left*. Motion picture, Roadshow Film Distributors, 2009.
The Incredible Hulk. Television series, Columbia Broadcasting System (CBS), 1978–82.
Kellogg, Ray, John Wayne, and Mervyn LeRoy. *The Green Berets*. 1968; DVD, Warner Home Video, 2007.
Krasinski, John. *A Quiet Place*. Motion picture, Paramount Pictures, 2018.
Kubrick, Stanley. *Full Metal Jacket*. 1987; DVD, Warner Home Video, 2001.
Lawrence, Francis. *I Am Legend*. Motion picture, Warner Bros. Pictures, 2007.
Leder, Mimi. *Deep Impact*. 1998; DVD, Paramount Home Entertainment, 2006.
Lee, Ang. *Billy Lynn's Long Halftime Walk*. Motion picture, TriStar Pictures, 2016.
Lee, Ang. *Brokeback Mountain*. 2005; DVD, Roadshow Entertainment, 2006.
Lee, Spike. *25th Hour*. 2002; DVD, Buena Vista Home Entertainment, 2003.

The Looming Tower. Television series, Hulu, 2018–.
Lourié, Eugène. *The Beast from 20,000 Fathoms*. 1953; DVD, Warner Home Video, 2006.
MacDonald, Peter. *Rambo III*. 1988; DVD, Lionsgate Home Entertainment, 2008.
MacDougall, Ranald. *The World, the Flesh and the Devil*. 1959; DVD, 2010 edition, Warner Home Video, 2010.
Mann, Michael. *Ali*. DVD, Columbia TriStar Home Video, 2001.
Maté, Rudolph. *When Worlds Collide*. 1951; DVD, Paramount Home Entertainment, 2002.
McTiernan, John. *Die Hard*. Motion picture, Twentieth Century Fox Home Entertainment, 1988.
Mendes, Sam. *Revolutionary Road*. Motion picture, Paramount Vantage, 2008.
Menzies, William Cameron. *Things to Come*. 1936; DVD, Network, 2007.
Montgomery, Robert. *Lady in the Lake*. 1947; DVD, Warner Home Video, 2006.
Moore, Michael. *Fahrenheit 9/11*. DVD, Columbia TriStar Home Entertainment, 2004.
Morel, Pierre. *Taken*. 2008; DVD, Twentieth Century Fox Home Entertainment, 2009.
Muccino, Gabriele. *The Pursuit of Happyness*. 2006; DVD, Sony Pictures Home Entertainment, 2007.
Myrick, Daniel, and Eduardo Sánchez. *The Blair Witch Project*. DVD, Becker Home Video, 1999.
Nichols, Jeff. *Take Shelter*. Motion picture, Sony Pictures Classics, 2011.
Nolan, Christopher. *The Dark Knight*. Motion picture, Warner Bros., 2008.
Nolan, Christopher. *The Dark Knight Rises*. Motion picture, Warner Bros., 2012.
Onah, Julius. *The Cloverfield Paradox*. Motion picture, Netflix, 2018.
Peckinpah, Sam. *Major Dundee*. 1965; DVD, RCA/Columbia Pictures Home Video, 2005.
Peli, Oren. *Paranormal Activity*. 2007; DVD, Paramount Home Video, 2009.
Petrie, Daniel. *Fort Apache: The Bronx*. DVD, Home Box Office Home Video (HBO), 1981.
Preminger, Otto. *In Harm's Way*. 1965; DVD, Paramount Home Entertainment, 2005.
Proyas, Alex. *I, Robot*. 2004; DVD, Twentieth Century Fox Home Entertainment, 2008.
Ragona, Ubaldo, and Sidney Salkow. *The Last Man on Earth*. 1964; DVD, Alpha Video, 2004.
Redford, Robert. *Lions for Lambs*. 2007; DVD, Twentieth Century Fox Home Entertainment, 2008.
Reeves, Matt. *Cloverfield*. Motion picture, Paramount Pictures, 2008.
Reitman, Jason. *Up in the Air*. Motion picture, Paramount Pictures, 2009.
Rescue Me. Television series, Sony Pictures Television, 2004–11.
Roberts, Johannes. *The Strangers: Prey at Night*. Motion picture, StudioCanal, 2018.
Robinson, Phil Alden. *The Sum of All Fears*. 2002; DVD, Paramount Home Entertainment, 2008.
Robson, Mark. *Earthquake*. 1974; DVD, Universal Home Entertainment, 2006.
Romero, George A. *Dawn of the Dead*. 1978; DVD, Umbrella Horror, 2003.
Romero, George A. *Diary of the Dead*. 2007; DVD, Genius Products, 2008.
Romero, George A. *Land of the Dead*. DVD, Universal Pictures 2005.
Romero, George A. *Night of the Living Dead*. 1968; DVD, Force Video, 1999.
Roth, Eli. *Hostel*. 2005; DVD, Sony Pictures Home Entertainment, 2006.
Sagal, Boris. *The Omega Man*. 1971; DVD, Warner Home Video, 2007.
Schepisi, Fred. *Six Degrees of Separation*. 1993; DVD, Twentieth Century Fox Home Entertainment, 2006.
Scorsese, Martin. *Cape Fear*. 1991; DVD, Columbia TriStar Home Entertainment Australia, 2002.
Scorsese, Martin. *Raging Bull*. 1980; DVD, MGM Home Entertainment, 2001.

Scott, Ridley. *Alien*. 1979; DVD, Twentieth Century Fox Home Entertainment, 2004.
Scott, Ridley. *Black Hawk Down*. Motion picture, Revolution Studios, 2001.
Shults, Trey Edward. *It Comes at Night*. Motion picture, Roadshow Films, 2017.
Siegel, Don. *Invasion of the Body Snatchers*. 1956; DVD, Artisan Home Entertainment, 2002.
Sirk, Douglas. *There's Always Tomorrow*. 1956; DVD, Madman Entertainment, 2006.
The Six Million Dollar Man. Television series, American Broadcasting Company (ABC), 1974–78.
Slade, David. *30 Days of Night*. Motion picture, Icon Film Distribution, 2007.
Snyder, Zack. *300*. Motion picture, Warner Bros. Pictures, 2006.
Soderbergh, Steven. *Magic Mike*. DVD, Roadshow Entertainment, 2012.
Sonnenfeld, Barry. *Men in Black*. 1997; DVD, Sony Pictures Home Entertainment 2005.
Spielberg, Steven. *Munich*. Motion picture, DreamWorks SKG, 2005.
Spielberg, Steven. *War of the Worlds*. DVD, Paramount Home Video, 2005.
Stanton, Andrew. *Wall-E*. DVD, Walt Disney Studios Home Entertainment, 2008.
Stevens, George. *Gunga Din*. 1939; DVD, Warner Home Video, 2004.
Stevens, George. *Shane*. 1953; DVD, Paramount Home Entertainment, 2003.
Stockwell, John. *Turistas*. 2006; DVD, Twentieth Century Fox Home Entertainment, 2007.
Stone, Oliver. *Born on the Fourth of July*. 1989; DVD, Universal Pictures, 1999.
Stone, Oliver. *JFK*. 1991; DVD, Warner Home Video, 2008.
Stone, Oliver. *Nixon*. 1995; DVD, Walt Disney Studios Home Entertainment, 2008.
Stone, Oliver. *Platoon*. 1986; DVD, Twentieth Century Fox Home Entertainment, 2007.
Stone, Oliver. *Wall Street*. 1987; DVD, Twentieth Century Fox Home Entertainment South Pacific Pty Ltd, 2007.
Stone, Oliver. *World Trade Center*. 2006; DVD, Paramount Home Entertainment, 2009.
Tourneur, Jacques. *Cat People*. 1942; DVD, Warner Home Video, 2005.
Tourneur, Jacques. *Curse of the Demon*. 1957; DVD, Columbia TriStar Home Entertainment, 2002.
Trachtenberg, Dan. *10 Cloverfield Lane*. Motion picture, Paramount Pictures, 2016.
Verhoeven, Paul. *Starship Troopers*. 1997; DVD, Buena Vista Home Entertainment, 1999.
Wadleigh, Michael. *Woodstock*. 1970; DVD, Warner Home Video, 2001.
Walsh, Raoul. *Objective, Burma!* 1945; DVD, Warner Home Video, 2006.
Wan, James. *Saw*. DVD, Lionsgate, 2004.
Wellman, William A. *Beau Geste. The Gary Cooper Collection*. 1939; DVD, Universal Studios Home Entertainment, 2005.
Zwick, Edward. *Courage under Fire*. DVD, Twentieth Century Fox Home Entertainment, 1996.
Zwick, Edward. *The Siege*. 1998; DVD, Twentieth Century Fox Home Entertainment, 2009.

WORKS CITED

Adelman, Rebecca A. "'Suffering? You Haven't Seen Anything Yet': Rating the Global War on Terror in American Film." *Jura Gentium Cinema*, "Dossier: Horror Politics," 2009.
Aguayo, Michelle. "Representations of Muslim Bodies in *The Kingdom*: Deconstructing Discourses in Hollywood." *Global Media Journal*, vol. 2, no. 2, 2009, pp. 41–56.
Alleva, Richard. "Passion Play: Oliver Stone's 'World Trade Center.'" *Commonweal*, vol. 133, no. 16, 2006, pp. 24–25.
Altman, Rick. *Film/Genre*. BFI Publications, 1999.
Anderson, Christopher Todd. "Post-Apocalyptic Nostalgia: *Wall-E*, Garbage, and American Ambivalence toward Manufactured Goods." *Lit: Literature Interpretation Theory*, vol. 23, no. 3, 2012, pp. 267–82.
Anderson, Mark. *Cowboy Imperialism and Hollywood Film*. Peter Lang, 2007.
Ansen, David. "The 'Legend' of Will Smith." *Newsweek*, 2007, http://www.thedailybeast.com/newsweek/2007/12/12/the-legend-of-will-smith.html.
Ansen, David. "Torrents of Arabia." *Newsweek*, 2007, http://www.thedailybeast.com/newsweek/2007/09/28/torrents-of-arabia.html.
Araujo, Susana. "Security Unlocked and Fictions of Terror." *Review of International American Studies*, vol. 3.3–4.1, 2008, pp. 5–14.
Aufderheide, Pat. "Good Soldiers." *Seeing through Movies*, edited by Mark Crispin Miller, Pantheon, 1990, pp. 81–111.
Avila, Eric. "Dark City: White Flight and the Urban Science Fiction Film in Postwar America." *Liquid Metal: The Science Fiction Film Reader*, edited by Sean Redmond, Wallflower Press, 2004, pp. 88–97.
Baishya, Anirban Kapil. "Trauma, Post-Apocalyptic Science Fiction and the Post-Human." *Wide Screen*, vol. 3, no. 1, 2011, pp. 1–25.
Baudrillard, Jean. *The Spirit of Terrorism, and Requiem for the Twin Towers*. Translated by Chris Turner, Verso, 2002.
Bauman, Zygmunt. "Modernity and Ambivalence." *Theory Culture Society*, vol. 7, 1990, pp. 143–69.
Bell-Metereau, Rebecca. "The How-To Manual, the Prequel, and the Sequel in Post-9/11 Cinema." *Film and Television after 9/11*, edited by Wheeler Winston Dixon, Southern Illinois University Press, 2004, pp. 142–62.
Berardinelli, James. "*Cloverfield*." *Reel Views*, 2008, http://www.reelviews.net/movies/c/cloverfield.html.
Berger, James. *After the End: Representations of Post-Apocalypse*. University of Minnesota Press, 1999.
Bertrand, Ina, and Peter Hughes. *Media Research Methods: Audiences, Institutions, Texts*. Palgrave Macmillan, 2005.

Birkenstein, Jeff, Anna Froula, and Karen Randell, editors. *Reframing 9/11: Film, Popular Culture and the "War on Terror."* Bloomsbury, 2010.

Booker, M. Keith. *Blue-Collar Pop Culture: From NASCAR to "Jersey Shore."* Praeger, 2012.

Borden, Diane M., and Eric P. Essman. "Manifest Landscape/Latent Ideology: Afterimages of Empire in the Western and 'Post-Western.'" *California History*, vol. 79, no. 1, 2000, pp. 30–41.

Bordwell, David. "A Behemoth from the Dead Zone." *Observations on Film Art*, edited by Kristin Thompson and David Bordwell, January 25, 2008, http://www.davidbordwell.net/blog/2008/01/25/a-behemoth-from-the-dead-zone.

Bordwell, David. "Intensified Continuity Revisited." *Observations on Film Art*, edited by Kristin Thompson and David Bordwell, May 27, 2007, http://www.davidbordwell.net/blog/2007/05/27/intensified-continuity-revisited.

Bordwell, David. "Return to Paranormalcy." *Observations on Film Art*, edited by Kristin Thompson and David Bordwell, November 13, 2012, http://www.davidbordwell.net/blog/2012/11/13/return-to-paranormalcy.

Bordwell, David. *The Way Hollywood Tells It*. University of California Press, 2006.

Boyle, Kirk. "*Children of Men* and *I Am Legend*: The Disaster-Capitalism Complex Hits Hollywood." *Jump Cut*, vol. 51, Spring 2009, http://www.ejumpcut.org/archive/jc51.2009/ChildrenMenLegend/index.html.

Bradley, Matthew R. *Richard Matheson on Screen: A History of the Filmed Works*. McFarland, 2010.

Bradshaw, Peter. "*The Kingdom*." *Guardian*, 2007, http://www.guardian.co.uk/film/2007/oct/05/actionandadventure.

Brayton, Sean. "The Racial Politics of Disaster and Dystopia in *I Am Legend*." *Velvet Light Trap*, vol. 67, Spring 2011, pp. 66–76.

Briefel, Aviva, and Sam J. Miller, editors. *Horror after 9/11: World of Fear, Cinema of Terror*. University of Texas Press, 2011.

Broderick, Mick. "Surviving Armageddon: Beyond the Imagination of Disaster." *Science Fiction Studies*, vol. 20, no. 3, 1993, http://www.depauw.edu/sfs/backissues/61/broderick61art.htm.

Brown, Wendy. *States of Injury: Power and Freedom in Late Modernity*. Princeton University Press, 1995.

Burns, Jeremy Joseph. *Alternate Endings: The Post-Apocalypse in American and British Film and Literature*. 2009. University of Arkansas, MA thesis.

Butler, Judith. *Bodies That Matter: On the Discursive Limits of "Sex."* Routledge, 1993.

Butler, Judith. *Gender Trouble: Feminism and the Subversion of Identity*. 2nd ed., Routledge, 1999.

Calefato, Patrick. "Signs of Order, Signs of Disorder: The Other Uniforms." *Uniform: Order and Disorder*, edited by Francesco Bonami et al., Charta, 2000, pp. 195–204.

Carroll, Noël. *The Philosophy of Horror, or Paradoxes of the Heart*. Routledge, 1990.

Carter, Sean, and Klaus Dodds. "Hollywood and the 'War on Terror': Genre-Geopolitics and 'Jacksonianism' in *The Kingdom*." *Environment and Planning D: Society and Space*, vol. 29, 2011, pp. 98–113.

Cettl, Robert. *Terrorism in American Cinema: An Analytical Filmography, 1960–2008*. McFarland, 2009.

Charles, Alec. "Extreme Renditions: Reflections upon the War on Terror in British and American Screen Science Fiction." *Political Studies Association Annual Conference*, April 7–9, 2009.

Chermak, Steven, Frankie Y. Bailey, and Michelle Brown, editors. *Media Representations of September 11*. Praeger, 2003.
Christiansen, Steen. "Ideological Fission: *Cloverfield* and Terrorism." *Monsters and the Monstrous: Myths and Metaphors of Enduring Evil Conference*, September 22–25, 2008, https://vbn.aau.dk/en/publications/ideological-fission-emcloverfieldem-and-terrorism.
Cieply, Michael. "*The Kingdom* Gambles That Entertainment Can Trump Politics." *New York Times*, June 19, 2007, https://www.nytimes.com/2007/06/19/movies/19king.html.
Clasen, Mathias. "Vampire Apocalypse: A Biocultural Critique of Richard Matheson's *I Am Legend*." *Philosophy and Literature*, vol. 34, 2010, pp. 314–28.
Clover, Carol J. *Men, Women, and Chain Saws: Gender in the Modern Horror Film*. Princeton University Press, 1992.
Clover, Joshua. "The End." *Film Quarterly*, vol. 61, no. 3, 2008, pp. 6–7.
Cohan, Steven, and Ina Rae Hark, editors. *Screening the Male: Exploring Masculinities in Hollywood Cinema*. Routledge, 1993.
Cohen, Jeffrey, editor. *Monster Theory: Reading Culture*. University of Minnesota Press, 1996.
Combe, Kirk. "Spielberg's Tale of Two Americas: Postmodern Monsters in *War of the Worlds*." *Journal of Popular Culture*, vol. 44, no. 5, 2011, pp. 934–53.
Combe, Kirk, and Brenda Boyle. *Masculinity and Monstrosity in Contemporary Hollywood Films*. Palgrave Macmillan, 2013.
Connell, R. W. *Masculinities*. 2nd ed., Allen and Unwin, 2005.
Connell, R. W. "Studying Men and Masculinity." *Resources for Feminist Research*, vol. 29, nos. 1–2, 2001, pp. 43–55.
Conrad, Dean. *Space Sirens, Scientists and Princesses: The Portrayal of Women in Science Fiction Cinema*. McFarland, 2018.
Copier, Laura. *Preposterous Revelations: Visions of Apocalypse and Martyrdom in Hollywood Cinema, 1980-2000*. 2008. University of Amsterdam, PhD dissertation.
Corliss, Richard. "Americans Win the War on Terror!" *Time*, September 28, 2007, http://www.time.com/time/arts/article/0,8599,1666758,00.html.
Corliss, Richard. "The Blair Witch Reject." *Time*, January 16, 2008, http://www.time.com/time/arts/article/0,8599,1704366,00.html.
Corliss, Richard. "Will Smith Gets Lost in His *Legend*." *Time*, December 14, 2007, http://www.time.com/time/arts/article/0,8599,1694609,00.html.
Corrigan, Timothy, editor. *American Cinema of the 2000s: Themes and Variations*. Rutgers University Press, 2012.
Courtney, Susan. *Hollywood and Fantasies of Miscegenation: Spectacular Narratives of Gender and Race, 1903-1967*. Princeton University Press, 2005.
Coyle, Rebecca. "Point of Audition: Sound and Music in *Cloverfield*." *Science Fiction Film and Television*, vol. 3, no. 2, 2010, pp. 217–38.
Craik, Jennifer. "The Cultural Politics of the Uniform." *Fashion Theory*, vol. 7, no. 2, 2003, pp. 127–48.
Craik, Jennifer. *Uniforms Exposed: From Conformity to Transgression*. English edition, Berg, 2005.
Creekmur, Corey K. "The Sound of the 'War on Terror.'" *Reframing 9/11: Film, Popular Culture and the War on Terror*, edited by Jeff Birkenstein et al., Continuum, 2010, pp. 83–93.
Crowe, Lori. "Masculinity, Militarism and Popular Culture: The Warrior Superhero in Hollywood." *Gender, Agency and Political Violence*, edited by Linda Åhäll and Laura J. Shepherd, Palgrave Macmillan, 2012, pp. 19–38.

Culcasi, Karen. "Geographical Record: Constructing and Naturalising the Middle East." *Geographical Review*, vol. 100, no. 4, 2010, pp. 583–97.

Dargis, Manohla. "Defiance under Fire: Paul Greengrass's Harrowing *United 93*." *New York Times*, April 28, 2006, http://movies.nytimes.com/2006/04/28/movies/28unit.html.

Dargis, Manohla. "We're All Gonna Die! Grab Your Video Camera." *New York Times*, January 18, 2008, http://movies.nytimes.com/2008/01/18/movies/18clov.html.

Dargis, Manohla, and A. O. Scott. "How the Movies Made a President." *New York Times*, January 16, 2009, http://www.nytimes.com/2009/01/18/movies/18darg.html.

Davis, Mike. *Ecology of Fear: Los Angeles and the Imagination of Disaster*. Metropolitan Books, 1998.

Dawes, Birgit. "Celluloid Recoveries: Cinematic Transformations of Ground Zero." *Transnational American Memories*, edited by Udo J. Hebel, Walter de Gruyter, 2009, pp. 285–309.

Deacon, David, Michael Pickering, Peter Golding, and Graham Murdock. *Researching Communications: A Practical Guide to Methods in Media and Cultural Analysis*. Arnold, 1999.

Deane, Cormac. "The Embedded Screen and the State of Exception: Counterterrorist Narratives and the War on Terror." *Refractory*, vol. 14, 2008, http://refractory.unimelb.edu.au/2008/12/27/the-embedded-screen-and-the-state-of-exception-counterterrorist-narratives-and-the-%E2%80%9Cwar-on-terror%E2%80%9D-%E2%80%93-cormac-deane.

Denby, David. "On Duty: *World Trade Center*." *New Yorker*, August 13, 2006, http://www.newyorker.com/archive/2006/08/21/060821crci_cinema.

Dennis, Jeffrey P. "Men, Masculinities and the Cave Man." *The Handbook of Gender, Sex and Media*, edited by Karen Ross, Wiley-Blackwell, 2011, pp. 107–17.

DeRosa, Aaron, and Stacey Peebles. "Enduring Operations: Narratives of the Contemporary Wars." *Modern Fiction Studies*, vol. 63, no. 2, 2017, pp. 203–24.

Dixon, Wheeler Winston,, editor. *Film and Television after 9/11*. Southern Illinois University Press, 2004.

Dixon, Wheeler Winston, *Visions of the Apocalypse: Spectacles of Destruction in American Cinema*. Wallflower, 2003.

Doane, Mary Ann. "Film and the Masquerade: Theorising the Female Spectator." *Screen*, vol. 23, nos. 3–4, 1982, pp. 74–88.

Dodds, Klaus. "Hollywood and the Popular Geopolitics of the War on Terror." *Third World Quarterly*, vol. 29, no. 8, 2008, pp. 1621–37.

Drew, Julie. "Identity Crisis: Gender, Public Discourse, and 9/11." *Women and Language*, vol. 27, no. 2, 2004, pp. 71–77.

Dudink, Stefan, Karen Hagemann, and John Tosh, editors. *Masculinities in Politics and War: Gendering Modern History*. Manchester University Press, 2004.

Duncombe, Constance. "Foreign Policy and the Politics of Representation: The West and Its Others." *Global Change, Peace and Security*, vol. 23, no. 1, 2011, pp. 31–46.

Durham, Christopher Louis. *Masculinity in the Post-War Western: John Wayne and Clint Eastwood*. 2004. University of Newcastle upon Tyne, PhD dissertation.

Ebert, Roger. "*Cloverfield*." *Chicago Sun-Times*, January 17, 2008, http://rogerebert.suntimes.com/apps/pbcs.dll/article?AID=/20080117/REVIEWS/801170302/1023.

Ebert, Roger. "*I Am Legend*." *Chicago Sun-Times*, December 13, 2007, http://rogerebert.suntimes.com/apps/pbcs.dll/article?AID=/20071213/REVIEWS/712130305.

Edelstein, David. "And Opening This Week . . ." *New York Magazine*, December 7, 2007, http://nymag.com/arts/cultureawards/2007/41824.

Edelstein, David. "*Cloverfield* Is a Kick—a Bruising One." *New York Magazine*, January 17, 2008, http://nymag.com/daily/movies/2008/01/cloverfield.html.
Edelstein, David. "*12 Strong* Is an Underwhelming Tribute to the 'Horse Soldiers' of the Afghan War." *Vulture*, January 20, 2018, http://www.vulture.com/2018/01/review-12-strong-is-an-underwhelming-tribute-to-soldiers.html.
Edelstein, David. "Up from the Ashes." *New York Magazine*, August 3, 2006, http://nymag.com/movies/reviews/18855.
Edwards, Tim. *Cultures of Masculinity*. Routledge, 2006.
England, Marcia. "Breached Bodies and Home Invasions: Horrific Representations of the Feminized Body and Home." *Gender, Place and Culture*, vol. 13, no. 4, 2006, pp. 353–63.
Faludi, Susan. *The Terror Dream: Fear and Fantasy in Post-9/11 America*. Scribe, 2008.
Ferraro, Michael. "*I Am Legend*." *Film Threat*, 2007, http://www.filmthreat.com/reviews/10461.
Fitzpatrick, Andrea. "The Movement of Vulnerability: Images of Falling and September 11." *Art Journal*, vol. 66, no. 4, 2007, pp. 84–102.
Flynn, Kevin, and Jim Dwyer. "Falling Bodies, a 9/11 Image Etched in Pain." *New York Times*, September 10, 2004, http://www.nytimes.com/2004/09/10/nyregion/10jumpers.html.
Ford, Elizabeth A., and Deborah C. Mitchell. *Apocalyptic Visions in 21st Century Films*. McFarland, 2018.
Foundas, Scott. "Legend Has It." *Village Voice*, December 4, 2007, http://www.villagevoice.com/2007-12-04/film/legend-has-it.
Franklin, Garth. "*Cloverfield*." *Dark Horizons*, January 18, 2008, http://www.darkhorizons.com/review-cloverfield.
Gallagher, Mark. *Action Figures*. Palgrave Macmillan, 2006.
Gallagher, Tag. "John Ford's Indians." *Film Comment*, vol. 29, no. 5, 1993, pp. 68–72.
Gentry, Ric. "Another Meditation on Death: An Interview with Oliver Stone." *Film Quarterly*, vol. 60, no. 4, 2007, pp. 54–60.
Gilligan, Sarah. "Fragmenting the Black Male Body: Will Smith, Masculinity, Clothing, and Desire." *Fashion Theory*, vol. 16, no. 2, 2012, pp. 171–92.
Godfrey, Sarah, and Hannah Hamad. "Save the Cheerleader, Save the Males: Resurgent Protective Paternalism in Popular Film and Television after 9/11." *The Handbook of Gender, Sex and Media*, edited by Karen Ross, Wiley-Blackwell, 2011, pp. 157–73.
Graham, Stephen. "Cities and the 'War on Terror.'" *International Journal of Urban and Regional Research*, vol. 30, no. 2, 2006, pp. 255–76.
Greco, Lorenzo. "Social Identity, Military Identity." *Uniform: Order and Disorder*, edited by Francesco Bonami et al., Charta, 2000, pp. 145–52.
Greenen, Kathryn. "Regular Movie Review: *The Kingdom*." *Journal of Feminist Family Therapy*, vol. 20, no. 1, 2008, pp. 94–98.
Greven, David. "Contemporary Hollywood Masculinity and the Double-Protagonist Film." *Cinema Journal*, vol. 48, no. 4, 2009, pp. 22–43.
Grusin, Richard. "Premediation." *Criticism*, vol. 46, no. 1, 2004, pp. 17–39.
Gunn, James. "Father Trouble: Staging Sovereignty in Spielberg's *War of the Worlds*." *Critical Studies in Media Communication*, vol. 25, no. 1, 2008, pp. 1–27.
Halberstam, Jack. *Female Masculinity*. Duke University Press, 1998.
Hannah, Matthew G. "Virility and Violation in the US 'War on Terrorism.'" *A Companion to Feminist Geography*, edited by Lise Nelson and Joni Seager, Blackwell, 2005, pp. 550–64.

Hantke, Steffen. *American Horror Film: The Genre at the Turn of the Millennium*. University Press of Mississippi, 2010.

Hantke, Steffen. "Bush's America and the Return of Cold War Science Fiction: Alien Invasion in *Invasion, Threshold*, and *Surface*." *Journal of Popular Film and Television*, vol. 38, no. 3, 2010, pp. 143–51.

Hantke, Steffen. "Historicizing the Bush Years: Politics, Horror Film and Francis Lawrence's *I Am Legend*." *Horror after 9/11: World of Fear, Cinema of Terror*, edited by Aviva Briefel and Sam J. Miller, University of Texas Press, 2011, pp. 165–85.

Hantke, Steffen. "On the Acceleration of the Undead: Paradigm Change in the American Zombie Film." *Jura Gentium Cinema*, "Cinema and Globalization," 2010.

Hantke, Steffen. "The Return of the Giant Creature: *Cloverfield* and Political Opposition to the War on Terror." *Extrapolation*, vol. 51, no. 2, 2010, pp. 235–57.

Hartlaub, Peter. "*Cloverfield* a Shaky Look at Monster Attacking New York." *San Francisco Chronicle*, January 17, 2008, http://www.sfgate.com/movies/article/Review-Cloverfield-a-shaky-look-at-monster-3232485.php.

Haschemi Yekani, Elahe. "Privileged Crises in the Wake of 9/11: Universalizing Masculinity in Ian McEwan's *Saturday* and Oliver Stone's *World Trade Center*." *Contemporary Masculinities in the UK and the US*, edited by Stefan Horlacher and Kevin Floyd, Palgrave Macmillan, 2017, pp. 57–74.

Hay, James, and Mark Andrejevic. "Introduction: Toward an Analytic of Governmental Experiments in These Times: Homeland Security as the New Social Security." *Cultural Studies*, vol. 20, nos. 4–5, 2006, pp. 331–48.

Heffernan, Jeanne. "'Poised between Savagery and Civilization': Forging Political Communities in Ford's Westerns." *Perspectives on Political Science*, vol. 28, no. 3, 1999, pp. 147–51.

Heyes, Michael E. "Fixing Ground Zero: Race and Religion in Francis Lawrence's *I Am Legend*." *Journal of Religion and Film*, vol. 21, no. 2, 2017, pp. 1–27.

Higson, Andrew. "The Concept of National Cinema." *Screen*, vol. 30, no. 4, 1989, pp. 36–47.

Hoberman, J. "Good Soldiers." *Village Voice*, August 1, 2006, http://www.villagevoice.com/2006-08-01/film/good-soldiers.

Hoberman, J. "Fight Them over There." *Village Voice*, September 18, 2007, http://www.villagevoice.com/2007-09-18/film/fight-them-over-there.

Holloway, David. *9/11 and the War on Terror*. Edinburgh University Press, 2008.

"Hollywood Takes On the Iraq War." Editorial, *Cineaste*, vol. 33, no. 1, 2007, p. 4.

Holmlund, Christine. *Impossible Bodies: Femininity and Masculinity at the Movies*. Psychology Press, 2002.

hooks, bell. *Reel to Real: Race, Class and Sex at the Movies*. Routledge, 1996.

Jaafar, Ali. "I'm Not a Political Filmmaker Goddamit!" *Sight and Sound*, 2006, http://www.bfi.org.uk/sightandsound/feature/49325.

Jackson, Kimberly. *Technology, Monstrosity and Reproduction in Twenty-First Century Horror*. Palgrave Macmillan, 2013.

Jacobs, Alan. "In the Garden." *Cabinet*, no. 31, 2008, http://www.cabinetmagazine.org/issues/31/jacobs.php.

Jancovich, Mark. *Horror, the Film Reader*. Routledge, 2002.

Jeffords, Susan. *Hard Bodies: Hollywood Masculinity in the Reagan Era*. Rutgers University Press, 1994.

Johnson, Brian. "Oliver Stone: Redemption in the Ruins." *Maclean's*, vol. 119, no. 31, 2006, pp. 49–51.

Johnson, Maryann. "*The Kingdom* (Review)." *Flick Filosopher*, September 27, 2007, http://www.flickfilosopher.com/blog/2007/09/the_kingdom_review.html#axzz1rspQ1ycO.
Jordan, John W. "Transcending Hollywood: The Referendum on *United 93* as Cinematic Memorial." *Critical Studies in Media Communication*, vol. 25, no. 2, 2008, pp. 196–223.
Joyce, Stephen. "The Endings of *I Am Legend*." *Transmedia Storytelling and the Apocalypse*, Palgrave Macmillan, 2018, pp. 57–76.
Joyce, Stephen. "Foreshadows of the Fall: Questioning 9/11's Impact on American Attitudes." *American Cinema in the Shadow of 9/11*, edited by Terence McSweeney, Edinburgh University Press, 2016.
Kakoudaki, Despina. "Spectacles of History: Race Relations, Melodrama, and the Science Fiction/Disaster Film." *Camera Obscura*, vol. 17, no. 2, 2002, pp. 108–53.
Kaplan, Amy. "Homeland Insecurities: Reflections on Language and Space." *Radical History Review*, no. 85, 2003, pp. 82–93.
Kaplan, E. Ann. *Trauma Culture: The Politics of Terror and Loss in Media and Literature*. Rutgers University Press, 2005.
Keane, Stephen. *Disaster Movies: The Cinema of Catastrophe*. 2nd ed., Wallflower, 2006.
Kehr, Dave. "Descending into a State of Nature." *New York Times*, January 13, 2013, http://www.nytimes.com/2013/01/13/movies/homevideo/new-on-dvd-ashanti-and-wake-in-fright.html?ref=davekehr&_r=0.
Kehr, Dave. "How the West Was Filled with Loss." *New York Times*, March 23, 2012, http://www.nytimes.com/2012/03/25/movies/homevideo/john-fords-fort-apache-on-blu-ray-from-warner-home-video.html.
Kellner, Douglas. *Cinema Wars: Hollywood Film and Politics in the Bush-Cheney Era*. John Wiley and Sons, 2009.
Kelly, Casey Ryan. "The Wounded Man: *Foxcatcher* and the Incoherence of White Masculine Victimhood." *Communication and Critical/Cultural Studies*, vol. 15, no. 2, 2018, 161–78.
Kendrick, James. "Representing the Unrepresentable: 9/11 on Film and Television." *Why We Fought: America's Wars in Film and History*, edited by Peter C. Rollins and John E. O'Connor, University Press of Kentucky, 2008, pp. 511–28.
Kim, Ju-Yon. "Media, Nation, Performance." Audio podcast, Stanford University, March 30, 2007, https://itunes.apple.com/au/itunes-u/film-studies/id385378336itunes.apple.com/au/itunes-u/film-studies/id385378336.
King, Claire Sisco. *Washed in Blood: Male Sacrifice, Trauma, and the Cinema*. Rutgers University Press, 2012.
King, Geoff. "'Just like a Movie'? 9/11 and Hollywood Spectacle." *Spectacle of the Real*, edited by Geoff King, Intellect Books, 2005, pp. 13–22.
King, Geoff. "Responding to Realities or Telling the Same Old Story? Mixing Real-World and Mythic Resonances in *The Kingdom* (2007) and *Zero Dark Thirty* (2012)." *American Cinema in the Shadow of 9/11*, edited by Terence McSweeney, Edinburgh University Press, 2016.
Klawans, Stuart. "Virtual Catastrophe." *Nation*, September 11, 2006, http://www.thenation.com/article/virtual-catastrophe.
Kord, Susanne, and Elisabeth Kimmer. *Contemporary Hollywood Masculinities: Gender, Genre, and Politics*. Palgrave Macmillan, 2011.
Kracauer, Siegfried. "Hollywood's Terror Films: Do They Reflect an American State of Mind?" *New German Critique*, vol. 89, 2003, pp. 105–11.

Lane, Anthony. "Monstrous Times." *New Yorker*, January 21, 2008, http://www.newyorker.com/arts/critics/cinema/2008/01/28/080128crci_cinema_lane.

Lane, Anthony. "Outlaws." *New Yorker*, September 24, 2007, http://www.newyorker.com/arts/critics/cinema/2007/10/01/071001crci_cinema_lane?currentPage=all.

Larrieux, Stéphanie. "The World, the Flesh, and the Devil: The Politics of Race, Gender, and Power in Post-Apocalyptic Hollywood Cinema." *Quarterly Review of Film and Video*, vol. 27, no. 2, 2010, pp. 133–43.

Lavoie, Dusty. *Marijuanatopia?—Placing Pot Media in the U.S. Social Imaginary: Surveillance, Consumption and Pleasure.* 2011. University of Maine, PhD dissertation.

Lee, Felicia. "9/11 on Big Screen, Ambivalence in Audience." *New York Times*, August 10, 2006, http://www.nytimes.com/2006/08/10/nyregion/10movi.html.

Lee, Nathan. "*Cloverfield* Is One Giant, Incredibly Entertaining 'Screw You!' to Yuppie New York." *Village Voice*, January 15, 2008, http://www.villagevoice.com/2008-01-15/film/cloverfield-is-one-giant-incredibly-entertaining-screw-you-to-yuppie-new-york.

Leigninger, Robert D. "The Western as Male Soap Opera: John Ford's *Rio Grande*." *Journal of Men's Studies*, vol. 6, no. 2, 1998, pp. 135–48.

Lewis, Michael. "Hollywood Does 9/11." *Commentary*, 2006, pp. 40–45.

Lichty, Lawrence, and Raymond Carroll. "Fragments of War: Oliver Stone's *Platoon*." *Why We Fought: America's Wars in Film and History*, edited by Peter C. Rollins and John E. O'Connor, University Press of Kentucky, 2008, pp. 390–403.

Liss, Rebecca. "Oliver Stone's *World Trade Center* Fiction." *Slate*, August 9, 2006, http://www.slate.com/id/2147350.

Lobalzo Wright, Julie. *Crossover Stardom: Popular Male Music Stars in American Cinema*. Bloomsbury, 2017.

Lumenick, Lou. "The King-Dumb." *New York Post*, September 28, 2007, https://nypost.com/2007/09/28/the-king-dumb.

MacDonald, James. "The Ideology of Disaster: *Godzilla*, Gorillas and Geopolitics in the Global 21st Century." *Giant Creatures in Our World: Essays on Kaiju and American Popular Culture*, edited by Camille D. G. Mustachio and Jason Barr, McFarland, 2017, pp. 161–77.

MacKinnon, Kenneth. *Love, Tears, and the Male Spectator*. Fairleigh Dickinson University Press, 2002.

Magill, David. "Celebrity Culture and Racial Masculinities: The Case of Will Smith." *Pimps, Wimps, Studs, Thugs and Gentlemen: Essays on Media Images of Masculinity*, edited by Elwood Watson, McFarland, 2009, pp. 126–37.

Mantoan, Lindsey. "War after the End: Post-Apocalyptic Narratives after 9/11." *War as Performance*, Palgrave Macmillan, 2018, pp. 163–211.

Marcks, Greg. "A Credible Witness." *Film Quarterly*, vol. 60, no. 1, 2006, p. 3.

Matheson, Richard. *I Am Legend*. Millennium, 1999.

McCarthy, Todd. "*Cloverfield*." *Variety*, January 16, 2008, http://www.variety.com/review/VE1117935799.

McCarthy, Todd. "*I Am Legend*." *Variety*, December 7, 2007, http://www.variety.com/review/VE1117935602.

McGillis, Roderick. *He Was Some Kind of a Man: Masculinities in the B-Western*. Wilfrid Laurier University Press, 2009.

McKee, Alan. *Textual Analysis: A Beginner's Guide*. Sage Publications, 2003.

McSweeney, Terence, editor. *American Cinema in the Shadow of 9/11*. Edinburgh University Press, 2016.

McSweeney, Terence. *The "War on Terror" and American Film: 9/11 Frames per Second*. Edinburgh University Press, 2014.

Melnick, Jeffrey. *9/11 Culture: America under Construction*. Wiley-Blackwell, 2009.

Mitchell, Kevin. "*I Am Legend*: Apocalypse Soon." *World Socialist Web Site*, January 8, 2008, http://www.wsws.org/articles/2008/jan2008/lege-j08.shtml.

Miller, Toby, and Marwan M. Kraidy. *Global Media Studies*. Polity Press, 2016.

Monahan, Barry. "Kant's Sublime and the Disaster Film after 9/11." *Rethinking Genre in Contemporary Global Cinema*, edited by Silvia Dibeltulo and Ciara Barrett, Palgrave Macmillan, 2018, pp. 181–95.

Moreman, Christopher M. "*I Am Legend*." *Journal of Religion and Film*, vol. 12, no. 1, 2008, https://digitalcommons.unomaha.edu/jrf/vol12/iss1/8.

Morgan, Michael. *On Shame*. Routledge, 2008.

Morgenstern, Joe. "Smith Shines, but Script Falters in *I Am Legend*." *Wall Street Journal*, December 14, 2007, http://online.wsj.com/article/SB119759112354128281.html.

Morris, Wesley. "Where There's a Will . . ." *Boston Globe*, 2007, http://archive.boston.com/news/globe/living/articles/2007/12/14/where_theres_a_will.

Movshovitz, Howard. "The Still Point: Women in the Westerns of John Ford." *Frontiers: A Journal of Women Studies*, vol. 7, no. 3, 1984, pp. 68–72.

Mulligan, Rikk. "*I Am Legend*." *SFRA Review*, vol. 286, Fall 2008, pp. 31–32.

Mulvey, Laura. "Visual Pleasure and Narrative Cinema." *Screen*, vol. 16, no. 3, 1975, pp. 6–18.

Muntean, Nick. "It Was Just like a Movie." *Journal of Popular Film and Television*, vol. 37, no. 2, 2009, pp. 50–59.

Nadel, Alan. *Containment Culture: American Narrative, Postmodernism, and the Atomic Age*. Duke University Press, 1995.

Nama, Adilifu. *Black Space: Imagining Race in Science Fiction Film*. University of Texas Press, 2008.

Natoli, Joseph. "The America Endangered in *The American*: A Dark Allegory." *Senses of Cinema*, no. 57, 2010, http://sensesofcinema.com/2010/feature-articles/the-america-endangered-in-the-american-a-dark-allegory.

Natoli, Joseph P. *This Is a Picture and Not the World: Movies and a Post-9/11 America*. State University of New York Press, 2007.

Nayak, Meghana. "Orientalism and 'Saving' US State Identity after 9/11." *International Feminist Journal of Politics*, vol. 8, no. 1, 2006, pp. 42–61.

Neale, Steve. *Genre and Hollywood*. Routledge, 2000.

Neale, Steve. "Masculinity as Spectacle." *Screen*, vol. 24, no. 6, 1983, pp. 2–17.

Negra, Diane, and Yvonne Tasker, editors. *Gendering the Recession*. Duke University Press, 2013.

Newman, Kim. "*I Am Legend*." *Sight and Sound*, vol. 18, no. 3, 2008, pp. 69–70.

Nilges, Mathias. "The Aesthetics of Destruction: Contemporary US Cinema and TV Culture." *Reframing 9/11: Film, Popular Culture and the War on Terror*, edited by Jeff Birkenstein et al., Continuum, 2010, pp. 23–33.

Nolley, Ken. "The Representation of Conquest: John Ford and the Hollywood Indian, 1939–1964." *Hollywood's Indian: The Portrayal of the Native American in Film*, edited by Peter C. Rollins and John E. O'Connor, University Press of Kentucky, 2010, pp. 73–90.

Norden, Martin F., editor. *The Changing Face of Evil in Film and Television*. Rodopi, 2007.

North, Daniel. "Evidence of Things Not Quite Seen: *Cloverfield*'s Obstructed Spectacle." *Film and History: An Interdisciplinary Journal of Film and Television Studies*, vol. 40, no. 1, 2010, pp. 75–92.

O'Connor, John E. "The White Man's Indian: An Institutional Approach." *Hollywood's Indian: The Portrayal of the Native American in Film*, edited by Peter C. Rollins and John E. O'Connor, University Press of Kentucky, 2010, pp. 27–38.

Overpeck, Deron. "'People Are Going to Want to Know What Really Went Down': *Cloverfield* and the Return to Innocence in Post-9/11 America." *Horror Studies*, vol. 3, no. 1, 2012, pp. 105–22.

Ozcan, Ceylan. "Oliver Stone's *World Trade Center* as a Representation of the Collective Trauma of 9/11." *Journal of Faculty of Letters*, vol. 25, no. 2, 2008, pp. 205–20.

Page, Max. "The Future of New York's Destruction: Fantasies, Fictions, and Premonitions after 9/11." *The New Blackwell Companion to the City*, edited by Gary Bridge and Sophie Watson, Wiley-Blackwell, 2011, pp. 305–16.

Pak, Chris. "Confronting or Sidestepping Race in SF Film Adaptations: *I, Robot* and *I Am Legend*." *US-China Foreign Language*, vol. 8, no. 1, 2010, pp. 59–64.

Palmer, Lorrie. "Black Man/White Machine: Will Smith Crosses Over." *Velvet Light Trap*, vol. 67, Spring 2011, pp. 28–40.

Paramount Pictures. "World Trade Center Production Notes," 2006, http://www.wtcmovie.com/main.html.

Patterson, Kathy Davis. "Echoes of *Dracula*: Racial Politics and the Failure of Segregated Spaces in Richard Matheson's *I Am Legend*." *Journal of Dracula Studies*, no. 7, 2005, pp. 19–27.

Peberdy, Donna. *Masculinity and Film Performance: Male Angst in Contemporary American Cinema*. Palgrave Macmillan, 2011.

Petersen, P. S. "9/11 and the Apocalyptic Enemy Within: Terrorist Scenarios in Postmodern American Fiction and Film." *Ninth Nordic Conference for English Studies*, May 27–29, 2004, http://www.hum.au.dk/engelsk/naes2004/papers.htmlhttp://www.hum.au.dk/engelsk/naes2004/papers.html.

Petersen, P. S. "9/11 and the 'Problem of Imagination.'" *Orbis Litterarum*, vol. 60, no. 2, 2005, pp. 133–44.

Pheasant-Kelly, Frances. "Abjection, Trauma, Catharsis: *World Trade Center* as Classic Narrative." *Southwest Texas Popular Culture and American Culture Association Conference*, February 10–13, 2010.

Pheasant-Kelly, Frances. "Authenticating the Reel: Simulation and Trauma in *United 93*." *International Journal of the Arts in Society*, vol. 4, no. 1, 2009, pp. 95–06.

Phillips, Michael. "*Cloverfield*." *Chicago Tribune*, January 16, 2008, https://web.archive.org/web/20080120105037/http://chicago.metromix.com/movies/movie_review/movie-review-cloverfield/286254.

Phillips, Michael. "*I Am Legend*." *Chicago Tribune*, December 13, 2007, https://www.chicagotribune.com/zap-story-iamlegend-story.html.

Pile, Steve. "Intensities of Feeling: *Cloverfield*, the Uncanny, and the Always Near Collapse of the City." *The New Blackwell Companion to the City*, edited by Gary Bridge and Sophie Watson, Wiley-Blackwell, 2011, pp. 288–303.

Pitetti, Connor. "Uses of the End of the World: Apocalypse and Postapocalypse as Narrative Modes." *Science Fiction Studies*, vol. 44, no. 3, 2017, pp. 437–54.

Pollard, Tom. *Hollywood 9/11: Superheroes, Supervillains, and Super Disasters*. Paradigm Publishers, 2011.

Price, Stuart. "Bureaucracy, Coercive Force and Individual Agency: The Gendered Protagonist in the 'War on Terror.'" *Review of International American Studies*, vols. 3.3–4.1, 2008, pp. 60–71.

Prince, Stephen. *Firestorm: American Film in the Age of Terrorism*. Columbia University Press, 2009.
Puig, Claudia. "Action Aces Cohesion in *The Kingdom*." *USA Today*, 2007, http://www.usatoday.com/life/movies/reviews/2007-09-27-kingdom_N.htm.
Puig, Claudia. "Will Smith Is Powerful as an Urban 'Legend.'" *USA Today*, 2007, http://www.usatoday.com/life/movies/reviews/2007-12-13-i-am-legend_N.htm.
Purse, Lisa. *Contemporary Action Cinema*. Edinburgh: Edinburgh University Press, 2011.
Rainer, Peter. "*The Kingdom* Plays like CSI: Riyadh." *Christian Science Monitor*, September 28, 2007, http://www.csmonitor.com/2007/0928/p11s01-almo.html.
Randell, Karen. "'It Was like a Movie': The Impossibility of Representation in Oliver Stone's *World Trade Center*." *Reframing 9/11: Film, Popular Culture and the War on Terror*, edited by Jeff Birkenstein et al., Continuum, 2010.
Ray, Robert B. "Real and Disguised Westerns." *A Certain Tendency of the Hollywood Cinema, 1930–1980*, Princeton University Press, 1985.
Redmond, Sean. "Nowhere Left to Zone in *Children of Men* (2006)." In *American Cinema in the Shadow of 9/11*, edited by Terence McSweeney, 291–306. Edinburgh: Edinburgh University Press, 2016.
Redmond, Sean. "When Planes Fell Out of the Sky: The War Body on Screen." *The War Body on Screen*, edited by Karen Randell and Sean Redmond, Continuum, 2008, pp. 22–35.
Reinhard, CarrieLynn D. "Gameplay Marketing Strategies as Audience Co-optation: The Story of *The Dark Knight*, the *Cloverfield* Monster, and Their Brethren." *International Journal of Communication*, vol. 5, 2011, pp. 51–77.
Renner, Karen J. "The Appeal of the Apocalypse." *Lit: Literature Interpretation Theory*, vol. 23, no. 3, 2012, pp. 203–11.
Reyes, Xavier Aldana. "Violence and Mediation: The Ethics of Spectatorship in the Twenty-First Century Horror." *Violence and the Limits of Representation*, edited by Graham Matthews and Sam Goodman, Palgrave, 2013, pp. 145–60.
Rich, B. Ruby. "Out of the Rubble." *Sight and Sound*, 2006, http://www.bfi.org.uk/sightandsound/feature/49320.
Richards, Olly. "*Cloverfield*." *Empire*, July, 6, 2007, https://www.empireonline.com/movies/reviews/cloverfield-review.
Rickli, Christina. "An Event 'Like a Movie'? Hollywood and 9/11." *COPAS*, vol. 10, 2009, https://copas.uni-regensburg.de/article/view/114/138.
Robinson, Sally. *Marked Men: White Masculinity in Crisis*. Columbia University Press, 2000.
Rollins, Peter C., and John E. O'Connor. "Introduction: The Study of Hollywood's Indian." *Hollywood's Indian: The Portrayal of the Native American in Film*, edited by Peter C. Rollins and John E. O'Connor, University Press of Kentucky, 2010, pp. 1–11.
Rosen, Elizabeth. *Apocalyptic Transformation: Apocalypse and the Postmodern Imagination*. Lexington Books, 2008.
Rosenbaum, Ron. "Hijacking the Hijacking: The Problem with the United 93 Films." *Slate*, April 27, 2006, http://www.slate.com/id/2140676.
Rosenblatt, Josh. "*I Am Legend*." *Austin Chronicle*, December 14, 2007, http://www.austinchronicle.com/calendar/film/2007-12-14/570388.
Said, Edward. *Orientalism*. 25th anniversary ed., Penguin, 2003.
Šakota-Kokot, Tanja. *My War, Your War: Understanding Conflict in Africa and the Middle East through Fiction Film; "Hotel Rwanda" and "The Kingdom."* 2010. University of the Witwatersrand, PhD dissertation.

Salle, Mick La. "*The Kingdom*: Hunt for Terrorists Abroad Proves Not So Easy." *San Francisco Chronicle*, September 27, 2007, http://www.sfgate.com/cgi-bin/article.cgi?f=/c/a/2007/09/27/DDBHSEIDK.DTL.

Sánchez-Escalonilla, Antonio. "Hollywood and the Rhetoric of Panic: The Popular Genres of Action and Fantasy in the Wake of the 9/11 Attacks." *Journal of Popular Film and Television*, vol. 38, no. 1, 2010, pp. 10–20.

Sardar, Ziauddin, and Merryl Wyn Davies. "Freeze Framing Muslims." *Interventions: International Journal of Postcolonial Studies*, vol. 12, no. 2, 2010, pp. 239–50.

Savlov, Marc. "*Cloverfield*." *Austin Chronicle*, January 18, 2008, http://www.austinchronicle.com/calendar/film/2008-01-18/581461.

Savran, David. *Taking It like a Man: White Masculinity, Masochism, and Contemporary American Culture*. Princeton University Press, 1998.

Schwarzbaum, Lisa. "*Cloverfield*." *Entertainment Weekly*, January 16, 2008, http://www.ew.com/ew/article/0,,20172122,00.html.

Schwarzbaum, Lisa. "*The Kingdom* (2007)." *Entertainment Weekly*, September 26, 2007, http://www.ew.com/ew/article/0,,20058666,00.html.

Scott, A. O. "F.B.I. Agents Solve the Terrorist Problem." *New York Times*, September 28, 2007, http://movies.nytimes.com/2007/09/28/movies/28king.html.

Scott, A. O. "Man about Town, and Very Alone." *New York Times*, November 14, 2007, http://movies.nytimes.com/2007/12/14/movies/14iege.html?_r=0.

Scott, A. O. "Pinned under the Weight of Skyscrapers and History in *World Trade Center*." *New York Times*, August 9, 2006, http://movies.nytimes.com/2006/08/09/movies/09worl.html.

Shaheen, Jack. "Stereotypes Reign in *The Kingdom*." *Washington Report on Middle Eastern Affairs*, December 2007, https://www.wrmea.org/007-december/stereotypes-reign-in-the-kingdom.html.

Shary, Timothy, editor. *Millennial Masculinity*. Wayne State University Press, 2013.

Shaw, Tony. *Cinematic Terror: A Global History of Terrorism on Film*. Bloomsbury, 2015.

Sherman, Daniel J., and Terry Nardin, editors. *Terror, Culture, Politics: Rethinking 9/11*. Indiana University Press, 2006.

Sherman, Fraser A. *Screen Enemies of the American Way: Political Paranoia about Nazis, Communists, Saboteurs, Terrorists and Body Snatching Aliens in Film and Television*. McFarland, 2010.

Silverman, Kaja. *Male Subjectivity at the Margins*. Routledge, 1992.

Slotkin, Richard. *Gunfighter Nation: The Myth of the Frontier in Twentieth-Century America*. Atheneum, 1992.

Slotkin, Richard. "Our Myths of Choice." *Chronicle of Higher Education*, September 28, 2001, http://chronicle.com/article/Our-Myths-of-Choice/29729.

Smith, Julian. *Looking Away: Hollywood and Vietnam*. Scribner, 1975.

Smith, Sid. "*The Kingdom*." *Chicago Tribune*, September 28, 2007.

Sobchack, Vivian C. *The Persistence of History: Cinema, Television, and the Modern Event*. Routledge, 1996.

Sontag, Susan. "The Imagination of Disaster." *Commentary* (October), 1965, pp. 42–48.

Staiger, Janet. "Hybrid or Inbred: The Purity Hypothesis and Hollywood Genre History." *Film Criticism*, vol. 22, no. 1, 1997, pp. 5–20.

Stevens, Dana. "*I Am Legend*." *Slate*, December 13, 2007, http://www.slate.com/articles/arts/movies/2007/12/i_am_legend.html.

Stevens, Dana. "Stone Cold." *Slate*, August 8, 2006, http://www.slate.com/id/2147347.

Stevens, Dana. "When Monsters Attack Pretty People." *Slate*, January 17, 2008, http://www.slate.com/articles/arts/movies/2008/01/when_monsters_attack_pretty_people.html.
Stewart, Garrett. *Closed Circuits: Screening Narrative Surveillance*. University of Chicago Press, 2015.
Stewart, Henry. "*Cloverfield*." Cinepinion, edited by Henry Stewart, January 24, 2008, http://cinepinion.blogspot.com.au/2008/01/cloverfield.html.
Sturken, Marita. *Tourists of History: Memory, Kitsch, and Consumerism from Oklahoma City to Ground Zero*. Duke University Press, 2007.
Subramanian, Janani. "Alienating Identification: Black Identity in *The Brother from Another Planet* and *I Am Legend*." *Science Fiction Film and Television*, vol. 3, no. 1, 2010, pp. 37–56.
Svendsen, Lars. *A Philosophy of Fear*. Reaktion Books, 2008.
Takacs, Stacy. "The Contemporary Politics of the Western Form: Bush, *Saving Jessica Lynch*, and *Deadwood*." *Reframing 9/11: Film, Popular Culture and the War on Terror*, edited by Jeff Birkenstein et al., Continuum, 2010.
Takacs, Stacy. "Jessica Lynch and American Identity Post 9/11." *Why We Fought: America's Wars in Film and History*, edited by Peter C. Rollins and John E. O'Connor, University Press of Kentucky, 2008.
Tasker, Yvonne. "Soldiers' Stories: Women and Military Masculinities in *Courage under Fire*." *Quarterly Review of Film and Video*, vol. 19, no. 3, 2002, pp. 209–22.
Tasker, Yvonne. *Spectacular Bodies: Gender, Genre and the Action Cinema*. 2nd ed., Routledge, 1995.
Taubin, Amy. "Going Down." *Sight and Sound*, 2003, http://www.bfi.org.uk/sightandsound/feature/47.
Thompson, Kirsten Moana. *Apocalyptic Dread: American Film at the Turn of the Millennium*. State University of New York Press, 2007.
Thomson, David. "Mission Intractable." *Sight and Sound*, vol. 16, no. 2, 2006, pp. 28–30.
Tolliver, Willie. "Will Smith's Defense of His Race: Pop Culture and Contemporary Racial Politics." Joseph R. Gladden Public Lecture, Agnes Scott College, Atlanta, GA, May 17, 2003, https://podcasts.apple.com/us/podcast/joseph-r-gladden-public-lecture/id381501502.
Tonchi, Stefano. "Military Dress, Modern Dress." *Uniform: Order and Disorder*, edited by Francesco Bonami et al., Charta, 2000, pp. 153–59.
Totaro, Donato. "*Cloverfield*: An Intimate Apocalypse." *Offscreen*, vol. 12, no. 2, 2008, http://www.offscreen.com/index.php/pages/essays/cloverfield_apocalypse.
Tudor, Andrew. *Monsters and Mad Scientists: A Cultural History of the Horror Movie*. 2nd ed., Basil Blackwell, 1991.
Valenti, Jack. "Cinema and War: Hollywood's Response to September 11." *Harvard International Review*, vol. 24, no. 2, 2002, pp. 78–80.
Vonder Haar, Pete. "*Cloverfield*." *Film Threat*, 2008, http://www.filmthreat.com/reviews/10705.
Vonder Haar, Pete. "*The Kingdom*." *Film Threat*, 2007, http://www.filmthreat.com/reviews/10311.
Wadenius, Adam. "In Violation of the Balance: Foreignness and the Post 9/11 Horror Film." *Jura Gentium Cinema*, "Dossier: Horror Politics," November 2009, http://www.apwadenius.com/ewExternalFiles/in.violation.of.the.balance-web.pdf.
Walliss, John, and James Aston. "Doomsday America: The Pessimistic Turn of Post-9/11 Apocalyptic Cinema." *Journal of Religion and Popular Culture*, vol. 23, no. 1, 2011, pp. 53–64.
Walsh, Fintan. *Male Trouble: Masculinity and the Performance of Crisis*. Palgrave Macmillan, 2010.

Walsh, Mike. "Book Review: *Post-Classical Hollywood: Film Industry, Style and Ideology since 1945* by Barry Langford." *Senses of Cinema*, no. 61, 2011, http://www.sensesofcinema.com/2011/book-reviews/post-classical-hollywood-film-industry-style-and-ideology-since-1945-by-barry-langford.

Walters, James. *Alternative Worlds in Hollywood Cinema: Resonance between Realms*. Intellect Books / University of Chicago Press, 2008.

Warner Bros. "*I Am Legend* Production Notes," 2007, http://iamlegend.warnerbros.com/media/images/productionNotes/IAL-productionNotes.pdf.

Warton, John. "*Cloverfield* (2008) and the Appropriation of Documentary Forms: A Critical Quandary over Scientific Inscription." *Ninth Interdisciplinary Global Conference on Monsters and the Monstrous*, September 2011.

Weaver, Roslyn. *Apocalypse in Australian Fiction and Film: A Critical Study*. McFarland, 2011.

Wessels, Emanuelle. *The Politics of Ethical Witnessing: The Participatory Networks of 9/11 Media Culture*. 2010. University of Minnesota, PhD dissertation.

Westwell, Guy. "Regarding the Pain of Others: Scenarios of Obligation in Post-9/11 US Cinema." *Journal of American Studies*, vol. 45, no. 4, 2011, pp. 815–34.

Wetmore, Kevin J. *Post-9/11 Horror in American Cinema*. Continuum, 2012.

Wilkins, Karin. "The Problem with Mediated Terrorism in US Action-Adventure Film: Explorations in Matters of Prejudice and Knowledge." *International Communication Association Annual Conference*, 2006, p. 26.

Wilkins, Karin, and John Downing. "Mediating Terrorism: Text and Protest in Interpretations of *The Siege*." *Critical Studies in Media Communication*, vol. 19, no. 4, 2002, pp. 419–37.

Williams, Linda. *Playing the Race Card: Melodramas of Black and White from Uncle Tom to O. J. Simpson*. Princeton University Press, 2001.

Williams, L. Susan, and Travis W. Linneman. "Scripting an Enemy: Portrayals of Arab Terrorists in American Film." *Cinematic Sociology: Social Life in Film*, edited by Jean-Anne Sutherland and Kathryn Feltey, Pine Forge Press, 2010, pp. 192–206.

Wood, Robin. *Hollywood from Vietnam to Reagan . . . and Beyond*. Expanded and rev. ed., Columbia University Press, 2003.

Zacharek, Stephanie. "*Cloverfield*." *Salon*, January 18, 2008, http://www.salon.com/2008/01/18/cloverfield.

Zacharek, Stephanie. "*I Am Legend*." *Salon*, December 14, 2007, http://www.salon.com/2007/12/14/legend.

Zacharek, Stephanie. "*The Kingdom*." *Salon*, September 28, 2007, https://www.salon.com/2007/09/28/kingdom.

Zacharek, Stephanie. "*World Trade Center*." *Salon*, August 9, 2006, https://www.salon.com/2006/08/09/wtc.

Žižek, Slavoj. *Welcome to the Desert of the Real! Five Essays on September 11 and Related Dates*. Verso, 2002.

INDEX

10 Cloverfield Lane, 201n4
12 Strong, 188–94, 197n12
25th Hour, 25, 56–57, 197n33, 201n45
30 Days of Night, 87
300, 211n38, 212n1
15:17 to Paris, The, 209n1
9/11, 56–57, 155–57; allusions to, in cinema, 20–21, 67–68, 73, 106, 201n11, 203n23; construction of, 3, 21; and Hollywood, 3–7, 9–13, 38–40; mediated experience of, 30, 38, 50, 67–68, 77–79. *See also* shame; spectacle
2012, 72–73, 76, 202n21

action film, 144, 155, 175–76, 181–82; 1980s action, 9–13, 23, 144–45, 186, 196n15; as melodrama, 7, 9, 72
Afghanistan, war in, 24, 38, 147, 178, 188, 190–92
Aguayo, Michelle, 157, 170, 171
Alamo, The (2004), 211n38
Ali, 117
Alias, 172
Alien, 145, 201n12
alien invasion/threat, 4–6, 11, 68–70, 73–74, 115, 136, 195n5
Alleva, Richard, 39
al Qaeda, 155–57, 182, 187–92
Altman, Rick, 21
amateur/personal camera, 27, 65–72, 77–80, 85, 91–99, 201n3, 201n10
America: as colony, 132, 134–36, 139–41; as feminized, 6, 10; as foreign space, 144, 146, 162–64; as insecure/vulnerable, 6, 13–15, 23, 91–92, 143–47, 183; and national anxieties, 68–70; as remasculinized, 57–61

American, The, 177
American mythology, 15, 143, 145, 152, 188
American Sniper, 188
Anderson, Christopher, 122
Anderson, Mark, 145, 188
Andrejevic, Mark, 15, 118–19
Ansen, David, 205n13, 206n20, 207n34, 211n39
"Arab/Muslims," 15, 25, 151, 157–60, 165–66, 171, 174, 209n8
Armageddon, 72
Aston, James, 201n11, 205n9
Avila, Eric, 195n5

battlefield, 14, 50, 54, 92, 109, 149
Battlestar Galactica, 197n28
Baudrillard, Jean, 6, 54, 195n3
Bauman, Zygmunt, 97–98
Beast from 20,000 Fathoms, The, 72, 201n6, 202n14
Beau Geste (Wellman, 1939), 160–61
Belafonte, Harry, 113–15, 206n15
Bell-Mertreau, Rebecca, 4
Berardinelli, James, 201n7, 201n12
Berg, Peter, 144, 147, 155, 163, 181–82, 209n3, 210n10, 211n39
Berger, James, 107–8
Billy Lynn's Long Halftime Walk, 188
bin Laden, Osama, 155, 178–79, 182, 191
Black Hawk Down, 145, 165, 176, 210n13, 210n19
blackness, 16, 115–18, 138, 141, 196n24
Blair Witch Project, The, 99, 202n18
Bloody Sunday, 198n13
blowback, 177–83, 212n40
Boardwalk Empire, 200n41
Book of Eli, The, 107, 121, 197n35, 207n36

borders/boundaries: blurring/collapse of, 13–14, 90–93; breach of, 14, 98, 145–48; transgressions/violation of, 15, 176, 201n11
Bordwell, David, 21, 68–70, 82, 201n10, 202nn17–19
Born on the Fourth of July, 39, 200n39
Boyle, Brenda, 187
Boyle, Kirk, 109, 134–35, 138
Bradley, Matthew R., 205n6, 207nn34–35
Bradshaw, Peter, 209n2, 211n37
Brayton, Sean, 109, 128, 133, 136, 140, 205n9, 206nn21–22, 207n32, 208n41, 208mn49–50
Broderick, Mick, 11, 107, 139, 197n26
Brokeback Mountain, 20
Brown, Wendy, 8
buddy film, 46, 165–70, 197n26, 200n31
Burns, Jeremy, 108
Bush administration, 7, 14, 25, 29, 108, 195n1, 195nn8–9, 196n16, 197n31, 206n23
Butler, Judith, 17–19, 59–60, 126

Cage, Nicolas, 40, 45, 199n17
Calefato, Patrick, 32, 54
Cape Fear (1990), 90
capitalist ideology, 112, 121–22, 204n39, 206n24
Carroll, Noël, 95, 111, 197n26, 200n39, 204n42
Carroll, Raymond, 200n39
Carter, Sean, 149, 151, 196n16, 197n31
Cat People (1942), 94
Cettl, Robert, 24–25
Charles, Alec, 45, 107, 197n28
Children of Men, 109
Christ figure, 132–36, 139–41
Christiansen, Steen, 69, 77, 95–97, 201n11
CIA (Central Intelligence Agency), 164, 177–78, 188, 191
Cieply, Michael, 166, 212n1
city, 4–6, 57, 90–93, 97, 128, 202n15; as battlefield, 14, 92, 210n19; post-apocalyptic, 112–14, 123, 136, 139–40, 208n52; as target, 67
class, 17–19, 57, 123; and Will Smith, 115–17, 206n19, 206n25, 207n27; working, 73–74, 113, 207n27

Clover, Carol, 71, 85–86, 99, 102, 197n26
Cloverfield, 65–87, 89–100, 189, 197n34, 204n2, 211n32
Cloverfield monster, 69, 91–98
Cloverfield Paradox The, 201n4
Cohan, Steven, 9–10
Cohen, Jeffrey, 16, 97
Cold War/1950s, 7, 10, 22, 97–98, 153–54, 196n23, 205n7. *See also* science fiction cinema
Combe, Kirk, 187
Connell, Raewyn, 17–19, 24, 196n12
Conrad, Dean, 203n22
conservative ideology/values, 11, 13; in *Cloverfield*, 86–87; in *I Am Legend*, 109, 121, 139–40; in *The Kingdom*, 155, 170; in *World Trade Center*, 43, 47
consumerism, 106, 111–13, 119, 121–27, 204n39, 206nn23–24
containment, strategies of, 22, 41, 48, 66, 76–80, 96, 117, 151–56. *See also* spectacle
Copier, Laura, 110, 114, 136, 138, 141
Corliss, Richard, 209n2
Courage Under Fire, 172, 211n31
Courtney, Susan, 113
Coyle, Rebecca, 68, 80, 201n12, 203n31
Craik, Jennifer, 31, 34, 52, 59
Creekmur, Corey, 157, 174
crisis: and Hollywood genre cinema, 7–13, 20, 23, 68–69, 106, 110; and masculinity, 7–13, 21, 36, 59, 198n11; national, 3, 7–14, 17, 20–21
Crowe, Lori, 72
Curse of the Demon, 94

Dargis, Manohla, 134, 202n17
Dark Passage, 72, 84–85
"Darkseekers," 130, 136–39, 208
Davies, Merryl Wyn, 160–61, 196n19
Davis, Mike, 4
Dawes, Birgit, 14, 41
Dawn of the Dead, 207n31
Day after Tomorrow, The, 67, 73
Day the Earth Stood Still, The (2008), 67, 203n22
Deep Impact, 107
Deepwater Horizon, 209n3

Deliverance, 86, 200n43
Deluge, 201n6
Denby, David, 199nn17–18, 200n40
Dennis, Jeffrey, 20
DeRosa, Aaron, 200n36
Diary of the Dead, 70
difference, 95–97, 109, 136–39, 149–50, 208nn50–51; erasure/annihilation of, 24, 46, 128, 169, 191; as positive, 32, 57
disaster movies, 4–5, 12, 14, 30, 39–45, 52–53, 65, 71–77, 85, 197n26; and 9/11, 3, 30
Dixon, Wheeler Winston, 195n3
documentary aesthetic, 65, 70–71, 78, 145, 157, 163, 202n18, 203n31
Dodds, Klaus, 149, 151, 164, 168, 175, 196n16, 197n31
Downing, John, 165
Drew, Julie, 6–7, 195n8, 196n14
Duncombe, Constance, 195n10, 196n20
Durham, Christopher, 23, 196n11

Earthquake, 66, 76
Ebert, Roger, 201n7, 201n12, 205n13, 207nn34–35
Edelstein, David, 192, 198n13, 199nn17–18, 200n40
Elektra, 172
emasculation, 35–37, 65, 85–86, 89–90, 155–57, 173
emergent hero, 71–72, 75–76
End of Days, 208n48
England, Marcia, 91
Entourage, 210n14
Escape from New York, 203n26
everyman, 26, 65–66, 71–77, 81, 96–100, 205n7

Fahrenheit 9/11, 155
Faludi, Susan, 11, 14, 74, 173, 196n14, 198n13
fatherhood, 12–13, 44–47, 73–74, 132–36
fathers, 41, 73–74, 90, 103–5, 118, 148–51, 168–69; redemption/recuperation of, 11–13, 132–41, 182–83, 188–91, 210n12; and return to the home, 47–51, 193–94
FBI (Federal Bureau of Investigation), 150–51, 159, 164–65, 209n10, 210n11
female: absence, 48, 188–89, 196n15, 199n27; masculinity, 170–74; maternal absence,
11, 13, 114, 150; as passive/helpless, 13, 44–51, 71–74, 173; as redeemer, 136–41
feminized males/heroes, 44, 85, 88, 101–2, 110–15, 152, 189
films noir, 23, 72–73, 84–85, 186
final girl, 86–89, 136, 173, 204n1
final man, 111–13, 110–15, 120–29, 206n24
Fitzpatrick, Andrea, 35
Ford, Elizabeth, 205n9
Ford, John, 177–78, 196n23, 209n6
Fort Apache, 28, 144, 145–46, 152, 153, 154, 161, 176, 177, 182
Fort Apache: The Bronx, 209n10
Franklin, Garth, 202n17
Fresh Prince of Bel Air, The, 206n19
frontier myth, 15, 145, 152, 164, 176–77, 188
Full Metal Jacket, 20, 145

Gallagher, Mark, 7, 9, 10, 18, 23, 196n15
Garner, Jennifer, 172
Gentry, Ric, 42, 48, 63, 199n26
Gilligan, Sarah, 112, 117–18
Godfrey, Sarah, 11, 13, 16, 31, 103, 151, 196n14
Godzilla, 69, 95, 201n6, 202n13, 202n20, 204n43
Gojira, 69, 95, 202nn14–15, 204n38
"good Indian," 166–70, 176, 211n28
Graham, Stephen, 162, 176
Green Berets, The, 145, 192
Ground Zero, 25, 29–31, 51–59, 108–9, 125, 199n27, 212n2; wreckage of, 35–36, 55
Gunga Din, 160, 163, 169–70, 176, 211n38
Gunn, James, 73–74

Halberstam, Jack, 171–73
Hamad, Hannah, 11, 13, 16, 31, 103, 151, 196n14
handheld camera. *See* amateur/personal camera
Hannah, Matthew, 6–7, 15, 152, 160, 176, 195n9
Hantke, Steffen, 16, 68–72, 76, 94, 110, 196n23, 197n26, 204n36, 208n50
Hark, Ina Rae, 9–10
Haschemi Yekani, Elahe, 198n11
Hay, James, 15, 118–19
Heffernan, Jeanne, 177

hegemonic/normative masculinity: and crisis, 8–9, 59, 103–4; and Hollywood, 7, 10, 186; and identity, 31–34, 51–56; and national identity, 3, 6, 10, 12, 187; and others, 16–17, 19–20, 24
Heston, Charlton, 23, 66, 117, 134–35, 206n15, 207n26
Heyes, Michael, 207n33, 208n41
Hoberman, J., 50, 199nn17–18, 211n37
Holloway, David, 159, 185–86
Hollywood cinema: 1990s, 12, 52–53, 106, 196n21; post–World War II, 23, 186; Vietnam/1970s, 23–24, 86, 106, 134, 162, 186, 197n29. *See also* Cold War/1950s; science fiction film
home: as breached, 13–14, 87–91, 189–90; as gendered space, 47–51, 209n7; as insecure, 13–14, 108, 146–48, 169, 196n17; as securitized, 118–21; and (symbolic) return, 44–52, 74, 132–33, 148–54, 193–94, 212n4
home invasion, 88–89, 100
homeland, 14, 31, 90, 119, 189
Homeland Security, 13–15, 118–19
horror film, 21, 67–68, 90, 94–97, 99, 102–3, 106–7, 196n17, 196n23, 197nn26–27, 203n35, 204n41; "discovered footage," 94; "home invasion," 26, 87; realist, 70–71; slasher, 70, 86–87, 95, 99, 202n17, 204n1; survival horror, 202n17, 204n2
Hurricane Katrina, 108, 128, 206n22
husbands, 31, 44, 47, 73, 88, 100–102, 189
hypermasculinity, 10–11, 60

I, Robot, 128
I Am Legend (film), 103–42, 197n35
I Am Legend (novella), 105, 123–24, 205nn5–7, 205n12
"imagination of disaster," 4–5, 30, 38, 42, 67, 107, 121
Incredible Hulk, The (TV series), 169
Independence Day, 115, 196n21
In Harm's Way, 201n44
Invasion, The, 69, 196n23
Invasion of the Body Snatchers (1956), 98
Iraq, war in, 20, 24, 147, 178, 188, 206n22

ISIS, 182, 186–87, 192
It Comes at Night, 107

Jaafar, Ali, 37, 40, 199n20, 201n46
Jackson, Kimberly, 92, 96, 98
Jacobs, Alan, 89, 100
Jancovich, Mark, 21
Jeffords, Susan, 10, 12
JFK, 39, 198n7
Johnson, Brian, 48, 50, 199n15, 199n19, 200n40
Johnson, Maryann, 209n4, 211n39
Jordan, John W., 5, 38
Joyce, Stephen, 25, 196n21, 208n50

Kakoudaki, Despina, 52–53, 72, 78–79, 197n26
Keane, Stephen, 30, 40, 42, 195n6
Kehr, Dave, 24, 146, 177
Kelly, Casey Ryan, 9
Kendrick, James, 58, 78, 199n16
Khatib, Lina, 146–47
Kimmer, Elisabeth, 12
King, Claire Sisco: on *I Am Legend*, 103–4, 106, 108–9, 133, 138, 206nn21–22; on "sacrificial" films, 20, 45, 141
King, Geoff, 145, 195n3
Kingdom, The, 143–84, 185, 189, 197n36
King Kong (1933), 202n14
Klawans, Stuart, 52, 199n15, 200n40
Kord, Susanne, 12
Kracauer, Siegfried, 97–98
Kraidy, Marwan M., 22

Lady in the Lake, 72, 84–85
Land of the Dead, 207n31
Lane, Anthony, 175, 201n7, 202n17
Last House on the Left, The (2009), 87
Last Man on Earth, The, 205n7, 205n12, 208n43
Lavoie, Dusty, 207n34
Lee, Nathan, 201n11
Leininger, Robert, 197n32, 210n12
Lewis, Michael, 43, 63, 199n15
Lichty, Lawrence, 200n39
Linneman, Travis, 147, 157, 169, 173, 196n19, 210n18, 210n22

Lions for Lambs, 38, 209n10
Liss, Rebecca, 200n40, 200n42
Lobalzo Wright, Julie, 206n16
Lone Survivor, 209n3
Looming Tower, The, 197n28
Los Angeles, 4, 106, 108, 112, 205n12
Lost Patrol, The, 147, 160, 162–63
Lumenick, Lou, 211n37

MacDonald, James, 201n12
MacKinnon, Kenneth, 60
Magill, David, 115, 206n17
Major Dundee, 147–48, 165, 170
male: agency, 44–51, 163–64, 170–75; as insecure/vulnerable, 35–36, 44–45, 65, 86, 98, 115, 119–22
male action genres, 7, 12, 20, 23, 143, 154, 162, 176, 191, 209n5

mannequins, 92, 121–28, 206n24, 207nn27–29
Mantoan, Lindsey, 106
Man Who Shot Liberty Valance, The, 206n14
masculinity, 6–7, 10, 17, 21, 23, 52, 63, 144, 153, 156, 173, 186–87; and Hollywood, 3, 7–13, 25, 145; as masochistic/wounded, 35–37; as overcivilized, 87–90; as renegotiated, 44, 48, 52, 60–63
masquerade, male, 57–61
Matheson, Richard, 105, 123–24, 205nn6–7, 205n12, 207n34
McCarthy, Todd, 202n17, 205n13
McGillis, Roderick, 53–54, 60
McKee, Alan, 22
McSweeney, Terence, 20, 25
Melnick, Jeffrey, 196n14
Men in Black, 115
militarized masculinity, 51–56, 132–36
Miller, Toby, 22
Missing, The, 165, 170, 177, 211n28
Mist, The, 73
Mitchell, Deborah, 205n9
Mitchell, Kevin, 206n22
Monahan, Barry, 68
monster: giant, 25–26, 65–71, 79–80, 85, 93–97, 204n43; as mirror, 122–24; as stranger, 93–100; as terrorist, 15–17

monster movie, 65, 68–71, 79, 85, 95, 97, 204n43
monstrous masculinity, 100–102, 129–32, 139–41, 180–83
Moreman, Christopher M., 208n49
Morgan, Michael, 88–89, 100
Morgenstern, Joe, 207n35
Movshovitz, Howard, 148
Mulligan, Rikk, 206n22
Mulvey, Laura, 9
Munich, 177–82, 197n36
Muntean, Nick, 5, 14, 30, 40–41, 80

Nadel, Alan, 22
Naked City, The, 97
Nama, Adilifu: on *I Am Legend*, 109, 117; on *The Omega Man*, 106, 129, 134; on science fiction cinema, 16, 23, 107, 115–16, 136, 138, 196n24
Nayak, Meghana, 15–16, 157, 159–61, 196n20, 208n37, 209n8
Neale, Steve, 9
Negra, Diane, 11
neoliberal ethos, 119–21
New York: as battlefield, 92–93, 201n8; as cinematic target, 4, 30, 67–68, 203n26; as site of trauma, 108, 111, 113, 123
Night of the Living Dead, 205n7
Nilges, Mathias, 12, 11, 195n10
Nixon, 39
Nolley, Ken, 196n20
North, Daniel, 94–95

Obama administration, 195n2
Objective Burma!, 157
O'Connor, John E., 164, 176
Omega Man, The, 105–14, 117, 120, 129–30, 134–36, 205n6, 205n12, 206n15, 207n29, 208n52
orientalist discourses, 15–16, 145, 157–66, 168, 183, 191, 196n20
otherness. See difference
outposts, 143, 145–48, 160–62, 176, 183, 211n38
Overpeck, Deron, 75–76
Ozcan, Ceylan, 35, 40, 47

Page, Max, 4, 6, 195n3, 195n7
Pak, Chris, 208n49
Palmer, Lorrie, 116–17
Paranormal Activity, 70, 99
paternalism/paternal, 11–13, 31–32, 44–51, 57, 71–74, 103–4, 126–27, 132–36, 148–51; failure, 73–74, 127, 132–33; guilt, 104–5, 109, 138; redemption, 13, 73–74, 141, 168; sacrifice, 136–37, 177–78
Patterson, Kathy Davis, 205n5
Pearl Harbor, 7, 15, 195n10, 198n5, 201n44
Peebles, Stacey, 200n36
Pheasant-Kelly, Frances, 39–40, 61
Phillips, Michael, 201n7
Pile, Steve, 79, 201n12
Pitetti, Connor, 108
Platoon, 39, 200n39
Pollard, Tom, 205n9
popular culture, American, 11, 169, 181
postapocalypse films, 105–15
Price, Stuart, 211n33
Prince, Stephen, 38, 196n23
professional-paternal masculinity, 44, 48, 103–4, 110, 118, 126, 133, 143, 150–51, 183, 190
Puig, Claudia, 205n13, 207n35, 211n37
Purse, Lisa, 173
Pursuit of Happyness, The, 114, 134

Quarantine, 69–70
Quiet Place, A, 69, 107

race, 16–17, 109–10, 115–17, 121–24, 136–40, 206n25, 207nn27–28
Rainer, Peter, 209n4
Rambo: First Blood Part II, 192
Rambo III, 144
Reagan era, 10, 11
Redmond, Sean, 12, 203n23
remasculinization, 7–13, 15–17, 55–61, 73–77, 86–93, 98–102, 143–46, 170–79, 188–94, 195n8
Rendition, 177, 209n10
Renner, Karen, 72, 106–7
Rescue Me, 198n6
revelation, 29, 45, 48, 64, 107
Revelation, Book of, 29

revenge. *See* vengeance
revenge fantasy, 144, 175, 181, 185
Revolutionary Road, 200n41
Reyes, Xavier Aldana, 77
Rich, B. Ruby, 41–42, 199n17, 200n40
Richards, Olly, 67–68
Rickli, Christina, 5
Road, The, 73, 107, 114, 207n36
Robinson, Sally, 8–9, 36–37, 61, 196n11, 196n13, 200n43
Romero, George A., 205n7, 207n31
Rosenbaum, Ron, 38–39, 41, 55
Rosenblatt, Josh, 207n35

Said, Edward, 159
Sardar, Ziauddin, 160–61, 196n19
Savlov, Marc, 201n11
Savran, David, 10, 196n11, 196n13
Saw, 87
Saw II, 87
Schwarzbaum, Lisa, 201n12, 202n17
Schwarzenegger, Arnold, 205n11, 206n18
science fiction film, 16, 21; apocalypses, 12, 65, 105–15; Cold War/1950s, 5, 68–69, 72, 93, 97–98, 106–7, 113, 196n23
Scott, A. O., 115, 134, 199nn17–18, 205n13, 207n35, 209n2, 209n4
Searchers, The, 53, 74, 146, 154, 161, 176–77, 181, 209n7, 209n9
security, discourses of, 118–21
self-sacrifice, male, 23, 46, 132–41, 204n40, 208n48
September 11. *See* 9/11
Shaheen, Jack, 166, 196n19, 209n2, 210n18, 210n22
shame: of 9/11, 7, 11, 87–90, 144; male, 87–90, 100–102, 127, 198n9
Shane, 209n7
Shannon, Michael, 58–59, 200n41
Shaw, Tony, 201n9
She Wore a Yellow Ribbon, 176, 209n6
Shrek, 126–27
Siege, The, 165, 196n21
Silverman, Kaja, 23, 36, 186, 196n13
Six Degrees of Separation, 206n25, 207n27
Slotkin, Richard, 7, 15, 145, 164, 175, 197n26
Smith, Julian, 186
Smith, Sid, 209n4

Smith, Will, 115–18, 120, 134, 140, 206nn17–20, 206n25, 207n29
sons, 148–49, 166–67, 182
Sontag, Susan, 5, 67, 107
space: as gendered, 148–51; as Orientalized, 157–65; public/private, 90–93; urban, 118–21
spectacle: of 9/11, 4–6, 30, 77–80; containment of, 22–23, 39–44, 185, 199n20; and Hollywood film, 3–7, 30, 67, 79, 121; of terror, 79, 163, 174
Stagecoach, 209n9
Staiger, Janet, 21–22
Stallone, Sylvester, 10
Starship Troopers, 145
Stevens, Dana, 199n15, 201n6, 205n13
Stewart, Garrett, 22–23
Stone, Oliver, 29–64, 198n7, 199nn16–17, 199n19, 199n23, 199n26, 199n29, 200n35, 200nn39–40, 200n42, 201n46
Strangers, The, 87–89, 100–102, 197n34, 203n35, 204n44
Strangers: Prey at Night, The, 203n35
"strong father," 3, 11–13, 17, 23, 88–89, 107
Sturken, Marita, 41, 195n9
Subramanian, Janani, 109, 115–16, 207n33, 208n49
Sully, 198n3
Svendsen, Lars, 196n18
Syriana, 157, 173, 209n10

Takacs, Stacy, 199n22
Taken, 13
Take Shelter, 200n41
Tasker, Yvonne, 10–11, 18, 118, 171–72, 196n13
Taubin, Amy, 56
television screens: as conduits for terror, 13–14, 77, 189–90, 203n30; to contain terror of 9/11, 13–14, 30, 38, 42–43, 50
terror, allusions to real-world imagery, 69, 173–74
terrorist-Other, 15, 178–79, 183, 210n24; as hidden/veiled, 32, 149, 162, 176, 191; perspective, 149, 163–64, 167, 183
terror-Other, 22, 25, 61–64, 70, 140–41; as monstrous mirror, 15–17, 127–30, 144, 181–83, 187
Texas Chain Saw Massacre, The, 71, 87

Them!, 71–72, 202n14, 204n40, 204n43
There's Always Tomorrow, 206n14
Thing, The (1981), 98, 201n12
Thomson, David, 181
Tolliver, Willie, 115–16, 206nn18–19, 206n25
Tonchi, Stefano, 52
Tora! Tora! Tora!, 198n5
Totaro, Donato, 202nn11–12, 202n17, 205n9
Tourneur, Jacques, 94
Trump era, 119, 159, 186–88, 212n6
Tudor, Andrew, 72
Twin Towers: in cinema, 198n3, 210n16; as symbol, 6, 56–57, 156, 180

uniformed masculinity, 31–34, 51–56
United 93, 5, 30, 38–40, 42, 45, 106, 197n33, 198n13, 199n14, 203n26
United Airlines Flight 93, 25, 30, 199n14

Vacancy, 87
Valenti, Jack, 195n4
vampire-zombies, 130, 136–39, 208
vengeance, 54, 74, 175–83, 185
Vietnam era, 10, 23, 24, 39, 54, 86, 106, 144, 162, 186, 192, 197n29, 205n7, 210n19
Vonder Haar, Peter, 211n34, 211n37

Walliss, John, 201n11, 205n9
Wall Street, 199
Walsh, Fintan, 8
war movies, 7, 54, 144–45, 155, 165, 175–76, 181–82, 209n5; Vietnam, 162; World War II combat, 145, 157, 162, 191–92
War of the Worlds (2005), 67, 69, 72–76, 197n34, 207n36
"war on terror": in cinema, 21–23, 30, 69, 144–45, 159, 185–86, 211n33; construction of, 3, 195n2, 195n11, 197n31; and gender, 13, 15, 21
Weaver, Roslyn, 107, 205n10
Wessels, Emanuelle, 96
westerns, 7, 11, 15–16, 20–21, 60, 143, 145–48, 152, 160–62, 164–65, 176–77, 195n17, 196n20, 196n25, 197n26, 209nn6–7; frontier western, 143, 145–48, 151–53, 160–63, 165, 176, 188, 209n10, 211n38; post–World War II, 23, 197n32
Westwell, Guy, 206n22, 208nn50–51

When Worlds Collide, 72, 201n6, 202n21
whiteness, 12, 70, 123, 129, 134–36, 140, 207n32
Wilkins, Karin, 165, 196n19
Williams, L. Susan, 147, 157, 169, 173, 196n19, 210n18, 210n22
Williams, Linda, 143, 209n5
Wood, Robin, 186, 197n26
World, the Flesh and the Devil, The, 110, 113–14, 121–23, 126, 206n15
World Trade Center, 30, 188, 212n12
World Trade Center (film), 29–64, 185, 189, 197n33, 212n4

Zacharek, Stephanie, 40, 67, 182, 199n18, 200n40, 205n13, 211n34
Zero Dark Thirty, 145, 177–79, 197n36
Žižek, Slavoj, 6, 45, 195n3

ABOUT THE AUTHOR

Credit: RMIT University

Glen Donnar is senior lecturer in the School of Media and Communication at RMIT University in Melbourne, Australia. His work has appeared in publications such as *Communication, Politics, and Culture Journal* and *Celebrity Studies*.

www.ingramcontent.com/pod-product-compliance
Lightning Source LLC
Chambersburg PA
CBHW030620230426
43661CB00053B/2073